MY
HUSBAND
AND I

MY HUSBAND AND I

The Inside Story of
70 Years of the Royal Marriage

INGRID SEWARD

**SIMON &
SCHUSTER**

London · New York · Sydney · Toronto · New Delhi

A CBS COMPANY

First published in Great Britain by Simon & Schuster UK Ltd, 2017
A CBS COMPANY

5 7 9 10 8 6

Simon & Schuster UK Ltd
1st Floor
222 Gray's Inn Road
London WC1X 8HB

www.simonandschuster.co.uk

Simon & Schuster Australia, Sydney
Simon & Schuster India, New Delhi

A CIP catalogue record for this book
is available from the British Library.

ISBN: 978-1-4711-5955-8
Trade paperback ISBN: 978-1-4711-5957-2
Ebook ISBN: 978-1-4711-5958-9

Typeset in Sabon by M Rules
Printed and bound by CPI Group (UK) Ltd, Croydon, CR0 4YY

FOR THELMA

Contents

Introduction   I

1   Wedding Celebrations   5
2   Childhood Contrasts   21
3   Growing Together Apart   37
4   Kissing Cousins   57
5   Changes   73
6   Parenthood   99
7   Philip and Albert   123
8   Bringing Up Andrew and Edward   141
9   Watching the Family Grow   159
10 Trials and Tribulations   179
11 The Death of Diana   197
12 Different Interests   221
13 From Banquets to Tea at the Palace   241
14 Defender of the Faith   257
15 Threescore Years and Ten   271

Acknowledgements   285
Bibliography   287
Index   291

Introduction

After many years writing about the royal family, among the questions I am most often asked are: 'What are the Queen and the Duke of Edinburgh like as a couple? How does their marriage work? How do they operate as parents and grandparents?' In short, when you strip away all the formality of royalty and the protocol that goes with it, what are they *really* like? With the success of the television series *The Crown*, interest in the personal side of their lives has been opened up to a whole new generation.

Having been around the Queen and the Duke for over thirty years, and met them both on many separate occasions, I feel able to provide a unique insight into their lives, which I hope I have achieved through the following pages. As they celebrate seventy years of marriage, there has never been a more important time to set their story in the context of the changing world they have lived through together.

Their story is as fascinating as it is improbable. How did an almost penniless prince of Greece win the heart of the world's most eligible princess? How did she persuade her father, a King Emperor over whose dominions the sun never set, to give his consent? She was a chaste child-woman, who went straight from her nursery to the marital bed. He was a handsome 25-year-old

naval officer, independent and charismatic, but without money
or estates to his name. He was born on a dining-room table in a
villa on the Greek island of Corfu; she was born in a grand house
in London's Mayfair with Home Secretary Sir William Joynson-
Hicks in attendance.

   In a world where appearances counted for everything, Philip of
Greece's upbringing was one of distinctly royal disorder. When his
engagement to Princess Elizabeth was announced two years after
the end of the war, the British people had very mixed feelings. To
many, Philip was regarded as an immigrant fortune hunter, with
distinctly German connections through his sisters. In 1947, any
hint of foreign blood was frowned upon, unless the owner came
swathed in riches like the great American heiresses who married
into the British aristocracy. Prince Philip ticked none of these boxes,
but although the princess was young and somewhat naïve, she was
stubborn and determined to conquer any opposition to the union
with the man she loved. She had an uphill struggle, because at the
time the establishment was able to wield great influence – and Philip
was very much not a part of it.

For the past seventy years, Prince Philip, the most fiercely competitive of men, has had to walk two paces behind his wife in public. It
could have been an impossible role for a man of his temperament,
but fortunately the Queen is the kind of traditionalist who believes
a man should be the master of his own home. She has always appreciated how difficult it is for someone so obsessed with his masculine
image as her husband to have a wife who always takes precedence
over him. If compromise is marriage's essential ingredient, it has
been especially vital to the Queen and Prince Philip. Theirs is a
surprisingly small world from which there is no escape. In their
personal affairs, they have only each other to turn to for comfort
and support. And, living on top of each other as they do, each must

make allowances for the other if life is not to become so claustrophobic as to be unbearable.

The Queen and Prince Philip made their accommodations early in their union and their marriage has been a success because of it. They remain close and, even after seven decades, the Queen's face lights up when Philip enters a room. When she first took the unexpected reins of the monarchy in 1952, she was overwhelmed by the masculine pressures of the court while struggling to come to terms with the untimely death of her father. Without appearing to do so, Prince Philip took on the unlikely role of champion to his wife and became both mother and father to their children, allowing the Queen to deal with the requirements of her position.

Until now, in the year he decided to announce he would give up his official duties, Prince Philip's contribution to the royal marriage and everything it entails has been largely unrecognised, and I hope this book will help redress that oversight.

Over the years, the Queen and Prince Philip have tried to keep control of the speculation and intrusion into their private lives and that of their family. However, they have often been faced with a press who seldom appear to worry if the stories are true – so long as they provide sensational headlines.

The failure of the marriage of their son and heir Prince Charles to the ingénue Lady Diana Spencer certainly did that. It was the lowest point of the Queen's long reign. Never had she envisaged she would be in the position of having to write to both her son and daughter-in-law saying a divorce was desirable. It went against everything she had been taught and rankled with her strong religious beliefs and position as Defender of the Christian Faith. It was made even worse by the death of Diana a year and a day after the divorce was finalised. Without the strong moral support of her husband, the Queen may well have crumbled, but she didn't. In November 1997, three months after Diana's death, they celebrated their golden wedding anniversary, and she paid tribute to her husband, saying he was 'her strength and stay all these years'. More personally, she spoke for the first time of his 'constant love and help'.

The seventy-year marriage of Elizabeth and Philip has transcended some of the most turbulent times in the history of Great Britain. From the dark days of post-war Britain to the similarly dark days of the age of terrorism in which we now live, the Queen and Prince Philip have seen it all. They watched in sadness as not one but three of their children's marriages ended in divorce, but they have lived long enough to see them all happily move on. They have enjoyed good enough health to see their many grandchildren grow up and can now watch their great-grandchildren begin that same process. No one can ask for more. The story of how they achieved this is the story of this book.

Chapter 1

WEDDING CELEBRATIONS

'Lilibet is the only thing in this world which is absolutely real to me and my ambition is to weld the two of us into a new combined existence . . .' So wrote the 26-year-old Prince Philip to his mother-in-law two weeks after his marriage on 20 November 1947. It was to be the blueprint for their life together and, such was the depth of his passion at the time, he went on to expand on his theme.

'Cherish Lilibet? I wonder if that word is enough to express what is in me. Does one cherish one's sense of humour or one's musical ear or one's eyes? I am not sure, but I know that I thank God for them and so, very humbly I thank God for Lilibet and for us.'

Two nights before the wedding, in the royal tradition, a grand ball was given by the King and Queen at Buckingham Palace. Philip's cousin Lady Pamela Mountbatten, who was among the 1200 guests, admitted her teenage memories of the wedding day were out-dazzled by the ball. It was certainly something to remember after all the years of wartime austerity. The royal estates provided plenty of game, which was prepared by the chefs, and the finest wines and champagnes were brought up from the cellars. The menu, which included lobster mayonnaise, turkey, vanilla soufflé and cherries in brandy, was eaten off state china and in the centre of each round table for eight stood a gold vase filled with pale yellow roses and carnations.

It was all too much for some of the guests and during the evening an Indian maharajah apparently became so drunk he took a swing at the Duke of Devonshire, but no one had a clue as to why. Towards the end of the evening, or more appropriately the following morning, the King led a conga line through the state apartments before the assembled company sat down for breakfast. Mr Carroll Gibbons, one of the King's favourite bandleaders, played below the organ loft in the ballroom with a programme of foxtrots, waltzes and rhumbas. Personal requests were sent by page to the bandleader, and when the Princess Elizabeth requested a tune that the band did not know there was a flutter of panic. Eventually Gibbons sat down at the piano with only his leading saxophonist. In a moment or two the ballroom was filled with the haunting strains of the tune played on the piano by Gibbons purely from memory, with the saxophonist at his side.

The princess was wearing a dress of vivid coral pink net and delighted in showing off her engagement ring, which had been redesigned by Philip himself from his mother Princess Alice's own heirloom stones. 'She looked wonderful,' said Lady Margaret Colville, the princess's lady-in-waiting that night. She was 'effervescent'.

'Lilibet was a lovely girl, very pretty, and they were in love,' remembers Lady Pamela Mountbatten, 'but the horror for him was that she would ultimately be Queen of England. That would put paid to his promising naval career. What would he do for the rest of his life, always two steps behind? I think he thought he was either being very foolish taking this on, or he would have to do it seriously – which is what he has done. The awful thing for them was that they weren't expecting to have to take on the job till they were in their fifties.'

As soon as the engagement was announced, Pamela's father, Lord Mountbatten, started giving Philip the benefit of his views on how the wedding should be arranged and how the couple's new household should be run. Elizabeth was aware of Mountbatten's interferingly ambitious plans and did not like it. This was a view shared by her mother, though not necessarily by her father.

Philip knew how to respond and cautioned his pushy uncle by letter: 'I am not being rude but it is apparent you like the idea of being General Manager of this little show, and I am rather afraid she might not take to the idea quite so docilely as I do. It is true I know what is good for me, but don't forget she [Elizabeth] has not had you as uncle loco parentis counsellor and friend as long as I have.'

By mid-October the wedding invitations to over two thousand guests had been sent out bearing the distinctive royal postmark, the cypher of the King. The most important invitees were, and still are, those known as 'the magic four hundred'. These consist of royalty from all over Europe, who must be invited regardless of whether they are still throned or deposed. And of course, there were their personal friends who make up the intimate circle.

As it was only two years after the end of the war, the King decided that there was no question of Prince Philip's sisters being invited, as their German connection was still too shaming (they had moved to that country from Paris in the early 1930s to marry German aristocrats and stayed there during the war). 'So soon after the war, you couldn't have "the Hun",' Lady Mountbatten recalled. 'I think Philip understood, but the sisters certainly didn't. For years afterwards, they'd say: "Why weren't we allowed to come to your wedding?" They weren't exactly Stormtroopers.'

It remained such a sensitive topic that it wasn't until 2006 that Prince Philip broke a sixty-year public silence about his family's

Nazi ties, when he gave an interview for a book entitled *Royals and the Reich* and explained how, like many other Germans, his family found Hitler's early attempts to restore Germany's power and prestige positive.

'There was a great improvement in things like trains running on time and building,' Philip explained. 'There was a sense of hope after the depressing chaos of the Weimar Republic. I can understand people latching onto something or somebody who appeared to be appealing to their patriotism and trying to get things going. You can understand how attractive it was.' He stressed, however, that he was never 'conscious' of anybody in the family expressing anti-Semitic views.

From his father's seven brothers and sisters, all but one had died, but Philip's Uncle George attended the wedding with his wife, Marie Bonaparte, and their daughter Eugenie alongside various cousins and cousins by marriage including Queen Helen of Romania, Queen Alexandra of Yugoslavia and Queen Frederica of Greece.

The wedding was billed as a symbol of hope for the future for a country ravaged by war. There still were bomb craters in many of the streets; buildings often collapsed on their own, or were propped up with scaffolding; and every week brought the discovery of another unexploded bomb. Whole streets had to be demolished and everywhere there were damaged houses where one or two of the floors were open to the elements. Bits of wallpaper blew in the wind and the detritus from a half-damaged room piled up against what was left of the walls. Although the coldest winter within living memory was about to descend, the day of the wedding, 20 November, recorded temperatures of 59° Fahrenheit (15° Centigrade) due to an unusual tropical airflow.

Even though the war had been over for some thirty months, the country was still subject to rationing. Bread, coal, sweets, clothes, furniture and soap were just a few of the things in short supply. As a special concession, it was agreed the Household Cavalry would be allowed to escort the princess to her wedding in full-dress uniform instead of their battledress. Because it was a period of such austerity, initially the wedding was going to be held quietly and privately in St George's Chapel at Windsor to avoid any ostentatious display, but then the Labour government relented and permitted the marriage to become a public occasion. They realised such a festivity could only light up the hearts of the war-weary people, who showed astonishing generosity when the news was announced. Women sent sugar and flour from their meagre rations to help towards the wedding cake; others sent precious nylon stockings and hoarded lengths of fabric. Some even sent their clothing coupons, but these had to be returned since it was illegal for them to be passed on.

The *Radio Times*, the most popular publication of the day, commemorated the wedding with a lavish cover. The magazine also described the wedding inside Westminster Abbey, the route of the royal procession and an order of service. As it was the first royal wedding to be extensively filmed and broadcast on television, it took great ingenuity from the Outside Broadcasting Unit to cover it all. The technical problems of televising the day were so great that it was decided to only advertise half of what the BBC intended to film in case things went wrong. This was how the magazine advertised the programme:

The Royal Wedding

THURSDAY, NOVEMBER 20
The Marriage of H.R.H. PRINCESS ELIZABETH with
     Lieutenant PHILIP MOUNTBATTEN, R.N. in
     Westminster Abbey
11.03 Procession of Her Majesty the Queen leaves Buckingham
     Palace.

11.16 Procession of His Majesty the King and Her Royal
　　　　Highness the Bride leaves Buckingham Palace.
11.30 THE SERVICE
12.30 Departure of the Bride and Bridegroom from Westminster
　　　　Abbey, and the return processions to Buckingham Palace.

COMMENTATORS:

Wynford Vaughan-Thomas (inside the Abbey)
Richard Dimbleby (outside the West Door of the Abbey)
Peter Scott (on the roof of St. Margaret's, Westminster)
Audrey Russell (near Admiralty Arch)
Frank Gillard (outside Buckingham Palace)
It is hoped to interrupt programmes during the afternoon for a
　　　　description of the departure of the Bride and Bridegroom
　　　　for their honeymoon.

THE WEDDING SERVICE:

Fanfare (Bax)
During the Procession of the Bride:
Hymn: Praise, My Soul, The King Of Heaven (Goss)
Introduction read by the Dean
Solemnisation of the Marriage by the Archbishop of Canterbury
Psalm 67 (Bairstow)
Lesser Litany, the Lord's Prayer, and Responses taken by the
　　　　Precentor
Prayers and Blessing by the Dean
Motet: We wait for thy loving kindness, O God (McKie)
Address by the Archbishop of York
Hymn: The Lord's My Shepherd (Crimond)
Final Prayer and Benediction by the Archbishop of Canterbury

Amen (Orlando Gibbons)
Fanfare (Bax)
The National Anthem
During the signing of the Register:
Anthem: Blessed by the God and Father (S. S. Wesley)
Fanfare (Bax)
Wedding March (Mendelssohn)

Fifty-five BBC microphones enabled listeners throughout the world to share in the excitement. Broadcasters along the route and outside the abbey told of the arrival of guests and from his position on the Victoria Memorial, Frank Gillard described the bride leaving her home with her father the King. Further down the Mall, Audrey Russell, who was positioned on the roof of the Admiralty Citadel, took over from Gillard. Then, while the Irish State Coach, with Princess Elizabeth inside, passed on its way down the full length of Whitehall, the programme switched to the inside of the abbey for Wynford Vaughan-Thomas's impression of the scene. As Vaughan-Thomas finished his description, Peter Scott took over from the roof of St Margaret's Church. He announced the bride's arrival in Parliament Square and a moment or two later renowned commentator Richard Dimbleby described the scene as the State Coach drew up to the West Door of the abbey.

Out of sight of all the movement in the abbey, the engineer in charge of the broadcast sat at his control panel. On it was marked some twenty-six microphone circuits and he had to decide when to change one circuit for another and when to blend, say, the abbey bells with the sound of crowds cheering as Princess Elizabeth and Lieutenant Mountbatten left the abbey.

At seven o'clock on the morning of the wedding, John Dean (Prince Philip's valet) had tapped on the Duke of Edinburgh's bedroom door at Kensington Palace where he was staying and entered with his tea. 'He woke at once and was plainly in great form, extremely cheerful and in no way nervous,' Dean recalled. 'There had been a wedding rehearsal the previous day so we all knew exactly what we had to do, and the split-second timings of the day's arrangements were clear in my mind.'

After Philip had dressed and breakfasted on coffee and toast, the valet gingerly handed him his sword, realising they were ready far too soon. 'How the Duke resisted the temptation to light a cigarette I do not know,' Dean recalled. 'He had given up the habit, as from the previous night, and did not complain.' Despite the early hour, Philip and David Milford Haven, his best man, or supporter as they are called in royal circles, downed a gin and tonic to toast the last moments of Philip's bachelorhood.

On the eve of their wedding, the King had admitted Lieutenant Mountbatten RN to the royal family by making him a Knight Companion of the Order of the Garter and authorising him to use the appellation of 'Royal Highness' that he had surrendered on his naturalisation as a British subject. The King had also granted him the Dukedom of Edinburgh, which had originally been created by George II in 1727 for Prince Frederick, his son and heir.

Back at Buckingham Palace, the princess's maid Margaret 'Bobo' MacDonald had for once not had to wake 'her little lady' as she always called her. The princess was already up and sitting in her dressing gown by the window looking at the crowds. 'I can't believe it's really happening, Crawfie,' she said to Marion Crawford, her old governess, who joined her by the window. 'I have to keep pinching myself.'

By 11.25, Prince Philip and David Milford Haven had taken their places inside the abbey to await the arrival of the bride and the King.

Eileen Parker was a guest with her slightly hungover husband Mike (he had been at Philip's stag party the night before), and she recalls the moment: 'As we sat down, the organ began to play Elgar's Concerto in C Major. Suddenly, the vast congregation stood again and I wondered whom it could be for. Princess Elizabeth was timed to leave the palace at 11.03 precisely to reach the abbey by 11.28. Turning around slightly, I could glimpse Winston Churchill with his wife walking slowly down the aisle. It was a thrilling experience to see them so close.'

Six kings and seven queens were among the 2500-strong congregation, the largest gathering of royalty, regnant and exiled, anyone could remember. As the sound of cheering outside the abbey rose from a rumble to a mighty roar, the rousing hymn, 'Praise My Soul, The King Of Heaven' provided the vocal backdrop to the entrance of the princess and the King. The young bride in her ivory satin Norman Hartnell gown held onto the arm of her father, who was dressed in the uniform of the Admiral of the Fleet. Directly behind them and three paces ahead of the other bridesmaids, in deference to her rank, Princess Margaret walked, alone.

The Archbishop of York had the right idea, but it must have sounded improbable when he told so much assembled finery – tiaras, top hats, long dresses, uniforms and robes – that the marriage was 'in all essentials the same as it would have been for any cottager who might be married this afternoon in some small country church in a remote village in the Dales'.

After the service, the Duchess of Edinburgh laid her bridal bouquet – which had briefly gone missing at the palace while everyone was getting ready – at the Tomb of the Unknown Warrior. When the newly-wed couple returned to Buckingham Palace in the Glass Coach, the police temporarily lost control and a crowd burst through the cordon into the palace forecourt.

The King, who had seemed on the verge of tears during the signing of the register, made no speech at the wedding breakfast, and simply raised his glass to 'the bride'. He had confided to the archbishop that giving away his daughter was a more moving thing than getting married yourself.

According to Crawfie's more simplistic view, the wedding break-fast was a 'merry lunch party': 'The tables were decorated with similax [a dark red berried green plant] and white carnations and at each of our places there was a little bunch of white heather, sent down from Balmoral. The famous gold plate and the scarlet-coated footmen gave a fairy-tale atmosphere to it all.'

In fact, the footmen are always left outside the firmly closed Bow Room doors, only appearing when rung for. Inside the sanctuary, the royal family and their guests ate their cold buffet, made the congratulatory toasts and cut the cake – with a sword – which can often lead to a lot of good-natured giggles.

A few days later, when she was back in Athens, Prince Philip's mother Alice wrote to him: 'How wonderfully everything went off and I was comforted to see the truly happy expression on your face and to feel your decision was right from every point of view.' Alice also wrote a detailed twenty-page description of the wedding itself, which she sent on to Philip's absent sisters.

The princess's father wrote a letter to his daughter, full of love and pride about how he contemplated his life without her:

> *I was so proud of you and thrilled at having you so close to me on our long walk in Westminster Abbey, but when I handed your hand to the Archbishop I felt that I had lost something very precious. You were very calm and composed during the Service and said your words with such conviction that I knew everything was all right.*
>
> *I am so glad you wrote and told Mummy that you think the long wait before your engagement and the long time before the wedding was for the best. I was rather afraid you thought I was being hard-hearted about it. I was so anxious for you to come to South Africa, as you knew. Our family, us four, the Royal Family must remain together, with additions of course*

at suitable moments!! I have watched you grow up all these years with pride under the skilful direction of Mummy, who as you know is the most marvellous person in the world in my eyes, and I can, I know, always count on you, and now Philip, to help in our work.

Your leaving us has left a great blank in our lives, but do remember that your old home is still yours and do come back to it as much and as often as possible. I can see that you are sublimely happy with Philip which is right, but don't forget us is the wish of

Your ever loving and devoted, Papa

Although years later she remembers the grand ball most vividly, Pamela Mountbatten was also moved by the wedding ceremony. The day itself, she says, passed in a happy blur. Her impression of the royal couple – both related to her – was of two people caught in a fairy tale.

'Philip was the fairy prince,' she said. 'Handsomer than a fairy prince because he was so masculine. And she, with that marvellous complexion, had absolute star quality. With the golden coach and beautiful horses, it was a kind of vision. It poured with rain but the crowd, in that very British way, ignored it and queued all night to get a place. Standing on the balcony afterwards, seeing the enormous crowd rush up to the gates of the palace, was an incredible feeling.'

She recalls the youngest bridesmaid, Princess Alexandra (the bride's cousin, aged twelve), running around boisterously while the older ones pretended to be appalled. Princess Margaret, being the chief bridesmaid, 'bossed' the others around and Queen Juliana of the Netherlands 'chuntered at how dirty everyone's jewellery was'.

To mark the day, Prince Philip gave the bridesmaids a silver and rose-gold powder compact that he had designed himself. In one of the very few interviews she ever gave, Lady Elizabeth Longman recalled Prince Philip's brusque way of giving the generous gift as if he was embarrassed, which he almost certainly was. Philip, she said, 'dealt them out like playing cards. When we compared them, we were very chuffed to see that each one was slightly different but with the initials E and P.'

Pamela Mountbatten added: 'Mine has six little sapphires down the middle. I used to have it in my bag all the time, but suddenly it's no longer safe when you're going on the bus or Tube or walking the streets.' However, she says the biggest let-down of the wedding day was when Prince Baudouin, heir to the Belgian throne, refused to join the bridesmaids at Ciro's nightclub, which was where the party moved on to. 'He was the only other young person around. We all thought: "Tall, dark and a future king." But he played safe. We thought he was stuffy beyond words for not coming.'

David Milford Haven, Philip's socialite cousin and best man, had decided on Ciro's because most of his friends wouldn't have been seen dead there and he thought the bridesmaids, being so young and unsophisticated, would feel more comfortable in its cosy interior.

As the newly-weds came hand in hand down the great curved staircase of Buckingham Palace to head off for their honeymoon, they were showered with rose petals. Outside, an open landau with two horses waited to take them to Waterloo station to catch the train to Broadlands in Hampshire, the home of Earl Mountbatten. Tucked under the plaid rugs and a couple of hot-water bottles, was the furry form of the Queen's pet corgi, Susan, who was to spend their honeymoon with them. The guests chased the carriage to the front gates of the palace quadrangle, and even the Queen picked up her skirts and ran to the railings to watch them disappear into the cheering crowds, who had waited so long.

The start of the honeymoon was not an outstanding success. The press did everything in their considerable powers to snatch photographs of the newly-weds. When they arrived at Romsey station, they were followed all eleven miles to the gates of the Broadlands estate. The Mountbattens were away in India, having overseen Partition there, and in their absence things were not run entirely smoothly. On the Sunday morning, when the couple arrived for the service at Romsey Abbey, photographers were so anxious to get a picture they placed stepladders against the walls to look through the windows into the abbey. It was a baptism of fire for the royal couple, but once they were at Birkhall in Scotland, they were left on their own in the most romantic setting possible.

The princess wrote to her mother telling her how happy she was, but also to say she realised how many changes marriage would bring to her life. She wanted to ask her mother's advice on how to deal with her husband's free spirit and the tradition of the old-fashioned formalities of the Court. 'Philip is terribly independent,' she wrote, 'and I quite understand the poor darling wanting to start off properly without everything being done [underlined] for us.' She knew it would be difficult for them both, with him so used to doing what he wanted, to be tied to a suite of rooms in a huge, old-fashioned palace where everything was subject to endless protocol. She already knew he found many of the courtiers pompous, ridiculously conservative and stuffy, while they in turn found him abrasive and rude. Clearly, it had to be looked at as a long-term strategy if he was to earn the respect his position demanded.

'It is so lovely and peaceful just now,' the princess continued with her letter. 'Philip is reading full length on the sofa, Susan is stretched out before the fire, Rummy is fast asleep in his box beside the fire, and I am busy writing this in one of the armchairs near the fire (you see how important the fire is!). It's heaven up here!'

'It was bitterly cold with heavy snow, but big log fires kept the house cosy,' Philip's valet John Dean remembered. Dean and the princess's maid, Bobo MacDonald, were thrown together by their position and Dean says he greatly enjoyed her company once she had 'thawed': 'She was a lovely dancer and very good fun with a nice sense of humour. But even when we were staying in some village and were out socially in the local pub, she always addressed me as Mr Dean.'

Bobo's presence in Prince Philip's life was much more of a problem. Philip and Lilibet were young lovers and wanted the privacy frequently denied them. The princess was used to being surrounded by staff and often ignored their presence, but Philip was not. He resented not being able to be alone with his wife when he wanted to be and did not expect to find Bobo at her mistress's side at all times, even when she was in the bathroom.

'Life at court was very frustrating for him at first,' explained Patricia Mountbatten's husband, Lord Brabourne. 'It was very stuffy. [Tommy] Lascelles [private secretary to the King] was impossible. They were bloody to him. They patronised him. They treated him as an outsider. It wasn't much fun. He laughed it off, of course, but it must have hurt. I'm not sure Princess Elizabeth noticed it. She probably didn't see it. In a way marriage hardly changed her life at all. She was able to carry on much as before. In getting married she didn't sacrifice anything. His life changed completely. He gave up everything.'

The prince couldn't escape from the royal protocol, as they even had to live with his in-laws at Buckingham Palace while Clarence House was being refurbished. The old guard at the palace found him difficult, but more than that, they worried he would not treat the princess with the sensitivity they felt she deserved and needed.

According to Rabbi Arthur Herzberg, a distinguished American writer who has spoken at length to Philip: 'He has lost his real identity. He once told me he thinks of himself as a cosmopolitan European.' Pamela Mountbatten confirmed that it was a problem for him: 'He knew he was going into the lions' den. He was very conscious of the way he'd been treated and how hard he would have to fight for his position and his independence [against the establishment]. What he didn't know was just how fearsome it was going to be.'

To help, the couple picked a small but loyal team. Jock Colville, diplomat and former Downing Street assistant private secretary to Neville Chamberlain, Churchill and Clement Attlee between 1939 and 1945, was recommended by Lascelles and became private secretary to Princess Elizabeth until 1949. But Philip chose Australian Mike Parker as his private secretary and he also became an equerry to the couple. The comptroller and treasurer to the Edinburgh household was Sir Frederick 'Boy' Browning, who was married to the novelist Daphne du Maurier and was the former chief of staff to Louis Mountbatten.

At that time, the establishment was certainly able to wield great personal influence, with problems often fixed over a few large whiskies or a rubber of bridge. Problems were seldom discussed openly, but solutions would be quietly found. Establishment figures were discreet, unruffled and unobtrusively powerful. They never admitted to mistakes, never complained of one another, never resigned and were never proved wrong. Prince Philip did not fit into this world one little bit. 'If one of the establishment aristocrats had married the Queen,' the former Bishop of London Richard Charteris observed, 'it would have bored everybody out of their minds. Whatever Philip might be, he was never going to be boring.'

Their first year of marriage, living at Buckingham Palace, was not easy, but eventually Clarence House became available. 'It was a shambles,' Mike Parker remembered. 'But it was got together very quickly, and they furnished it with a lot of their wedding presents.' After his turbulent childhood, it was the first proper home Prince Philip had ever had. He had finally found real happiness and stability with the woman he loved, but it was to be short-lived.

Chapter 2

CHILDHOOD CONTRASTS

Princess Elizabeth, the future Queen of England, and Prince Philip of Greece were born in an age when it was almost unthinkable for a member of any of the royal families of Europe to marry a commoner. Princes married princesses, royal cousins married royal cousins. When Queen Victoria married her first cousin, twenty-year-old Prince Albert of Saxe-Coburg and Gotha in 1840, a dynasty came into being that linked the thrones of Britain, Denmark, Greece and Russia with the Grand Duchies of Prussia.

Princess Elizabeth arrived in the world at 2.40am in 17 Bruton Street on 21 April 1926 in the heart of London's Mayfair. At the time, London was the largest, most polluted and dirtiest city in the world with a population of nearly 8 million. Sheep were still allowed in Hyde Park, their fleeces covered with soot from the smoke-filled air, but they kept the grass under control and shepherds competed to be allowed to graze their woolly flocks in the London parks.

The British aristocracy, with their fine, large houses and estates, enjoyed immense privilege, and although the First World War had altered the domestic class structure, their lives still revolved around the sporting calendar. In Mayfair, most of the five-storey houses were privately owned and boasted magnificent ballrooms. They usually stood empty during the shooting and hunting seasons – the furniture covered with dust sheets only to be brought to life again during the London season. The smartest department stores were Harrods, which boasted a magnificent food hall and whose present building was completed in 1905, and Selfridges, which opened in 1909. Despite this, there were very few grand hotels, such as the Savoy and the Ritz, with the Grosvenor House not opening until 1929. The little princess learnt to ice skate there aged seven as they had a skating rink in the Great Room, the mechanics of which are still in place below.

The house where the princess was born was the London home of her grandparents, the Earl and Countess of Strathmore, who also owned a Scottish estate (Glamis Castle) and a country house in Walden Bury, Hertfordshire. The pillared, double-fronted house in Bruton Street no longer exists, but opposite, at number 10, the 1930s façade of Norman Hartnell's showrooms bears testimony to the grandeur of the area.

At the time, a pint of milk cost 3d and the average house cost just £619 as opposed to £290,000 today. In an era when most people smoked, a packet of twenty cigarettes cost less than a shilling. The big craze of the year was newspaper crosswords, as after the *Sunday Express* began to print them in 1924 the other papers soon caught on. 'It would be a little unwise even for superior folks to affect any marked degree of scorn for the present crossword puzzle craze. After all, the vocabularies of most of us are rather uncomfortably limited,' the *Yorkshire Observer* wrote.

The British public were also hooked on reading exciting thrillers and detective stories, with *Daily Express* writer Edgar Wallace the most popular author of the time. No fewer than eighteen Wallace novels appeared that year, and in the second half of 1926 his sales topped an incredible 750,000. Among his devotees were King George V and Prime Minister Stanley Baldwin. Wallace was a celebrity of the age and his views were sought on a wide range of issues. 'Simply monstrous' was how he described in the *Daily Express* the government's introduction of a betting tax in November.

The year came to an end with the British Broadcasting Company becoming the British Broadcasting Corporation on 1 January 1927. The first broadcast was a Happy New Year Ball, beginning with the tune 'The More We Are Together'. At the theatre, opening nights were strictly black-tie affairs, with ladies in evening gowns, and even in many middle-class homes, the family was expected to change for dinner into black tie and were waited upon.

However, not everyone lived such privileged lifestyles. There was also desperate social unrest and, twelve days after the royal princess was born, there was a general strike for the first time in British history. The strike, which bought the country to a standstill, was precipitated by the government's withdrawal of subsidy to the coal industry and a dispute between the mine owners and the miners against a proposed reduction in their wages at a time when the whole country relied on coal.

Many people, including King George V, had some sympathies with the miners and how they had been treated by the owners, but for a while there seemed to be a serious threat to public order. People pulled together to do the essential tasks that the strikers had abandoned, such as unloading food ships at the docks, conducting and driving buses and so on. Meanwhile, society girls acted as waitresses to help feed the stand-in workforce.

It was into this world of social unrest and unemployment on one hand and immense privilege on the other that the princess was born. Her father, the Duke of York, was the second eldest of four brothers, the sons of King George V and Queen Mary, and second in line to the throne. Her mother, Lady Elizabeth Bowes-Lyon, was the daughter of the Earl and Countess of Strathmore, and one of those wonderful people who light up a room with their energy when they enter. Elizabeth had at first refused the duke's proposal of marriage, anxious she would not enjoy the rigours of royal life, but he was persistent and she finally accepted. On 26 April 1923, she became the first commoner in 300 years to marry into the royal family.

Almost three years later to the day, the duchess went into labour on a dark and dismal April night, with the rain lashing at the windows of the upstairs bedroom, which had been converted into an operating theatre for the birth. The doctors in attendance were Sir Henry Simpson and Walter Jagger and, in the early hours of the morning of 21 April, Sir Henry decided to perform a Caesarean section as the baby was in the breech position. As was the custom then, Home Secretary Sir William Joynson-Hicks was present and sent a message to the Lord Mayor of London to advise him of the imminent birth. Nothing was mentioned about the Caesarean.

A few hours later, it was officially announced that 'Her Royal Highness the Duchess of York was safely delivered of a Princess at 2.40am this morning'. The Court Circular recorded that the King and Queen, who were in residence at Windsor, 'received with great pleasure the news that the Duchess of York gave birth to a daughter this morning'.

Many of the national newspapers were able to run the news of the birth as part of their headline news the same day and the *Morning Post* reported the scene: 'Outside the big grey façade of 17 Bruton Street a crowd stood, oblivious of the heavy showers of rain, waiting . . . Presently a neat, efficient nurse came and looked down into the street. The upturned faces must have all asked a question, for it was with a nod and the most reassuring smile that the owner of the uniform withdrew.'

'I must have been one of the first people outside members of the family to see the princess,' recalls Mabell, Countess of Airlie, in her memoirs. 'I called at 17 Bruton Street on 22 April, the day after her birth: although I little thought then I was paying homage to the future Queen of England, for in those days there was every expectation that the Prince of Wales (who was holidaying in Biarritz) would marry within the next year or two.'

At the time of her birth, the little princess was third in line to the throne, immediately after her father and his glamorous elder brother, the Prince of Wales. Behind her were her uncles Prince Henry, who was later the Duke of Gloucester, and Prince George, later the Duke of Kent, and her aunt Mary, who became the Princess Royal.

British *Vogue* hailed the birth of the new princess, although the Prince of Wales was their biggest pin-up, with his extreme good looks winning him film-star status. He hunted with the Quorn, played polo and steeplechased; he dined at Ciro's in Paris; he danced at the Embassy Club in London and set fashions in dress in much the same way as the Duchess of Cambridge does today. His plus fours, Prince of Wales checks, Fair Isle sweaters and Breton berets and straw boaters all helped the fashion business and, added to that, his expressions of sympathy for the unemployed made him even more popular.

The Yorks, by contrast, represented domestic bliss. According to *Vogue*, the duchess's dictum – 'I want her to be a frilly baby' – had been taken up by nannies throughout Mayfair at the time of the princess's birth. An approved account by a former member of the household bears testimony to this, when the author describes the baby princess's wardrobe changes. 'White frocks for the morning. For the afternoons – a waisted frock with a simple bodice, short sleeves and the all-important little skirt composed of tiny flouncy frills. Londoners were charmed to catch glimpses of her driving in the park in a pink frock with an old-world sun-bonnet and gravely holding above her head the smallest of pink parasols.'

Like most small children, she was fond of animals and when she was tiny played with her grandmother Lady Strathmore's two chows, whom she loved to stroke and would clap and chuckle, beating her heels on the floor when she saw them. Her other greatest delight was to pat her father's large hunters and see him ride away in his hunting kit from Naseby Hall in Northamptonshire. The duke and duchess took this house for the hunting season and the princess spent much of the winter there with her nanny, Clare Knight, in attendance. She also loved her grandfather King George V's grey parrot Charlotte and used to select lumps of sugar to give to the bird while her grandfather was ill.

Later, when the duke and duchess moved from the Strathmore residence in Bruton Street to their own home at 145 Piccadilly, the soot-covered nursery windows held a great fascination for the little princess. Not only could she see the working horses pulling their heavy carts outside, but when she heard the clop of multiple hooves, she knew she would catch sight of the soldiers and horses threading their way under the arch that led to Constitution Hill.

Her christening took place on 29 May in the private chapel at Buckingham Palace, which was later destroyed by a bomb. It was presided over by Archbishop of York Cosmo Gordon Lang, and her godparents were Lady Elphinstone (her aunt); Arthur, Duke of Connaught (great-great-uncle); Queen Mary and King George V (paternal grandparents); the Earl of Strathmore (maternal grandfather); and Princess Mary, Viscountess Lascelles (aunt). The occasion was described by Mabell Airlie, who was in attendance to Queen Mary as one of her ladies of the bedchamber on that day: 'She was a lovely baby although she cried so much all through the ceremony that immediately after it her old-fashioned nurse [Clara Knight] dosed her well from a bottle of dill water – to the surprise of the modern young mothers present and to the amusement of her uncle, the Prince of Wales.'

The baby was named Elizabeth Alexandra Mary – after her mother, her great grandmother and her grandmother – and she wore the gown of cream satin Honiton lace that had been worn by all of Queen Victoria's nine children and subsequently by every royal child until 2004. She was baptised with water from the River Jordan, which had been sent from the Holy Land for the christening. The bottle of holy water was delivered by Mabell Airlie to Bruton Street the day after the general strike ended, and she had to push through the crowds outside to gain entrance. 'There are always a few people waiting to see her,' the Duke of York told her when she finally got through, 'but there have never been so many as today.'

It was a pattern that was to last her whole life. But in the 1920s and for much of the 1930s, the idea that Princess Elizabeth might become Queen was hardly considered, least of all by the Yorks, who were looking forward to gradually expanding their family. They expected to be pushed down the line of succession by the children from any union the Prince of Wales might make, little realising what was to come.

Although Prince Philip once described himself as 'a discredited Balkan prince of no particular merit or distinction', the blood in his veins is royal on both his mother and father's side and they could claim royal connections going back generations. Both he and Princess Elizabeth were great-great-grandchildren of Queen Victoria and as such were distant cousins. Philip's father, Prince Andrea, was the son of King George I of Greece, a Prince of Denmark who had been handed the Greek throne. The family were Danish rather than Greek, if they were anything, though it would be more accurate to describe him as a member of the inter-related tribe of German princelings who had come to occupy many of the thrones of Europe. One of the King's sisters, Alexandra, married the Prince of Wales, later King Edward VII, and another married Alexander III, the Emperor of Russia. Philip's mother, Princess Alice of Battenberg, was born in the Tapestry Room at Windsor Castle in the presence of her great-grandmother Queen Victoria and died some eighty-four years later at Buckingham Palace.

Prince Philip's father was tall, handsome and intelligent and an officer in the Greek army. He had four brothers who loved playing practical jokes on each other. Prince Philip recalled: 'Anything could happen when you got a few of them together. It was like the Marx brothers.'

When Philip's parents got engaged in 1903, the Prince and Princess of Wales (later King George V and Queen Mary) gave a party for them at Marlborough House in London attended by King Edward VII, who declared that 'no throne in Europe was too good for Alice'. Their wedding in the Grand Duchy of Hesse-Darmstadt, the ancestral home of the Battenbergs, was a lavish affair that October, attended by royalty from across Europe, including Queen Alexandra of England and a great gathering of European grand dukes, princes and princesses.

For days before the ceremony, there were spectacular parties in Darmstadt. Tsar Nicholas II of Russia brought the Russian Imperial Choir with him from St Petersburg to entertain the congregation. At the Russian Orthodox ceremony, the second of three the couple went through, Alice, who had been born profoundly deaf, misheard the questions. She said 'no' instead of 'yes' when asked if she freely agreed to the marriage and said 'yes' instead of 'no' when asked if she had promised her hand to another. Although she could lip read, on this occasion she was thwarted by the voluminous facial hair of the Russian priest.

The formalities completed, there was a family banquet at which Tsar Nicholas over-indulged himself to such an extent that he hit Alice in the face with a satin shoe as she drove away in the royal carriage. She managed to catch the shoe and hit the Tsar over the head with it, leaving him in the road roaring with laughter.

After a brief honeymoon in Schloss Heiligenberg, one of several castles the Battenberg family owned, the couple sailed to Greece on the royal yacht *Amphitrite*. Alice was now a member of the Greek royal family, although she had never set foot in Greece, having been brought up with her parents in England. After a short stay in the royal palaces in Athens, Alice and Andrea moved to Corfu.

Their family home was called Mon Repos, a substantial villa built in the classical style in the 1820s by the British High Commissioner, Sir Frederick Adam, for his Greek wife. Although lacking in services such as gas and electricity, it was a palatial home by the standards of Corfu. Standing in grounds thick with orange and lemon trees and gardens scented with eucalyptus and pines with views across the Ionian Sea, it would eventually be inherited by Andrea from his father in 1913. He referred to Mon Repos as his 'royal chateau'.

The island was Homer's 'beautiful and rich land' and Odysseus's last stop on his journey home to Ithaca. Mon Repos is on the Kanoni Peninsula south of Corfu town on the site of the ancient capital, Corcyra. The residence is shabby but the rooms are beautifully proportioned and it is not hard to imagine how lovely it once was. A small plaque on the outside gates is all there is to say it was the birthplace of Prince Philip, as the interior is now a museum and the dining room where he was supposed to have been born is empty, apart from a few glass cases with displays on the history of the Mon Repos estate.

Andrea and Alice had four daughters between 1905 and 1914 before, after a gap of seven years, Prince Philip was born on 28 May 1921 (later adjusted to 10 June when Greece adopted the Gregorian calendar). The family doctor decreed that the dining-room table was the most suitable place in the house for the delivery. As an officer in the Greek army, Andrea was away fighting the Turks at the time of the birth, so Philip's first few months were spent in the company of adoring females who doted on him.

The housekeeper, Agnes Blower, when interviewed many years later, said that Philip with his blue eyes and blond hair was 'the sweetest, prettiest baby'. She added that the family were 'as poor as church mice'. Perhaps her memory was failing, as Andrea employed (in addition to the housekeeper) an English nanny, Miss Roose, a Greek cook, an English couple and some local footmen. While the four daughters were growing up, there was also a French governess. Even in exile years later, Andrea had a valet serving him until his dying day. The house was well stocked with baby food and clothes, which Nanny Roose ordered from London.

Philip was three months old when he made his first visit to England with his mother and sisters. In spite of the long journey, they wanted to attend the funeral of Philip's maternal grandfather, Admiral of the Fleet Prince Louis of Battenberg, by then the Marquis of Milford Haven. The family travelled by train to London from Athens via Rome and Paris. Nanny Roose, a maid for Alice and Andrea's valet made up the party.

The family may have lived in relatively straitened circumstances, but there were always funds for travel. One month later in Corfu, Andrea, back from the front, summoned the local mayor to Mon Repos for the official registration of Philip's birth. With the Queen Mother Olga of Greece as his godmother, he was given the name of 'Philippos' in the registry of births. This was followed by a formal christening in the Orthodox church in Corfu City. Cheering crowds lined the streets leading to the church where a band played and the city officials watched the baby Philip being immersed in the font.

In July 1922, the family and their entourage travelled to London again for the wedding of Alice's younger brother Lord Louis Mountbatten (Uncle Dickie to Philip) to the heiress Edwina Ashley. The grand wedding took place at St Margaret's, Westminster, with the glamorous Prince of Wales as best man and King George V leading the congregation of royalty from all across Europe. All four of Philip's sisters were bridesmaids, dressed in white and delphinium blue. Philip was deemed too young to attend and remained with Nanny Roose at Spencer House where they were all staying.

But this relatively settled life was about to be thrown into chaos, as the ongoing Greco-Turkish War was about to take a decisive turn after three years of fighting in the aftermath of the First World War. One month later, the Greek forces were routed by the Turks at Smyrna. Greek casualties were heavy and more than a million Greeks became refugees.

The earlier Greek advance, in which Andrea had participated, had turned into a crushing Turkish victory, and by the autumn of 1922 the Greeks had been driven out of Asia Minor, so ending a presence there which dated back 2500 years. Smyrna, the main Greek town on the Asian mainland, was sacked, and a young Aristotle Onassis was among those who escaped and he fled to Argentina to start his own meteoric social climb.

Meanwhile, there had been growing opposition to the war in Greece, and immediately after the fall of Smyrna the nation rose in revolution. Prince Andrea was arrested, charged with treason and faced death by firing squad, a fate that had befallen several of his fellow officers.

'How many children do you have?' Greece's new military leader, General Theodoros Pangalos, asked his royal prisoner.

'Five,' Andrea replied.

'Poor little orphans,' the general said.

The only advantage Andrea had at that time was that he was a relation of the British royal family, and that might have proved no advantage at all had George V not been consumed by the memory of what had happened to his other royal relations, the Romanovs, three years earlier. As Marion Crawford, governess of Philip's future wife, made a point of explaining, history is 'the doings not of a lot of dusty lay figures in the past, but of real people with all their problems and bothers'. Even if Crawfie did not apprise the young Elizabeth of the fatal part her grandfather had played in their tragic outcome, the King himself was all too aware.

In February 1917, Russia had fallen to the Bolsheviks and Tsar Nicholas II had been deposed. He was George V's first cousin (their mothers were sisters); the two men knew each other well and were on friendly terms, sometimes meeting and frequently exchanging letters. They even looked alike. 'Exactly like a skinny Duke of York [the future George V] – the image of him,' one of Queen Victoria's ladies-in-waiting once observed of Nicholas. When Nicholas appealed to his cousin for asylum in Britain, George V made it his personal business to ensure that it was refused. Where would he stay, the King wanted to know? And who was going to pay for his upkeep?

The prime minister, David Lloyd George, had initially offered the imperial family the sanctuary they sought. The King, however, aware of the social instability and the corresponding upsurge in republicanism the First World War had generated in Britain, was concerned that Nicholas would bring Russia's revolutionary chaos with him. Sacrificing family blood on the altar of expediency, he ordered his private secretary, Lord Stamfordham, to write to the foreign secretary, Lord Balfour: 'The residence in this country of the ex-Emperor and his Empress ... would undoubtedly compromise the position of the King and Queen.'

The offer was duly withdrawn, and on 16 July 1918 Tsar Nicholas, his wife Alexandra, their four daughters and their young son were shot and bayoneted to death in a cellar in Ekaterinburg in the Urals. There is no record of George V having expressed sorrow, much less contrition, at his own role in the tragedy.

But now another royal relation – and one who also had a wife, four daughters and a young son – was facing execution. It was a matter the King could not ignore. Andrea, like the murdered Tsar, was also a first cousin; his father, George I of Greece, was the brother of George and Nicholas's mothers. There were other connections. As we have seen, Andrea's wife was the daughter of the former First Sea Lord, the first Marquis of Milford Haven. Alice was a first cousin once removed of George V himself.

As part of the Greek royal family and an officer of the Greek army, Andrea had to accept a large part of the responsibility for the final disaster that seemed set to befall him and his family. During the hostilities with Turkey in 1921, he was a major-general with command of a division stationed in Asia Minor. His troops, he declared, were 'riff-raff', his officers useless, the high command incapable. His assessment was accurate but hardly diplomatic. Nor was it the height of military professionalism to disobey the clear and direct order to advance and instead ask to be relieved of his command. When Smyrna fell and the royal family were again ousted – a regular occurrence since they had first been invited onto the throne of Greece in 1863 – Andrea provided the new military rulers with a made-to-measure scapegoat with his actions the year before. He was arrested, tried and sentenced by a jury of junior officers who, said Princess Alice, 'had previously decided that he must be shot'.

George V had been prepared to leave the Romanovs to their fate, but the idea of allowing another batch of close relations to fall to the executioner's blade or bullet clearly proved too much to stomach, even for a monarch as imperious as this. Following appeals by Princess Alice through her younger brother, Louis, the future Earl Mountbatten of Burma, the King personally ordered that his incautious relation was for saving.

Commander Gerald Talbot, Britain's former naval attaché in Athens, now employed as a secret agent in Geneva, was duly dispatched, in disguise and travelling under false papers, to open negotiations with Pangalos. Things did not go well until the cruiser HMS *Calypso* sailed in, her guns raised, to help concentrate the military government's thoughts. Which it did: while Andrea's fellow officers were duly being executed, he was driven to the harbour by Pangalos himself and put aboard the *Calypso*, where his wife was waiting for him.

The warship then steamed to Corfu to pick up eighteen-month-old Philip and his four sisters. The family seemed quite philosophical about being exiled, 'for they frequently are', as the *Calypso*'s captain, Herbert Buchanan-Wollaston, observed. Philip's sister, Princess Sophie, eight at the time, was not so sanguine. She later recalled her abiding memory of leaving Mon Repos was the smell of smoke from the grates in every fireplace. Alice had ordered her daughters to burn everything: letters, papers and documents and leave nothing behind.

'It was a terrible business, absolute chaos,' she later recalled. The crossing to Brindisi in Italy was a rough one and the family, along with their Greek lady-in-waiting, French governess and English nanny, were all seasick.

Once ashore they took the train from Brindisi to Rome and then to Paris. Philip spent much of the journey crawling around on the floor, blackening himself from head to toe and even licking the windowpanes. His mother tried to restrain him, but Nanny Roose – 'A divine person, much nicer than all the other nannies, we adored her,' Princess Sophie recalled – kindly advised, 'Leave him alone.' From Paris, the family took the boat train across the English Channel and arrived in London, where they were given temporary shelter in Kensington Palace by Alice's mother, the Dowager Countess of Milford Haven.

Thus, Philip left Greece for good at the age of eighteen months. He never lived there again and never learned to speak Greek, although as a young man he signed his name 'Philip of Greece'. In reply to his official biographer Basil Boothroyd's question about spending his childhood in the unsettled and unhappy circumstances of exile, Prince Philip dismissed it: 'I don't think it necessarily was particularly unhappy. It wasn't all that unsettled.'

As far as he was concerned, he lacked for nothing and accepted his nomadic existence as completely normal, and his parents soon set up home on the outskirts of Paris. He had a strong family unit in the shape of four adoring sisters. Later, when he went to school in England and his sisters were married, he spent the long summer holidays with them in various German castles, often with his father. As a result, Philip saw much more of his father than anyone would suppose. Until the age of nine, when he was sent to school in England and his father closed the house in Paris and his mother was committed to a hospital in Switzerland after suffering a nervous breakdown, he never felt particularly different.

He was not. In those days, many wealthy mothers were deprived of the chance to look after their children and often retired neurotic and depressed to be 'ill' in their bedrooms for years. At that time, almost everyone that could afford a private education for their children sent them away to boarding school, particularly boys. Parents who lived abroad seldom saw their offspring, except for the long summer holidays, and did not play a hands-on role in bringing them up. Children can be so adaptable, accepting what happens to them as the norm and yet still idealise the remote figures of their parents. Philip seems to have been no different, but his move to an English school was going to open up a whole new path in his life.

Chapter 3

GROWING TOGETHER APART

As King George V grew older, he became increasingly alarmed at his son and heir's behaviour. The Prince of Wales exchanged one married mistress for another and eventually took up with the most undesirable one of all – Mrs Wallis Simpson, an American divorcee. His wilful reluctance to find himself an appropriate girl-friend who would make a suitable wife inevitably focused attention on the heir presumptive, the young Princess Elizabeth. But, in the regal manner, nobody in any of the royal households broke the code of discretion and referred to the looming crisis. 'Maybe the general hope was that if nothing was said the whole business would blow over,' the princess's governess, Marion Crawford, said.

Given the increasing possibility that the princess would eventually ascend to the throne, Queen Mary believed it was vital that Elizabeth should study genealogy to understand that comedy of bloodlines descended from Queen Victoria, which provided Europe with its royal houses. She insisted that history, too, was important, as was poetry ('wonderful memory training') and a knowledge of the geography of the British Empire. But maths?

'Was arithmetic really more valuable,' the Queen wanted to know, 'than history?' Money is not a subject of practical concern to the royal family, so Elizabeth, the Queen observed with telling foresight, would probably never have to do her own household accounts. Crawfie took note. 'Queen Mary's practical suggestions were most welcome and I revised the schoolroom schedule for Princess Elizabeth accordingly.'

Whether the Duchess of York ever knew about this, and if she did, whether she cared, is not recorded. The answer in both cases is probably not. The Yorks, so determinedly bourgeois in all other things, simply did not consider a full and rounded education a matter of any great importance for their children's welfare. 'No one ever had employers who interfered so little,' the governess noted. Fortunately, the princess was able to learn by experience. Before she was ten years old she was present at the celebration of her grandparents' Silver Jubilee in 1935 and the weddings of her uncles George Duke of Kent and Henry of Gloucester, at which she was a bridesmaid.

Of far greater concern to the Yorks was the Prince of Wales's affair with Wallis Simpson. It was a liaison scored with the hallmark of catastrophe – for the country, for the crown and most particularly for the Yorks themselves. When George V died on 20 January 1936 (by the hand of his doctor, it transpired, who killed him with a lethal injection of cocaine to ensure that the announcement of his death would make the next morning's edition of *The Times* and not the less respectable evening papers), it meant that the princess's Uncle David was now King Edward VIII. His hold on the crown, however, was less than Wallis Simpson's hold on him and later that year he would let go of his birthright 'for the woman I love'.

The Duke of York, or Bertie as he was known, afflicted with a bad stammer and frail of health, did not want to shoulder the responsibility of kingship. He did not believe he was up to it. He had not been trained for it, he complained. A number of senior government advisers agreed and, when it became clear that a new king was going to have to be found, there was a serious suggestion, recorded in 1947 'by gracious permission of His Majesty the King', by Dermot Morrah, Fellow of All Souls College, Oxford, that the crown should go to his younger brother, the sexually adventurous Duke of Kent.

'This is absolutely desperate,' Bertie cried to his cousin, the future Earl Mountbatten of Burma. 'I've never even seen a State paper.' (Another cousin, Nicholas II, expressed the same sentiments in noticeably similar words when the imperial crown of Russia came to him: 'What's going to happen to me? I'm not prepared to be a czar. I never wanted to become one. I know nothing of the business of ruling. I have no idea of even how to talk to the ministers.') The only real solution to the crisis threatening to engulf the House of Windsor was to pass the crown to the next in line, however reluctant he might be to accept it. Some order had to be made of the chaos David's ill-considered affair had caused.

When the news was broken to Bertie by his mother that the uncrowned Edward VIII had done the unthinkable and abdicated the throne in December and passed his responsibilities to him, he recalled, 'I broke down and sobbed like a child.' The Queen was highly embarrassed by this display of weakness in yet another of her sons. 'Really!' she was heard to complain in the middle of the crisis. 'This might be Rumania.'

The Duchess of York had not been quite the support she might have been as events moved towards their denouement. As the abdication approached, she retired to bed ill. Faced with a situation from which there was no retreat, however, the new Queen Consort showed her mettle. She had not wanted to be Queen, but when the role was thrust upon her she assumed its mantle with grace and natural poise. When the news came through, Margaret turned to her sister in the nursery at 145 Piccadilly and asked, 'Does that mean you will have to be the next Queen?'

'Yes, some day,' the ten-year-old Elizabeth gravely replied.

Back came the riposte: 'Poor you.'

There was a dark personal side to this apparently blossoming public face. Bertie, now transmogrified into George VI, had always been prone to tantrums, known to his family as 'gnashes'. The confusion and fear engendered by this dramatic change in his position and by the later worries caused by the war only served to exacerbate his unsteady and sometimes violent temperament. His father had been subject to similar temper fits. His married life was less than blissful, and King and Queen sometimes found it so difficult to communicate that they had to write letters to each other instead.

Late in his life, Edward VIII, then Duke of Windsor, told James Pope-Hennessy: 'Off the record, my father had a most horrible temper. He was foully rude to my mother. Why, I've seen her leave the table because he was so rude to her, and we children would all follow her out.' He then added, 'Not when staff are present, of course.' But staff have a way of finding out about such things. George V's behaviour was well-discussed in the servants' quarters, although scenes of such private unhappiness and frustration were never played out in public.

As far as it was possible to contain them, such outbursts were not allowed to intrude up onto the nursery floor. 'We want our children to have a happy childhood which they can always look back on,' Queen Elizabeth would insist. But the happy family idyll had been damaged. The family were forced to move out of 145 Piccadilly and into Buckingham Palace, a cold, impersonal building with endless corridors which could take a whole morning to navigate. Couldn't they build a tunnel back to Piccadilly, Elizabeth wistfully suggested? But this new world, with its domestic upsets and feuds and subtleties of status and inexorable duty, could not be locked out. Bath time with their parents, always such a ritual, had to be cancelled because the King and Queen, who before had spent most of their evenings at home, were now out almost every night at official functions.

Princess Margaret, then six, and the older Elizabeth could not but be aware of the tensions and the strain events had caused their father, of the way their mother, once so relaxed and easy-going, now looked drawn and older. There had also been a change in Elizabeth's own status. As a little girl, she had been taught to curtsey to her grandparents whenever she visited them. The aura of majesty had now fallen on her parents and she was instructed by Crawfie that henceforth they had to curtsey to Papa and Mummy.

'Margaret too?' Elizabeth asked.

'Margaret also,' was the answer. 'And try not to topple over.'

The King and his Queen Consort quickly put a stop to that. The princess was not in any doubt about what her position was, though – and hadn't been for some years. Elizabeth, Crawfie insisted, was a 'special' child: neat, courteous, conscientious, unusually well behaved and 'very shy'. She was aware from the earliest age, however, of just where she stood in the pecking order. Her parents wanted their daughter to feel herself a 'member of the community' but, as Crawfie remarked, 'just how difficult this is to achieve, if you live in a palace, is hard to explain. A glass curtain seems to come down between you and the outer world, between the hard realities of life and those who dwell in a court.'

When she played in Hamilton Gardens, crowds of people would often gather to peer at her through the railings, as if they were contemplating some exotic creature at the zoo. When she went for walks through Hyde Park, she was often recognised. 'Ignore them,' her nurse, Clara Knight, known as 'Allah', ordered, following her own advice and striding purposefully past the gaping onlookers, looking neither to the left nor right. With Allah as her trainer, Elizabeth's ability to completely disregard the stares of the inquisitive soon became second nature. But she knew why they were looking.

When she was seven years old, Elizabeth was addressed by the Lord Chamberlain with a cheery, 'Good morning, little lady.'

'I'm not a little lady,' came the imperious reply. 'I'm Princess Elizabeth!'

This display of regal asperity proved too much for Queen Mary, who promptly marched her granddaughter into the Lord Chamberlain's office and said, 'This is Princess Elizabeth, who one day hopes to be a lady.'

But princess she certainly was and, with her uncle gone and the likelihood of her parents producing a son and heir apparent receding with each passing year, a queen she was ever more likely to become. And the impact of that impending burden only hardened her emotional restraint. The death of George V had provoked no outward display of emotion, only the question of whether it was right that she should continue playing with her toy horses (Crawfie said it was). After she was taken to see her grandfather lying in state in Westminster Hall, she remarked: 'Uncle David was there and he never moved at all. Not even an eyelid. It was wonderful. And everyone was so quiet. As if the King were asleep.'

'She was reserved and quiet about her feelings,' Crawfie noted. And it was something the Queen herself would acknowledge in later years, when she remarked: 'I've been trained since childhood never to show emotion in public.'

The girls spent the day looking down the stairwell at the comings and goings of the prime minister and his ministers, and then rushing to the windows to stare at the thousands of people gathered outside. When a letter was delivered addressed to Her Majesty the Queen, Elizabeth turned to Lady Cynthia Asquith. '"That's Mummy now," she said, with a tremor in her awestruck voice.'

Whatever awe she felt was offset by her inherent composure and her remarkable sense of responsibility. She was not worldly and has not become so. It was never intended that she should. The practice of keeping her emotions to herself in public acquired the force of habit in private. She does not like being touched. She raises her voice rarely; anger and temperament have no part to play in this lifetime's exercise in self-control. Instead, she shows her displeasure by icy silence. If that makes her incomplete as a person — and there is an element of the child in her inability to address the sometimes-wayward behaviour of her own family — there is also a regality about her which is both reassuring and intimidating. The aura of majesty comes naturally to her. It was as if she always knew she was destined to be Queen and set about from the earliest age acquiring the necessary skills, always trying hard to do 'what she felt was expected of her'.

She did not join Margaret in those practical jokes that are such a tradition in the royal family (as long ago as 1860, Lord Clarendon was saying that he never told them his best jokes because pretending to pinch his finger in the door amused them more). When Margaret hid the gardener's rake or threatened to sound the bell at Windsor which brought out the guard, Elizabeth would hide with embarrassment. Order always had to be maintained. She was, said Crawfie, 'neat and methodical beyond words. She would sometimes get up in the middle of the night to make sure her shoes were neatly stowed.'

Self-control was essential. At the Coronation of their father in Westminster Abbey, she said of her little sister, 'I do hope she won't disgrace us all by falling asleep in the middle.' And when their parents set sail for the propaganda tour of Canada and the United States just before the outbreak of the Second World War, and Margaret told her that she had her handkerchief ready, Elizabeth sternly warned her, 'To wave, not to cry.'

Despite this emotional reserve, she was compassionate. During the war the two princesses were moved to the comparative safety of Windsor Castle. They were subjected to the occasional air raid but never to the full force of the Blitz. Even so, Elizabeth took a keen and caring interest in the welfare of those more directly affected by the carnage. When the battleship *Royal Oak* was torpedoed by a German U-boat that had slipped through the defences of the northern naval base Scapa Flow in October 1939, with the loss of 800 lives, she exclaimed: 'It can't be! All those nice sailors.' That Christmas the deaths were still on her mind, as she remarked: 'Perhaps we are too happy. I keep thinking of those sailors and what Christmas must have been like in their homes.' And when she read the name of someone she knew who had died in combat, usually an officer who had been briefly stationed at the castle, she would write to the mother 'and give her a little picture of how much she had appreciated him at Windsor and what they had talked about,' said Crawfie. 'That was entirely her own idea.' More mundanely but very much in character, she would instruct her more rumbustious sister not to point and laugh at anyone wearing a 'funny hat'.

She subscribed to Louis XIV's view that punctuality is the politeness of princes (and princesses) and was always on time. She was obedient – her only transgression of any note, apart from the occasional nursery scrap with her sister, was when she, aged seven or eight years old, turned an ornamental inkpot over the head of the mademoiselle employed to teach her French.

She was discreet. When the King flew to Italy in 1944, he told his daughter where he was going. His trip was classified as top secret and Elizabeth kept the information to herself and didn't even share it with those women – Allah, Bobo MacDonald and Crawfie – who she was so close to. She also acquired the royal family habit of banishing unpleasant thoughts and people from her mind. Uncle David was not dead, but he might as well have been. The Duke of Windsor had been particularly fond of his niece. He had been a frequent visitor to the house in Piccadilly and took a childish delight in joining her in her games, but since the abdication he had ceased to exist. 'In the palace and the castle his name was never mentioned,' Crawfie noted.

With the crown now all but certain to pass to her, her father, from the day he became George VI, started taking his daughter into his confidence, 'speaking to her as an equal'. By war's end she was attending council meetings, taking the counsel of Prime Minister Winston Churchill, and discussing the affairs of state with her father daily. Given her new status as heir to the throne, Queen Elizabeth enhanced her interest in her daughter's education and it was on her instigation that she was sent to study constitutional history under Sir Henry Marten, the vice-provost of Eton College just across the river Thames from Windsor.

Yet, for all her maturity, she remained in many ways a child. Her polished manners and grown-up conversation concealed a wealth of inexperience. Throughout her childhood and almost all of her teens, she was dressed in the same clothes as her sister, despite the fact that Margaret was four years her junior. She also shared her nursery classroom with Margaret. She never had to hone her talents on the grindstone of the competition of contemporaries of her own age.

Isolated behind that glass curtain, she enjoyed minimal social life of her own. What little she did have she left it to her mother to organise. It was not until a special Girl Guide troop was formed for her that her circle widened out to include children from beyond her own privileged background. Several Cockney evacuees from the East End joined the royal troop at Windsor and it was 'no doubt very instructive', so Crawfie remarked, for Elizabeth to mix with young-sters who did not have a 'tendency to let them have an advantage, win a game, or be relieved of the more sordid tasks', as the children of the court had.

Now, said Crawfie, 'it was each for himself'. The princess was not comfortable in this competitive environment. She liked the security of the safe and simple routine of royal life. Ever since she was a little girl, she had shared her bedroom with Bobo, the Scotswoman twenty-two years her senior who became and remained her closest friend. She found the informal intimacy of a guide camp difficult to deal with. 'She was getting older, and had been brought up so much alone, I could understand why she did not want to undress before a lot of children all of a sudden, and spend the night with them,' Crawfie said.

When it came to dealing with boys, she was even more inhibited. Boys of any kind, Crawfie remarked, were strange creatures out of another world to the princess and her young sister. But whereas Margaret was instinctively flirtatious when in the company of the opposite sex, Elizabeth, fundamentally shy, was always much more reserved in their rare company. 'That unsophisticated air of hers has always been part of her charm,' her governess remarked.

When she was under the tutelage of Sir Henry Marten in his study at Eton, his regular pupils would sometimes look in, but they, with typical Etonian insouciance, feigned not to know who she was and, after politely raising their top hats, would speedily withdraw again. Elizabeth, for her part, pretended not to notice the interruptions.

She was thirteen when war broke out, but that did not mean there were more openings for her. At the age of almost eighteen, she had not yet, her father's equerry, Group Captain Peter Townsend, noted, 'attained the full allure of an adult. She was shy, occasionally to the point of gaucheness.'

No real attempt was made to put her more at ease with young men. Miss Betty Vacani, the London dancing mistress who would also teach the next royal generation their steps, was called out to Windsor during the war to organise dance classes for the princesses. By royal instructions they were for little girls only. 'The princesses did not understand the antics of little boys, and this did not seem the moment to teach them,' Crawfie said.

Despite all that, there was one boy Elizabeth did notice, however. He was tall and blond, with 'Viking' good looks. His name was Prince Philip of Greece, and she was dazzled by him from the first moment she saw him, when she was just thirteen and he was eighteen. They were married eight years later, and he was the only man she had ever known.

It wasn't entirely inevitable that they would meet. Prince Philip's parents Andrea and Alice arrived in London from Corfu in 1922 with their five children and retinue of six servants. King George V's diary entry for 19 December reads: 'Andrea came to see me, he has just arrived from Athens where he was tried and very nearly shot.' On arrival they were given temporary shelter by the Dowager Marchioness of Milford Haven at Kensington Palace, where in later years as a schoolboy Philip maintained a base where he could keep his belongings and school trunk in the holidays.

Andrea still owned his house in Corfu while Alice had an allowance from the Mountbatten family, but by royal standards they were not well-off. However, it cannot be said that Philip's childhood was spent in impoverished circumstances; Andrea was fortunate in that he had two brothers who had married heiresses and who proved to be generous with financial assistance.

Although deprived of Greek nationality, Andrea and his family were free to travel on Danish passports. When his son William became King George I of Greece, King Christian of Denmark had insisted that his descendants maintain Danish nationality. Soon after their arrival in London, Andrea and Alice sailed to New York as guests of Andrea's brother Christopher, who had married an American tin-plate heiress complete with a yacht and homes in California and Florida. Christopher was later to provide funds for Philip's school fees. Meanwhile, Philip was left in the charge of Nanny Roose, who took him on a daily pram ride round Kensington Gardens.

Andrea's elder brother George was married to Princess Marie Bonaparte, the great-granddaughter of Napoleon's brother, whose mother had inherited a fortune from the family which founded Monte Carlo casino. George invited Andrea to bring his family to Paris, where George owned several properties. Uncle George provided a house for the family in the Paris suburb of St Cloud where Aunt Marie paid all the household expenses.

It was Nanny Roose who bore the responsibility for Philip's upbringing and had the greatest influence over him. She taught him British nursery rhymes and, despite the lack of funds, insisted on dressing him in clothes sent over from London. And she made certain that he spoke English and was brought up with English customs. 'Nobody's allowed to spank me but my own nanny,' Philip informed a friend's nanny who was about to discipline him for breaking an expensive vase. His nanny was obliged to have such a central role in his upbringing, because his mother Alice had been profoundly deaf since birth and communicated with the outside world by sign language, which Philip did learn.

Nanny Roose remained with the family until arthritis forced her to retire to the warmer climate of South Africa. In her letters to Philip's sisters, she once wrote that Philip told her that he loved her 'as much as pineapple'. In another letter that Philip wrote to 'Roosie', as he called her, he reminded her of the time one Easter morning when she told him to get up quickly as they were late. While Roosie was out of the room, Philip dressed and got back under the covers, only to spring out fully dressed when Roosie came to scold him. 'Full of fun' was how she fondly remembered him.

One of Philip's closest friends was Hélène Foufounis, at whose palatial family villa near Le Touquet Philip spent several summer holidays. Like Philip, she too eventually moved to Britain where, as Hélène Cordet, she became a London cabaret singer and nightclub owner, and remained one of his closest confidantes. 'He was like an English boy rather than a Greek or German. He had an English nanny. Everyone adored him so much, particularly my mother, because he was so good looking,' Hélène Cordet recalled.

Holidays were spent rattling across Europe by train to stay with relations, many of whom had managed to retain royal estates and lived in style. To Romania, for instance, where his aunt Missy was Queen (she wore a tiara at dinner every evening) and where Philip's cousin Queen Alexandra of Yugoslavia remembered 'our nannies all cheerfully sitting down to tea with bowls of caviar'. The young boy whose own means were straitened was allowed no such extravagance. He was trained, Alexandra says, 'to save and economise better than other children, so much so that he acquired a reputation for being mean.' Other holidays were spent in England at Lynden Manor in Berkshire, the country estate of Philip's uncle George Milford Haven. There he found a best friend in his cousin David, who years later would be best man at Philip's wedding.

'He had such unbelievable charm,' said his sister, Sophie. 'He had a tremendous sense of humour.' He was also a real boy with an adventurous, outgoing personality, fond of climbing trees, forever testing himself against the elements and his playmates. 'It was always Philip,' Alexandra said, 'who ventured out of his depth' at the seaside, 'or who rounded up other boys encountered on the beach and organised an intensive castle-building brigade.' He was given a Box Brownie and took up photography, which remained a lifetime's hobby. He had a boy's interest in motorcars.

That humour his sister mentioned was of a somewhat rumbustious kind. 'He was a great show-off, he would always stand on his head when visitors came,' one of his sisters remarked. On one occasion, when staying with another aunt, Queen Sophie of Greece, and her sister, the Landgravine of Hesse, Alexandra recalled him releasing a sty of pigs and stampeding them through the ladies' elegant garden tea party.

He could be kind-hearted. When a rich cousin, who was very taken with Philip, once bought him a toy, she cruelly said to Hélène's nine-year-old sister Ria, who was stricken with a diseased hip, 'I didn't buy you anything because you can't play.'

'Philip went very red and ran out of the room,' Hélène said. 'He came back with an armful of his own toys, and the new one, thrust them on the bed and said, "These are for you."'

Philip's early education was not notable for its classroom successes. At the age of five he was sent to The Elms, the exclusive American school in Paris. Philip rode there on a bicycle he had bought himself with savings that had started with the pound his uncle, the King of Sweden, sent him every year. His school report called him 'a rugged, boisterous boy, but always remarkably polite'.

These early years in St Cloud were happy ones, but as time went by Philip's family began a gradual dispersal. His mother became deeply obsessed with religion and eventually had to be committed to a sanatorium in 1930, while his father Andrea, for lack of anything better to do, became a socialite eventually settling in Monte Carlo. Philip's sisters gravitated towards their German relations, where they each found husbands.

When Philip was eight, George Milford Haven entered him as a boarder for Cheam School in Surrey, one of England's oldest preparatory schools, where David Milford Haven was a pupil. From that time onwards it was George and his wife who acted *in loco parentis*. George was a Cheam old boy himself and regularly attended sports days and prize-givings. George had recently left the navy to enter the world of business and became a director of several public companies. His interest in gadgets of all kinds and his inventiveness are traits that he passed on to Philip. As a young officer in the navy, George invented an automatic tea-maker to rouse him in the mornings and he air-conditioned his quarters with a system of fans. Years later, Philip went one better with the invention of a boot remover and cleaner which was commercially marketed.

Cousin Alexandra had been sent to Heathfield School near Ascot at the same time as Philip entered Cheam and they kept up a correspondence with each other. Alexandra tells of some of the high-spirited adventures Philip shared with his cousin David. On one occasion the boys cycled to a scout camp from Lynden Manor in Bray to Dover, a journey of some 120 miles. They arrived extremely saddle sore, but elated. Anxious to avoid having to ride home, they stowed away in the hold of a barge in Dover Harbour that was bound for London docks. They spent two nights sleeping on sacks of grain and lived off some rock cakes they had bought with them.

At Cheam, Philip excelled at sports. He won the school diving competition, came equal first in the high jump, won the under-12 hurdles and became a promising cricketer. Although he showed a keen interest in history, he did not shine academically at all. He did win the Form III French prize, but as his cousin Alexandra told him, so he should have, 'after all the years he had lived in Paris'. In common with similar schools of the day, life for the boys was tough, with cold baths, bad food, hard beds and the cane for punishment. Philip believed his regime to be character forming, and in due course sent his son Prince Charles to Cheam, where he had an unhappy time.

When Philip turned twelve it was time to move from Cheam. He might have been expected to enter one of the great fee-paying schools in England, but the German side of his family intervened. His sister Theodora had married Berthold, the Margrave of Baden, in 1931. Her father-in-law Prince Max of Baden, the last Imperial Chancellor of Germany, had founded Salem School with the help of his personal secretary, Dr Kurt Hahn, in 1920 in his family home in Germany. By 1933, when Philip arrived, there were 420 pupils, and Salem was considered one of the finest schools in Europe.

The curriculum was rigorous, being based on physical fitness and self-reliance, and Theodora succeeded in persuading the Milford Havens that Philip should go to Salem.

But the timing could not have been worse. In January of that year, Hitler had come to power as chancellor, and the Nazis quickly established control over every aspect of life there. Soon Kurt Hahn, a Jew, was in trouble with the authorities. The Nazis could not allow a Jew to educate the youth of Germany, so he was arrested and imprisoned. Influential people from all over Europe, including British Prime Minister Ramsay MacDonald, petitioned Hitler to set Hahn free. As a result, he was allowed to emigrate to Britain where he set about establishing a new school in Scotland – Gordonstoun.

Philip lasted less than a year at Salem. He got into trouble for mocking the Nazi salute and when the Hitler Youth began to infiltrate the school, Theodora agreed he should return to England and Gordonstoun. The school was in its infancy when Philip arrived in the autumn term of 1934. There were only twenty-six pupils, but such were Hahn's abilities that the numbers grew to 156 by the time Philip left in 1939.

Hahn took an immediate liking to Philip. 'When Philip came to the school,' he wrote, 'his most marked trait was his undefeatable spirit . . . his laughter was heard everywhere . . . In his schoolwork he showed a lively intelligence. In community life, once he had made a task his own, he showed meticulous attention to detail and pride of workmanship which was never content with mediocre results.'

It was Hahn's belief that every pupil should learn seamanship and the subject Philip enjoyed most was sailing under the guidance of a retired naval officer, Commander Lewty, who led expeditions to the Shetland Islands and to the coast of Norway. Among Philip's duties on board was that of ship's cook. It was said he had a heavy hand with the butter when making scrambled eggs, but an interest in cooking and food has remained with him for the rest of his life. Not only did Philip greatly enjoy his days at Gordonstoun, he has given full credit to Hahn for the Duke of Edinburgh's Award Scheme. He said: 'It was Hahn's idea though not in all its details. I would never have started it but for Hahn, certainly not. He suggested I ought to do it and I fought against it for quite a long time.'

The situation on mainland Europe continued to develop. In 1935, the monarchy was restored in Greece. As part of the arrangements that followed, the bodies of the royal family who had died in exile were returned to Greece for reburial in the family vault. For this ceremony of state, Philip was given leave of absence from Gordonstoun and joined his extended family in Athens, where he saw his mother and father together for the first time since he had left St Cloud. He spent time with his mother, who had settled into a house in Athens where she remained throughout the war, dressed always in her nun's habit. There was a great gathering in Athens of all branches of the royal house of Greece. Cousin Alexandra reported that Philip wanted to know exactly who was who and that he was surprised to learn that he was third in line of succession to King George II of Greece, who was back on the throne after being deposed in 1924. Andrea was pressed to enter Philip for the Greek Naval College but would not contemplate it on account of the treatment he had received when banished from Greece; Philip's future, it appeared, lay in England.

There was further trauma in Philip's life when, in April 1938, Hahn had to break the news to Philip that George Milford Haven had died of cancer at the age of forty-five. His death had a profound effect on Philip's life as his uncle Lord Louis 'Dickie' Mountbatten, the younger brother of Milford Haven, stepped in to take George's place as a friend and adviser.

That summer, the year before Philip left Gordonstoun, he spent the holidays in Venice with cousin Alexandra as the guest of her mother Aspasia, widow of King Alexander of Greece. Aspasia was under strict instructions from Andrea to keep Philip out of trouble. The summer was a continuous round of parties and Philip was showered with invitations. There was no shortage of lovely young things eager for Philip to escort them home at the end of the evening. In the words of Alexandra: 'Blondes, brunettes and redhead charmers, Philip gallantly and, I think, quite impartially, squired them all.'

It is probable that Philip first fell in love that summer in Venice. The object of his affections was Cobina Wright, a beautiful American debutante, who won the title of Miss Manhattan the following year. For three weeks Philip escorted Cobina around Venice, followed by a week in London dining and dancing. When she returned to New York, Philip vowed to follow her one day to America, but it never happened. In 1973, in a *Town and Country* magazine interview, Cobina confirmed that she had met Philip in Venice and that she had photographs in her bedroom of the three loves of her life, one of them being Philip. She said they were still good friends and wrote to each other often.

In his final year at school, Philip rose to be head boy or 'guardian', he captained the cricket XI and the hockey team and represented Gordonstoun at the Scottish Schools Athletics championship. He wrote to Alexandra about Uncle Dickie having the fastest lift in London and a dining room that could turn into a cinema in his house in Upper Brook Street where Philip sometimes stayed in the holidays. Dickie was already part-way through a hugely successful naval career, and it was on his bidding that Philip took the entry exam to Dartmouth Royal Naval College.

Kurt Hahn's leaving report for Philip in 1939 was highly complimentary. He wrote: 'Prince Philip is universally trusted, liked and respected. He has the greatest sense of service of all the boys in the school. He is a born leader, but will need the exacting demands of a great service to do justice to himself. His best is outstanding; his second best is not good enough. He will make his mark in any profession where he will have to prove himself in a full trial of strength . . . His public spirit is exemplary; his sense of justice never failing; he demonstrated unusual courage and endurance in the face of discomforts and hardships; he had the making of a first-class organiser and was both kind and firm; his physical endurance was quite outstanding.'

Prince Philip's enthusiasm for Gordonstoun was no less complimentary. He said: 'I must confess I enjoyed my days at Gordonstoun. I would like as many boys as possible to enjoy their schooldays as much as I did.' Years later, Prince Philip, as Chancellor of Edinburgh University, when making Kurt Hahn an Honorary Doctor of Law, added: 'It cannot be given to many to have the opportunity and desire to heap honours upon their former headmasters.'

To prepare for the Dartmouth entrance examination, on Uncle Dickie's advice, Philip went to stay with the Mercers, a retired naval officer and his wife, in Cheltenham. During several weeks of extreme cramming, his hosts found him hard-working, eager to get on and quite without 'side'. He passed the examination sixteenth of the thirty-four entrants, most of whom were from naval schools. In May 1939, Philip entered the Royal Naval College at Dartmouth as a cadet, following in the footsteps of the three most recent Kings of England: George V, Edward VIII and George VI.

Within months of starting there, war would break out. Philip, like Elizabeth in her very different way, had been learning the importance of doing his duty. They had seen the results of what happened when people put their own interests first, as with Edward VIII's abdication, and from their mentors they had developed a keen public spirit, even at this early age. The war years would not only reinforce that message – they would draw them together.

Chapter 4

KISSING COUSINS

A letter written by the Queen in 1947 describing how, as a young Princess Elizabeth, she fell in love with Prince Philip, was sold in 2016 for £14,400 at Chippenham Auction Rooms in Wiltshire. It far exceeded the pre-auction estimate of £1200. The two-page letter was written to the author Betty Shew, who was compiling a book called *Royal Wedding* as a souvenir of the marriage, and the young princess agreed to share details of her relationship with her naval officer fiancé. The letter is written in ink on headed notepaper from Balmoral Castle.

In it, Princess Elizabeth recalls how she first met Prince Philip in 1939, talks about her engagement ring and wedding band and how the couple danced at nightclubs Ciro's and Quaglino's in London. The Queen wrote:

The first time I remember meeting Philip was at the Royal Naval College Dartmouth, in July 1939, just before the war. (We may have met before at the Coronation or the Duchess of Kent's wedding, but I don't remember).

I was 13 years of age and he was 18 and a cadet just due to leave. He joined the Navy at the outbreak of war, and I only saw him very occasionally when he was on leave – I suppose about twice in three years.

Then when his uncle and aunt, Lord and Lady Mount-batten, were away he spent various weekends away with us at Windsor. Then he went to the Pacific and Far East for two years as everyone there will know.

We first started seeing more of each other when Philip went for a two-year job to the RN Petty Officers' School at Corsham – before that we hardly knew each other. He'd spend weekends with us, and when the school was closed he spent six weeks at Balmoral – it was great luck his getting a shore job first then! We both love dancing – we have danced at Ciro's and Quaglino's as well as at parties.

She said of her engagement ring: 'I don't know the history of the stone, except that it is a very fine old cutting. It was given to me not long before the engagement was announced.'

She also wrote: 'Philip enjoys driving and does it fast! He has his own tiny MG which he is very proud of – he has taken me about in it, once up to London, which was great fun, only it was like sitting on the road, and the wheels are almost as high as one's head. On that one and only occasion we were chased by a photographer which was disappointing.'

The engagement ring was made by the jewellers Philip Antrobus of Old Bond Street using diamonds from a tiara belonging to Philip's mother, Princess Alice of Greece. Philip designed it himself using a 3-carat diamond solitaire as a centrepiece, flanked by five smaller diamonds on each side, all set in platinum. The wedding band was made from a nugget of Welsh gold that came from the Clogau St David's mine, near Dolgellau.

Although Philip had been a guest at Windsor Castle several times when Princess Elizabeth was a child, their romance may never have blossomed had it not fallen to him to escort the thirteen-year-old Princess Elizabeth and her younger sister Margaret around Dartmouth Naval College in July 1939. The royal family were on an official visit on the royal yacht *Victoria and Albert*. The Court Circular for that day reads: 'His Majesty the King and Her Majesty the Queen, Her Royal Highness Princess Elizabeth and Her Royal Highness Princess Margaret visited the Royal Naval College, Dartmouth. Captain Lord Louis Mountbatten RN was in attendance.'

The plan had been for the family to attend morning chapel at the college, but because there had been an outbreak of mumps and chicken pox among the cadets it was decided that the princesses should not attend the service. Philip's uncle Dickie Mountbatten was present in his role as aide-de-camp to the King. There is little doubt that Mountbatten had more than a hand in ensuring that Philip was picked over the other cadet captains to look after the princesses during the chapel service, as his dynastic ambitions had few bounds.

The following day he procured an invitation for Philip to lunch aboard the royal yacht. According to the account penned by governess Marion Crawford, Princess Elizabeth asked Philip what he would like to eat. Philip proceeded to gobble down several plates of shrimp and a banana split. In her book of memoirs about Philip, Queen Alexandra of Yugoslavia (formerly Princess Alexandra of Greece) says that years later, when the Queen and Prince Philip were trying to recall their meeting, she heard Philip say to the Queen: 'You were so shy. I could not get a word out of you.'

In any event, it seems that Prince Philip made a favourable impression on the young Princess Elizabeth and an exchange of correspondence began between the two of them. No one can remember exactly when, but no doubt Marion Crawford prompted Elizabeth to write a letter of thanks to Philip for entertaining her and her sister during the royal visit and the distant cousins continued their correspondence throughout the war years.

Princess Alexandra wrote in June 1941 that when Philip was on shore leave in Cape Town, she found him writing a letter. 'Who is it to?' she asked. 'Lilibet . . . Princess Elizabeth in England.' Alexandra surmised that Philip was angling for invitations and she may have been right. By October that year, Philip had spent the first of several leave weekends at Windsor Castle. King George VI wrote to Philip's grandmother Victoria Milford Haven: 'Philip came here for a weekend the other day. What a charming boy he is and I am glad he is remaining on in my Navy.'

On one of his Windsor weekends, he and David Milford Haven (later to be his best man) rolled back the carpets three nights running and took the sisters Elizabeth and Margaret for their partners, treating them as though they were grown-up ladies of fashion in a London ballroom, instead of two schoolgirls incarcerated in an ancient castle with thick stone walls surrounded by wire. But, however gloomy Windsor Castle might have appeared to others, they loved the place. 'Lilibet and I loved Windsor the best of all our homes,' Princess Margaret later recalled. 'It has such atmosphere.'

Prince Philip obviously liked it too as, despite dismissing his time there with typical insouciance, he spent several spectacular Christmases there with the royal family. The King and Queen had some concerns – not because they didn't like Philip, because they did, but they thought their daughter was too young to become too involved with anyone, let alone someone as dashing and macho as the virtually penniless prince.

In December 1943, the King and Queen held a small dance at Windsor Castle for both their daughters. The King felt Elizabeth had missed out on the kind of socialising she should have had during her teenage years, and because of the war she hadn't been able to have much fun. The Queen was impressed by the good manners of most of the young men invited, although Philip wasn't one of them as he was confined to bed in Claridges Hotel (of all gloomy places the Queen noted).

Much to both the princesses' delight, he was well enough to come to their pantomime and stay for the rest of the weekend. To raise funds for charity during the war and keep everyone entertained, the King had devised the idea of staging a pantomime every Christmas. That year it was *Aladdin*, with Princess Elizabeth as the principal boy. According to Crawfie, Princess Elizabeth acted better than she had ever done before. 'I have never known Lilibet more animated. There was a sparkle about her that none of us had ever seen before.' She went on to say: 'Prince Philip was falling out of his seat with laughter.' He then spent Christmas with them and was joined by his cousin David Milford Haven. According to Princess Elizabeth, 'we had a gay time, with a film, dinner parties and dancing to the gramophone.' The King's private secretary, Tommy Lascelles, recalled 'they frisked and capered away till near 1am'.

Looking back years later, Prince Philip described his wartime friendship with the royal family in a typically dismissive way: 'I went to the theatre with them once, something like that. And then during the war, if I was here, I would call in and have a meal. I once or twice spent Christmas at Windsor, because I'd nowhere particular to go. I thought not all that much about it, I think. We used to correspond occasionally . . . But if you are related – I mean I knew half the people here, they were all relations – it isn't so extraordinary to be on kind of family relationship terms. You don't necessarily have to think about marriage.'

In his thank-you letter to the Queen after Christmas, Philip wrote he hoped that his behaviour 'did not get too out of hand'. He added that he also hoped – if it was not too presumptuous – he could add

Windsor to Broadlands (the Mountbatten home) and Coppins (the country home of the Duke and Duchess of Kent) to his favourite places: 'That may give you some small idea of how much I appreciated the few days you were kind enough to let me spend with you.'

Despite their misgivings, there was little doubt that the King and Queen did little to dissuade Princess Elizabeth from seeing Philip. 'He is intelligent, he has a good sense of humour and thinks about things the right way,' the King wrote to his mother, Queen Mary. He added, however, that both he and the Queen thought her 'too young for that now, as she has never met any young men of her own age'.

At Dartmouth, Prince Philip had excelled. He won the King's Dirk as the best all-round cadet of his first term and capped it with the best cadet of the year. This was an exceptional performance as most of his contemporaries had already been at Dartmouth for several years while he was at Gordonstoun. He spent his book token prize on a copy of Liddell Hart's *The Defence of Britain*, a significant choice as war with Germany was looming despite Prime Minister Neville Chamberlain's promise of 'peace in our time'. On 3 September 1939, war with Germany was declared.

Prince Philip's first posting as a midshipman was to the battleship HMS *Ramillies* in January 1940 in the South Pacific. Philip spent the few days of his shore leave in Australia, working on a sheep farm rather than joining his shipmates who were having fun in the bars of Sydney. Over the course of several months, Philip was posted from ship to ship and, as a midshipman, was required to keep a log of anything of interest aboard each vessel. His journal has been praised for the detailed observations of technical matters, illustrated with plans, maps and diagrams and the occasional humorous note. According to the log, Durban was a favourite port of call and is mentioned several times with exclamation marks added – no doubt code for some good times had there.

Prince Philip's fourth posting was to HMS *Valiant* in the

Mediterranean fleet, where he first saw action at the bombardment of Bardia on the coast of Libya. His log records, 'The whole action was a spectacular affair.' He then spent two days in Athens where he saw his mother, Princess Alice, and cousin Alexandra among other Greek relatives. At a party there on 21 January, he caught the eye of the politician and diarist Sir Henry 'Chips' Channon, whose entry for that day reads: 'Prince Philip of Greece was there. He is extraordinarily handsome ... He is to be our Prince Consort, and that is why he is serving in our Navy.'

This may have been an inspired guess or perhaps it was wishful thinking on the part of Princess Nicholas of Greece, with whom Chips had been chatting earlier. Prince Philip's comment on the diary entry years later was that he must have been on the list of eligible young men, but one only had to say that for someone like Chips Channon to go one step further and say it is already decided. Chips also picked up some gossip about Philip's parents. He said his mother Alice 'was eccentric to say the least', while his father Andrea 'philanders on the Riviera'.

In March 1941, Prince Philip on board *Valiant* was caught up in the Battle of Cape Matapan off the south-west coast of the Peloponnesian peninsula, where the Italian navy was intercepted. Philip was in control of the ship's searchlights. 'My orders were that if any ship illuminated a target, I was to switch on and illuminate it for the rest of the fleet.' He caught two Italian cruisers in the beam of his searchlight, allowing the *Valiant* to sink them both. For his part in the action, Philip was mentioned in the commander of the British Mediterranean fleet Admiral Cunningham's despatches. Not long after, Philip got some shore leave in Alexandria, where he met up with David Milford Haven and his cousin Alexandra.

'Philip used to talk at this time of a home of his own, a country house in England,' she recalled. She found it rather touching that was what he wanted, but she knew with no family fortune coming his way and only his pay in the navy to live off, Philip would need to marry exceptionally well to achieve his dream objective.

By June of 1941, Prince Philip was due to return to England to sit for his sub-lieutenant's examinations. His ship home sailed via Halifax, Nova Scotia, to pick up some Canadian troops and later, while refuelling in the Caribbean, several of the Chinese stokers jumped ship and disappeared. For the rest of the voyage, Philip and the other midshipmen toiled in the fiery heat of the boiler room shovelling tons of coal into the furnaces. For this he was given a certificate as a qualified boiler trimmer. According to Princess Alexandra, the certificate had a place of honour among his cherished souvenirs, along with the receipted bill for his wife's bridal bouquet.

The examinations at Portsmouth were passed with distinction and Philip was soon back at sea as a sub-lieutenant on HMS *Wallace*. It was around this time that he first met Australian Mike Parker. At first, they were rivals, later the best of friends and they happened to be the two youngest first lieutenants in the navy. Parker recalled: 'We were highly competitive. We both wanted to show we had the most efficient, cleanest and best ships in the navy.' Mike's girlfriend Eileen, whom he later married, met Philip when he and Mike were stationed at Rosyth naval base on the Firth of Forth in Scotland.

'I recollect so well, thinking at the time, what a handsome man Philip of Greece was,' Eileen noted. 'Tall with piercing blue eyes and a shock of blond hair swept back from his forehead. I was not at all surprised to hear that every unmarried Wren on the base had her sights on him.' She went on to say that it was inconceivable that such an eligible young officer didn't have a sweetheart somewhere, but nobody ever came close enough to him to find out who it might be.

Eileen was right about Philip having, if not a sweetheart, then at least a girlfriend. Osla Benning was a beautiful Canadian-born

debutante whom Philip first met in 1939, when she shared a flat with
Sarah Baring, a god-daughter of Dickie Mountbatten, who asked
her to introduce Philip to a nice girl. Osla and Philip became close
friends and used to go dancing at the 400 Club, which was housed
in a cellar in Leicester Square and was described by a newspaper
as 'the night-time headquarters of society'. It had an eighteen-piece
orchestra, which always played softly to avoid drowning out conversation. There was a minute dancefloor and food, but no menu.
If guests wanted to eat, they simply ordered whatever they wished
and it was served promptly, which was no mean feat at that time.
According to Sarah Baring, the couple kept in touch when Philip was
at sea, as Osla showed Sarah letters from Philip saying how much
he was looking forward to seeing her when he got back. Evidently
Philip was a busy letter writer.

'I do know that he was her first love,' said Osla's daughter Janie
Spring years later. 'She never told me about him for years. She just
said: "I fell in love with a naval officer." Then I found a wonderful
picture of Philip, very young-looking, with his hair all tousled,
quite curly ... I could see why they got on. They were both very
much outsiders with no roots in the English milieu in which they
moved. Neither of them had experienced much emotional warmth
or security as children. Probably unconsciously, they recognised this
similarity in each other and this is what gave them a special bond.'

Their relationship wasn't to last, however, and once Philip had
spent time at Windsor Castle and set his sights on the young Princess
Elizabeth, Osla and he went their separate ways, although they
remained friends and Philip later became a godfather to Osla's son.

It may well be that the thought of marriage to Princess Elizabeth
did not enter Philip's head at that time, but the subject was not far
from other people's thoughts. In London in March 1944, Princess
Alexandra married King Peter of Yugoslavia and King George VI
was Peter's best man. King George II of Greece gave the bride away

and took the opportunity to raise the subject of Philip and Lilibet with the King. George VI admitted he was not happy with the idea as she was far too young. She was not yet eighteen and Philip was only twenty-two. The King promised to consider the matter, but soon he advised George of Greece that 'Philip had better not think any more about it for the present.'

After another visit to Windsor in July, Philip wrote to the Queen of 'the simple enjoyment of family pleasures and amusements and the feeling that I am welcome to share them. I am afraid I am not capable of putting all this into the right words and I am certainly incapable of showing you the gratitude that I feel.'

Prince Philip became first lieutenant of a new destroyer HMS *Whelp*. While the construction of the new ship was being completed, Prince Philip was a frequent guest at Coppins, the home of his cousin Marina Duchess of Kent, whose husband had been tragically killed in a plane crash in Scotland in 1942. By the summer, tongues were wagging about a possible royal marriage. Socialite and Lord Lieutenant of Caernarvonshire Sir Michael Duff reported to his cousin Lady Desborough: 'The Duchess of Kent came to dinner bringing Prince Philip of Greece who is charming and I consider just right to perform the role of Consort for Princess Elizabeth. He has everything in his favour, he is good looking, intelligent, a good sailor and he speaks only English ... I gather he goes to Windsor quite a lot. He is 24 and ripe for the job.'

By August 1944, Philip's ship was fully commissioned and ready for service. Both *Whelp* and Mike Parker's ship HMS *Wessex* were sent to join the Pacific fleet. Philip and Mike met up at the Australian base of the fleet. On shore leave, Mike organised society parties in both Sydney and Melbourne where every eligible young heiress wanted to meet the handsome prince. By then both Mike and Philip had grown luxuriant beards. They used to joke at parties that Mike was the prince and vice versa. Many girls flung themselves at Philip, but Mike claimed that nothing serious ever went on with the 'armfuls of girls ... we were young, we had fun, we had a few drinks, we might have gone dancing and that was it'.

By then, not only were Philip and Princess Elizabeth corresponding regularly but they each had photographs of the other on display. The princess had a picture of Philip with his beard on her dressing table and for his part her photo was on display in his cabin aboard ship. His service in the Far East would keep him away from England for some time yet, however, delaying any further developments in their relationship and giving it its first test.

Meanwhile, back in England, in February 1945 Princess Elizabeth joined the Auxiliary Territorial Service as a driver and car maintenance expert. She would proudly wear the ATS uniform of a junior commander on Remembrance Day 1945, the first to be observed for six years, when she placed her own wreath upon the Cenotaph.

By that stage, people realised that the war in Europe was coming to an end. Elizabeth could move back into her old apartments in Buckingham Palace. Her bedroom was her favourite shade of pink, with chintz covers for the chairs (she still loves these) and although she had her own sitting room, she still had breakfast every morning in the old nursery with Margaret. Their childhood string of horses on wheels were still on the landing, almost as though the last six years had never happened.

Her father was right to urge caution on the subject of marriage. Elizabeth was still partly a child as she had been shut away in Windsor Castle for much of the war. Although she had a deeply developed sense of duty, which made her appear more sophisticated than she really was, she was still very innocent and lacked experience of many normal events. Throughout the war, she hadn't been able to see a play or one single concert that she so loved. All her music and entertainment came to her, as it did to many others, through the medium of the radio. The whole royal family sat together and listened to Tommy Handley, in the comedy show *ITMA* ('It's That Man Again').

Finally, on 8 May 1945, Victory in Europe day, the war in Europe was over. Princess Elizabeth and Margaret slipped out of the palace to join the crowds singing in the streets. 'It was one of the most memorable nights of my life,' Princess Elizabeth said later. 'It was most exciting – we went everywhere,' Princess Margaret recalled.

Philip was not with them, as he was still at sea onboard *Whelp* steaming for Tokyo Bay. He witnessed the Japanese surrender in August aboard *Missouri*, the flagship of the US fleet, and did not return to England until January 1946. *Whelp* was decommissioned before being offered to South Africa, meanwhile Prince Philip was posted as a lecturer to the officers' training school at Corsham near Bath.

Whenever he had leave he would drive up to London in his MG sports car to stay at the Mountbattens' house in Chester Street, Belgravia. John Dean, who later became Philip's valet, wrote: 'He was so considerate, so anxious to avoid giving trouble to people who, after all, were paid to look after the family, that we all thought the world of him and looked forward to his visits.'

Dean remarked that Philip did not have much in the way of civilian clothing and often did not even have a clean shirt. 'At night, after he had gone to bed, I washed his shorts and socks and had them ready for him in the morning. I also did his mending. He was very easy to look after, and never asked for things like that to be done for him, but I liked him so much I did it anyway. Whenever Prince Philip brought a weekend bag and I unpacked it, I always found a small photograph in a battered leather frame – a photograph of Princess Elizabeth.'

Because of the rigid rules of court etiquette, apart from the odd occasion when Philip managed to synchronise his leave with invitations for the same parties as the princess, they had to be patient, which of course Philip wasn't. He could hardly turn up at the palace without a personal invitation, and if Elizabeth invited him for a pre-dinner drink in her suite of rooms, there always had to be a chaperone in the room. Princess Margaret was often there, but demanded just as much attention from Philip as if he were her own admirer. If they got invited to the same parties, all they could hope for were a couple of dances together. If there had been more, people would have started talking even more than they already were, as rumours of the royal romance began to appear in the press, after Prince Philip and Princess Elizabeth were seen together at the theatre and dancing at nightclubs.

Whatever their feelings for one another, there were still some obstacles. The King was concerned that his daughter had not had a proper opportunity to meet other eligible young men, and therefore organised parties at Windsor to which suitably classy Guards officers were invited. He was anxious to ensure that she knew she was making the right decision. There was also the question of Philip's nationality. Some courtiers were concerned that Philip might be compromised by his German relatives.

Princess Elizabeth had no such doubts and in August 1946 Philip was invited to spend part of the summer holiday at Balmoral for grouse shooting and stalking. According to Prince Philip, it was not until then that things became serious. He said: 'I suppose one thing led to another. I suppose I began to think about it seriously, oh, let me think now, when I got back in forty-six and went to Balmoral. It was probably then that we, that it became, you know, that we began to think about it seriously, and even talk about it.'

At some point during the holiday at Balmoral, Prince Philip proposed to Elizabeth and was accepted. It was to be an unofficial engagement with no public announcement. There was to be a royal tour of South Africa early in 1947 and the King did not want public attention diverted from the tour by any announcement. Princess

Elizabeth accepted that it was her duty to forget her personal wishes until after the tour had been completed. George VI later wrote to her: 'I was rather afraid you had thought I was being very hard-hearted about it.'

In his thank-you letter to Queen Elizabeth dated 14 September 1946, Prince Philip wrote: 'I am sure I do not deserve all the good things which have happened to me. To have been spared in the war and seen victory. To have fallen in love completely and unreservedly makes all one's personal and even the world's troubles seem small and petty. I only realise now what a difference those few weeks, which seem to flash past, have made to me. The generous hospitality and warm friendliness did much to restore my faith in permanent values and brighten up a rather warped view of life. Naturally there is one circumstance which has done more for me than anything else in my life.'

Two days before the royal tour of South Africa was due to depart, Dickie Mountbatten gave a small dinner party at Chester Street. The King and Queen were present, though Princess Margaret was absent with a chill. The guests toasted Philip and Elizabeth with champagne, except for the King, who always drank whisky. John Dean says that the royal engagement was in the air that night. The royal family set sail on 1 February 1947 in a new battleship, HMS *Vanguard*, on a tour that was to last until the middle of May.

The princess and Philip wrote to each other regularly and the enforced separation did nothing to dampen their love. On the contrary, it intensified it. Luckily for her, the trip was packed with engagements, and her days and evenings were filled with receptions, dinners, train journeys and welcomes, culminating in her twenty-first birthday speech in Cape Town, given in the gardens of Government House. It was crafted by leader writer and court correspondent of *The Times*, Dermot Morrah. The princess spoke from her heart to the youth of the whole Empire and her words had the impact they were intended to make: 'I declare before you all that my whole life, whether it be long or short, shall be devoted to your service and the service of our great imperial family to which we all belong. I shall not have the strength to carry out this resolution alone unless you join with me, as now I invite you to do.' Queen Mary was so moved by her granddaughter's words she confessed she 'wept' when she heard it on the radio.

After the family's return, Prince Philip told the Queen that although he realised she had been right to persuade them to delay the announcement, now he and the princess wanted to start their new life together, and in their absence he had been doing all he could to ensure that all objections were removed. In February, he had become a naturalised British subject, thus Prince Philip of Greece became Lieutenant Mountbatten RN. The Archbishop of Canterbury wrote to the King suggesting that Philip, who had been baptised in the Greek Orthodox Church, be officially received into the Church of England, and by October that was concluded.

Even so, the princess's parents still admitted to their concerns, as is typical for anyone when the time comes to give away their daughter in marriage. 'You can imagine what emotion this engagement has given me,' the Queen wrote to Tommy Lascelles. 'It is one of the things that has been in the forefront of all one's hopes and plans for a daughter who has such a burden to carry, and one can only pray that she has made the right decision, I think she has – but he is untried yet.'

In July, the Queen wrote to her sister, May (Lady Mary Elphinstone, mother of the Hon. Margaret Rhodes), to tell her very secretly that Lilibet had 'made up her mind' to become engaged to Philip Mountbatten. 'As you know she has known him since she was 12 and I think she is really fond of him and I do pray she will be happy.' They were keeping it 'a deadly secret' because she didn't want the press finding out and 'ruining everything'.

The actual date was fixed when Philip heard from the jewellers Antrobus that the ring was ready. On Wednesday 9 July 1947, the day before a Buckingham Palace garden party, so the couple could make their first joint public appearance, there was an announcement from Buckingham Palace: 'It is with the greatest pleasure that the King and Queen announce the betrothal of their dearly beloved daughter the Princess Elizabeth to Lieutenant Philip Mountbatten RN son of the late Prince Andrew of Greece and Princess Andrew [Princess Alice of Battenberg] to which union the King has gladly given his consent.'

Queen Mary sent a message of congratulation to Philip's mother Alice, who replied, 'The young couple seem very devoted to each other. They have had time to think such a serious decision over and I pray they will find happiness and great *friendship* in their future married life. Lilibet has a wonderful character and I think Philip is very lucky to have won her love.'

With their wedding scheduled for later in the year, Elizabeth and Philip were about to bring their relationship into the full glare of public attention as they began to plan for the rest of their lives together. It was a journey that would last for more than seventy years.

Chapter 5

CHANGES

In the spring before the announcement of the royal engagement seventy years ago, Britain experienced its most catastrophic river flooding in recorded history. The country had already suffered a long, hard freeze in the snowiest winter of the twentieth century and by early March 1947 snowdrifts towered up to 16ft high in some places. The country was in chaos – rail and road transport came to a standstill, chronic shortages of coal led to nationwide power cuts and food rationing was worse than in the war. At Corsham Naval Training Base, Prince Philip had to lecture his students by candlelight and wearing his naval greatcoat. When the temperatures shot up, melting the snow onto the frozen ground, a ferocious wind whipped up the floodwater, especially through the dykes in East Anglia around Sandringham, and 100 square miles of fens were turned into an inland sea.

The conditions created a brief spike in unemployment but, despite the return of thousands of ex-servicemen seeking work, this did not become a problem on anything like the scale of the interwar years, and by the autumn unemployment would be around 3 per cent of the work force. Although the war had ended almost two years previously, all basic foods were rationed, as were clothes, coal, furniture and petrol. London was scarred with bomb sites from the blitz. Between the announcement of the engagement in July 1947 and the wedding in November, things worsened for many people; the meat ration was reduced and potatoes became scarce as a result of the poor harvest. Austerity was the order of the day.

Elizabeth had promised her parents that she would be patient and make certain she still felt the same about Philip on her return from South Africa as she did before. Of course, their passion was intensified, but they still had to wait another two months before their betrothal was officially proclaimed in the court circular on 10 July. As if it were a taste of things to come, on the evening of the announcement the couple could not be together. Philip was on duty at Corsham and Elizabeth was a guest at a private dance at Apsley House, Hyde Park Corner, where successive Dukes of Wellington had lived since a grateful nation had presented the property to the victor of the Battle of Waterloo.

Across the country and the world, thousands of newspapers and magazines published photographs of the smiling couple. Winston Churchill, the then leader of the opposition, having lost the election in 1945 to Clement Attlee's Labour Party, said that the engagement was 'a flash of colour on the hard road we have to travel'. There was some opposition to a lavish wedding in those austere times. In a letter addressed to King George VI, the Camden Town branch of the Amalgamated Society of Woodworkers wrote: 'Any banqueting and display of wealth at your daughter's wedding will be an insult to the British people at the present time. You would be well advised to order a very quiet wedding in keeping with the times.'

But most others responded in a more positive way. Among the thousands of congratulatory messages sent to Prince Philip and Princess Elizabeth was one from Mike Parker, his close friend from his earlier naval days. To Mike's surprise, in Prince Philip's letter of thanks he wrote: 'I would like to mention that I am considering getting some staff together and would like you to join this as general nanny and factotum.' Philip's new staff included a secretary, a private detective and a valet, John Dean. To this group was added Parker as equerry-in-waiting.

In keeping with his new standing, Philip went to live at Kensington Palace with his grandmother the Dowager Marchioness of Milford Haven. He was later joined by his best-man-to-be David Milford Haven. John Dean duly arrived at Kensington Palace at eight every morning to wake Philip and David with cups of tea and to clean their shoes and see to their clothes. Philip was a heavy smoker and kept John busy refilling the cigarette boxes and emptying ashtrays. But out of sheer willpower, which he was still displaying in his nineties, when he gets up at 5am to be ready for an early start, Philip gave up smoking on his wedding day, at the request of his bride to be.

Despite the valet's best efforts, it took Philip, who showed little interest in his appearance, some time to accept Savile Row suits and shoes handmade at Lobb of St James's Street. At the garden party held at Buckingham Palace immediately after the engagement was announced, Philip appeared in a well-worn and shabby naval uniform. A week later, Philip accompanied his fiancée to Edinburgh, where she was to receive the Freedom of the City. As the princess made her acceptance speech, Prince Philip stood dutifully two steps behind, a position he would have to take many thousands of times over the coming years. It was the first time he saw the physical symbol of how his status would always be secondary to his future wife.

That evening in Edinburgh at a ball held in their honour, the couple danced a complicated eightsome reel. Philip had been wise enough to take some Scottish dancing lessons from Princess Margaret before the trip to Edinburgh and performed well. When the King heard about the evening in Edinburgh, he sent a message to King Paul of Greece saying: 'Philip is making out well.'

Prince Philip was still based at Corsham, but whenever he had time off he drove in his MG sports car to London to see Princess Elizabeth. His record time for the 98-mile journey from Corsham to London was one hour and forty minutes. In the autumn of 1947, he had a narrow escape when his car crashed into a tree, leaving him with a twisted knee. It didn't put him off his love of driving, and he used to take the princess in the MG to Richmond Park. To avoid unwanted attention from the public, she disguised herself with a scarf over her head, while Philip wore his normal prescription dark glasses. A staff car with the ever-present detective would follow discreetly behind.

Considering the dire straits of the country's finances after the heavy cost of the war, Parliament took a generous view in voting £50,000 for the refurbishment of Clarence House, a stone's throw from Buckingham Palace, which was to be the new palatial home for the couple after the wedding. In addition, Philip was granted a £10,000-a-year allowance and Elizabeth's was fixed at £50,000 a year. Philip took a great interest in every detail of the plans for Clarence House; he even consulted with the staff so that their quarters were efficiently laid out. His greatest delight was his fully equipped miniature cinema in the basement, a wedding present from the Mountbattens.

After the wedding, the couple lived in Elizabeth's apartments at Buckingham Palace while the works at Clarence House were completed. General Sir Frederick 'Boy' Browning, the husband of the novelist Daphne du Maurier, was appointed as comptroller and treasurer of their joint household. He was a former Guards officer who had been Dickie Mountbatten's chief of staff.

Because Prince Philip did not want to spend all his time in the palace, Browning found them a country house to rent at Windlesham

Moor in Surrey, where Philip immediately turned the grass tennis court into a cricket pitch. He was always health conscious and somewhat vain about his weight. If he thought he had gained any, he would put on two or three sweaters and run around the grounds until he worked up a sweat. He would come in exhausted and lie down and then have a bath to recover. This amused the princess, who thought he was quite mad, but he has kept his trim figure to this day – another example of his mental discipline.

Windlesham was also where they could entertain their friends rather less formally than in London, and they had supper parties and cricket parties. In the 50 acres of grounds, there was a miniature golf course with bunkers and undulating greens, and locals would be invited to play. Here, and later at Clarence House, Philip was the man of the house. It was he, rather than Elizabeth, who reviewed the menus and decided on the meals for the day, and the staff deferred to him on domestic matters. Life would be very different at Buckingham Palace after Elizabeth acceded to the throne.

For the princess, Windlesham was the smallest house she had ever lived in, but the household was still regal. There were six resident domestic staff, plus Elizabeth's dresser Bobo and Philip's valet when they were in residence. Even the dogs were given the royal treatment. At four thirty every afternoon, a footman brought in a tray laid with a cloth, silver spoons and forks, a plate each of biscuits and chopped meat and a jug of rich gravy. Elizabeth then gave each dog an individual serving in its own special bowl.

For the first few months of married life, Philip was given a desk job at the Admiralty, which he did not relish. 'I was just a dogsbody, shuffling ships around' was how he described it. Later he was posted to a residential staff course at the Royal Naval College in Greenwich. The demanding course was designed to prepare officers for high rank and involved Philip living at Greenwich during the week and returning to the palace at weekends. In addition, Philip had to find time for public duties, including an official visit to Paris with the then pregnant Elizabeth in May 1948.

Soon after the birth of Prince Charles in November, the King, on the advice of his doctors, cancelled a planned tour of Australia and New Zealand. His poor health meant he had to cut down on his public appearances. The burden of these official functions now fell on Elizabeth and Philip. At the same time, Philip was adding to his workload by taking on the presidency of the National Playing Fields Association, along with other organisations of which he accepted to become patron.

No matter how busy he was, Philip found time to have some fun at the Thursday Club, which had weekly meetings in a private room at Wheeler's fish restaurant in Soho. The club had been started by 'Baron' Nahum, who was an official photographer at the royal wedding. On an average evening at the Thursday Club there would be ten or fifteen members present. In addition to Philip and Baron, the actors David Niven and James Robertson Justice, Peter Ustinov and John Betjeman, Cecil Beaton, David Milford Haven, Iain MacLeod (later Chancellor of the Exchequer) and some newspaper editors might be present, as well as the occasional roguish figure. Philip would always be accompanied by Mike Parker.

Princess Elizabeth referred to this motley crew as 'Philip's funny friends'. There were rumours of wild parties, even of orgies, but exactly what went on at the club has never been substantiated. 'We've been given the reputation of being wild,' said Parker, 'but the truth is we enjoyed fun and going around with people who knew what was going on ... the idea that it was a drunken orgy is absolute rubbish. People got very merry but never drunk. As far as being wild, not guilty. As far as hanging around women, not guilty.'

Eileen Parker, who thought Philip's friends were 'distinctly odd', had known him for several years before he married the future Queen. From the very first, she said, 'He was a real loner. He was very good looking; tall, with that blond hair and those piercing blue eyes. You would turn and say, "Who's that?" "Oh, that's Prince Philip of Greece, but he never has anything to do with anybody."'

Marriage had not mellowed him. He was a man of his time and background, just as his wife was a woman of hers. Very much a man's man, he enjoyed drinking and jesting with his cronies and continued to keep to a bachelor routine. On one occasion, he and Parker were so late back to Clarence House that he found the gates locked and had to climb in over them. 'Serves them both right,' his wife commented drily.

Parker remembered those early years as 'incredibly happy, just gorgeous'. He oversaw all the prince's engagements and the pair picked up each other's phrases, copied each other's mannerisms and shared each other's jokes. They became well known for their elabo-rate practical jokes, and on one occasion during an RAF manoeuvre at the palace, they telephoned the Air Ministry and played a tape of a Battle of Britain dogfight down the line then shouted: 'Help! One of your pilots has gone berserk and he's strafing the palace!'

The palace old guard did not approve. They were most con-cerned with his apparent desire to continue bachelor friendships with people of somewhat dubious reputation. Their attitude, rather than reining him back, seemed only to spur Philip on his own way. Independent and single-minded, he disliked the constraints imposed by his membership of the royal family. Learning to fly a helicopter proved difficult, even though he had already earned his 'wings' in 1953. When Prime Minister Winston Churchill heard that Philip was learning to become a helicopter pilot as well, he summoned Parker to Downing Street, kept him standing in silence for several minutes while he carried on working at his desk, then gave him 'a long accusing stare' and coldly asked: 'Is your objective the destruc-tion of the whole of the royal family?'

In the spring of 1949, Elizabeth and Philip toured Lancashire by train followed by a tour of the Channel Islands on the training battleship HMS *Anson* and at last were able to move into Clarence House. Under Philip's supervision, Clarence House had been fitted out with the latest household gadgets including an intercom system, washing machines in the laundry and an electric trouser press for Philip's valet. The servants' quarters had a radio in every bedroom and a television, still something of a novelty, was in the staff sitting room. Much of the furniture and fittings in the house had been wedding presents. Both Elizabeth and Philip had offices next door at St James's Palace, to which Clarence House was connected by a passage on the first floor leading into the state apartments. The staff were mainly young and Parker described the atmosphere as being full of fun, very different from Buckingham Palace where, according to Parker, 'Philip didn't have many friends and helpers'.

The King's health improved in the summer, not enough for him to take on an arduous overseas tour, but sufficient for him to allow Philip to return to active service in the navy. Philip was posted as first lieutenant to HMS *Chequers*, the lead ship of the Mediterranean destroyer fleet based in Malta. The advantage of Malta was that Elizabeth could fly out to join her husband for lengthy stays.

While *Chequers* was being refitted in the dockyards in Malta, Philip stayed with Dickie Mountbatten in the villa he had rented while commander of the First Cruiser Squadron. Elizabeth joined them for her second wedding anniversary in November. Her time in Malta has been described as the only time in her life when she could live like an ordinary naval wife, driving herself, going to the hairdresser and shopping. It was a life less ordinary.

The villa Guardamangia had a staff of nineteen and Elizabeth usually had her lady-in-waiting and detective in tow. A governor's ball was held in her honour and she was soon called upon to perform civic duties, visiting schools and hospitals. Dickie Mountbatten wrote to his daughter Patricia in December: 'Lilibet is quite enchanting and I've lost whatever of my heart is left to spare entirely to her. She dances quite divinely and always wants a samba when we dance together and has said some very nice things about my dancing.' The princess made several trips to Malta, the longest being for eleven weeks, during which time baby Prince Charles was left behind with his grandparents, so the family was rarely in one place together. Mike Parker commuted regularly between Clarence House and Malta, keeping Philip up to date with his new interests at home, such as the National Playing Fields Association.

Prince Philip was in his element back on board ship. He was a strict disciplinarian and drove the crew hard in any sporting contests. In off-duty moments, he took up polo and soon became proficient, playing on the same team as his uncle Dickie. There was a minor blip in Philip's naval progression when he failed an oral section of his command examination. It is thought that he had fallen foul of the examiner on the polo field, who took the opportunity to get even by failing Philip. According to Mike Parker, Philip's commander-in-chief, Admiral Sir Arthur Power, wanted to over-rule the examiner. Philip would have none of it, stating: 'If they try to fix it I quit the navy for good.' He re-sat the exam and passed with flying colours. Soon after, in July 1950, Philip was promoted to lieutenant-commander and appointed to his first command, the frigate HMS *Magpie*. Before he was piped aboard his new ship, Philip returned to Clarence House for the birth of his daughter Princess Anne the following month.

Philip made sure that his ship became the best in the fleet. He was tough and fair and it brought results. *Magpie* excelled at manoeuvres and carried off six of ten events in the annual regatta. As 'cock o' the fleet', a red plywood rooster was hoisted aloft. *Magpie*'s tour of duty was a combination of naval exercises and ceremonial visits. In Gibraltar, he represented the King at the opening of their legislative council; *Magpie* sailed to Jordan, Turkey, Egypt and Iran on courtesy visits. When Elizabeth had recovered from the birth of Princess Anne, she again flew out to Malta in November, leaving the children with their grandparents. As *Magpie* did not have suitable accommodation for Elizabeth, the Admiral of the Fleet put another vessel, HMS *Surprise*, at her disposal. With Philip on his own ship, there was much fun had with the exchange of signals, the best-known being:

> *Surprise to Magpie*: Princess full of beans
> *Magpie to Surprise*: Can't you give her something better for breakfast?

The royal couple paid an unofficial visit to Greece to stay with Philip's cousin King Paul. They stayed in the royal palace in Athens where the Parthenon was floodlit in their honour. According to cousin Alexandra, when Philip took King Paul aboard *Magpie* he was astonished to find that Philip's quarters were full of papers on which Philip was working, including preparations for the Festival of Britain and the overseas tour of Canada. Philip had an interest in the festival as a showpiece for the inventiveness of British scientists and for British technology. It was planned for the centenary of the Great Exhibition, in which Prince Albert had played such an important role.

Although frail, George VI opened the festival on 3 May 1951, but he was soon struck down with a bug he could not shake off. His doctors ordered complete rest and cancellation of all public engagements; Elizabeth and Philip would have to take over. In July, Philip left Malta 'on indefinite leave'. As the crew of *Magpie* lined the decks to cheer him off, he said: 'I have kept my promise to make HMS *Magpie* one of the finest ships in the fleet. The past eleven months have been the happiest of my sailor life.' Back at Clarence House, he looked sadly at his white naval uniforms and said to John Dean: 'It will be a long time before I want those again.'

During the summer, Elizabeth stood in for her father at many public engagements, including Trooping the Colour. Detailed plans had been made for Elizabeth and Philip to pay an official state visit to Canada in September, but the King had been advised by his doctors that he should have an operation to remove his left lung, which was duly performed. Rather than set sail for Canada in the days after the operation, Philip persuaded the government that he and the princess should travel by air to avoid delaying the start of the tour.

When they landed, a nervous 25-year-old Princess Elizabeth stepped out onto the airplane gangway in Montreal on 8 October 1951, a crowd of 15,000 before her on the tarmac. She was about to begin her first major royal visit, during which she would be the centre of attention. The tour lasted thirty-three days during which time the royal couple travelled from coast to coast and back again. The tour was a great success, with hugely enthusiastic crowds at every stop.

The Canadian authorities had taken the greatest care to ensure that everyone involved, including the press, behaved impeccably. The same cannot be said of the American press when the royal couple made a short side trip to visit President Truman in Washington. Once back in Canada, Elizabeth displayed her skill at mimicry when she mocked the US photographers while she was doing some filming of her own. Pointing the camera at her husband, she cried out in a nasally American voice, 'Hey! You there! Hey, Dook! Look this way a sec! Dat's it! Thanks a lot!'

Elizabeth had this to say about Canada, once she was back in the UK: 'I am sure that nowhere under the sun could one find a land more full of hope, of happiness and of fine, loyal, generous-hearted people. They have placed in our hearts a love for their country and its people which will never grow cold and which will always draw us to their shores.'

The news at home was better. The King had progressed well

since his operation, so much so that it seemed possible that Philip would again be able to return to active service as the commander of his own destroyer. Winston Churchill was prime minster again, the Conservatives having won a general election in late October with a moderate majority of seventeen. Christmas was spent at Sandringham, with the King going out shooting on several days.

When they returned to London, the royal family went to see the musical *South Pacific* at the Drury Lane Theatre. The following day, on 31 January, the King waved goodbye to Elizabeth and Philip at London Airport as they set off on the first leg of their Commonwealth tour on a flight to Nairobi. The princess had few doubts that she would see her father again – after all, he had appeared to have made a good recovery from the operation, and she wanted to believe he would get better. As a precaution, however, the princess was given a sealed dossier containing the draft Accession Declaration, to be opened in the event of the King's death. A Royal Standard was also tucked away in the luggage, as were black mourning clothes.

Lord Chandos, the colonial secretary, described the scene at the airport as Elizabeth and Prince Philip left Heathrow: 'The King and Queen came to see them take off . . . I was shocked by the King's appearance. I was familiar with his look and mien, but he seemed much altered and strained. I had the feeling of doom, which grew as the minutes before the time of departure ebbed away. The King went on to the roof of the building to wave goodbye. The high wind blew his hair into disorder. I felt with foreboding that this would be the last time he was to see his daughter, and that he thought so himself.'

It had been agreed they could travel despite the tense situation in Kenya, which was facing the beginning of the Mau Mau uprising. The highlight of that leg of their tour was to spend a night at Treetops, a renowned game-viewing lodge in the Aberdare Forest game reserve, 100 miles from Nairobi. The lodge was built in the branches of an enormous tree, accessible only by ladder, overlooking a lake with a salt lick, a favourite watering hole for big game.

A dining area and three narrow bedrooms led onto the elevated viewing platform where the royal party, including the princess's maid Bobo MacDonald, lady-in-waiting Lady Pamela Mountbatten and Prince Philip's equerry Mike Parker, were to spend the night. They had been warned there was a possibility of being charged by an elephant on the way to the lodge, but unsurprisingly Prince Philip wanted to continue, and the group moved as silently as they could. There was a fifty-yard run of comparative open ground to cross before reaching the narrow wooden struts of a ladder into the tree. The princess did not falter and walked straight towards the ladder, ignoring the nearest elephant, which was standing right underneath, flapping her ears menacingly.

Once in the tree, the princess filmed the unfolding scene with her cine camera and couldn't be drawn from the array of game that gathered at the water hole. When the sunset had faded and it was no longer possible to use the cameras, the group talked in hushed voices about the game they had seen and what they might expect later. Concern was expressed for the princess's father, who had stood hatless at London airport on a bitterly cold day to wave her goodbye. Eric Sherbrooke Walker, the owner, recalls in his book, *Treetops Hotel*, that the princess replied warmly: 'He is like that. He never thinks of himself.'

'She then referred to her father's long illness and the family's great pleasure when it was believed he had reached the turning point. She told us that one day he raised his walking stick to his shoulder and declared, "I believe I could shoot now." She was closely informed of her father's plans and was able to say he was planning to shoot on the following day. Clearly from the tone of her conversation when she said good-bye to her father, she was hoping for a complete recovery.'

At sunrise, the princess – or the Queen, as she had unknowingly become during the night – was out on the balcony with her cine camera adjusting the light filter to film a rhino, silhouetted against the African dawn, at the salt lick. Prince Philip was keeping an eye on another rhino, which arrived at the scene puffing and blowing as if a bitter battle might ensue. Mike Parker went onto the balcony and believed he was with the Queen when the new reign began, as they looked at the dawn coming up over the jungle and saw an eagle hovering over their heads.

'I never thought about it until later,' he recalled, 'but that was roughly the time when the King died.'

After a breakfast of bacon and eggs cooked over the wood-burning stove, they all climbed down from the tree and walked back through the clearing, this time without incident. Mindful of the previous afternoon, Walker turned to the princess and said rather pompously, but still unaware of what had happened in London, 'If you have the same courage, Ma'am, in facing what the future sends you as you have at facing an elephant at eight yards, we are going to be very fortunate indeed.'

As the princess drove away, she waved and called, 'I will come again!' After Kenya became a republic within the Commonwealth in 1964, it was to be another twenty years before she returned.

Four hours later, the royal party were resting back at Sagana Lodge some twenty miles away when the editor of the *East African Standard* telephoned the princess's private secretary, Martin Charteris, who was staying at the only local hotel. The editor anxiously enquired if the teleprinter reports coming in from London about the King's death were true. It was news to Charteris. By a twist of fate, a telegram sent to Government House in Nairobi had not been decoded because the keys to the safe holding the codebook had been misplaced. A thoroughly unnerved Charteris checked the news with Buckingham Palace and immediately contacted Sagana

Lodge. He spoke to Mike Parker, who turned on his shortwave radio and heard the announcement from the BBC. He then woke a slumbering Prince Philip to tell him of the news. It was 2.45pm local time and already 11.45am in London.

According to Parker, Philip looked as if the whole world had dropped on his shoulders. 'He took the Queen up to the garden and they walked up and down the lawn while he talked and talked to her.' Pamela Mountbatten, who had known Philip since he was a child and had come to stay with her family, remembers his reaction: 'It was as though the world had fallen on him. I mean, he put a newspaper over his face and just remained like that for about five minutes. And then he pulled himself together and said he must go and find the princess ... she was having a rest in her bedroom ... and so they went for a walk in the garden and you could tell, walking up and down, up and down, that he was telling her. And then she came back to the Lodge – and one just thought, this poor girl who really adored her father, they were very close. And I think I gave her a hug and said how sorry I was. And then suddenly, I thought, my God, but she's Queen!'

The Queen has never spoken about her reaction to her father's sudden death except to say, 'My father died much too young and so it was all very sudden kind of taking on and making the best job you can.' She was in shock as she had not expected it. As Princess Margaret said, 'He died as he was getting better.' Three months later, there is a clue to her feelings in a touching letter to her father's assistant, Sir Eric Miéville.

'It all seems so unbelievable still,' she wrote, 'that my father is no longer here and it is only after some time has passed one begins to realise how much he is missed.' She added: 'My mother and sister have been wonderful, for they have lost so much – I do have my own family to help me.'

In the following hours, when preparations were made to return to

England as quickly as possible, the Queen calmly and mechanically wrote letters and telegrams while Philip sat beside her. 'She was sitting erect fully accepting her destiny,' Martin Charteris recalled. 'I asked her what name she would take and she said, "My own of course."'

'Poor guy,' Parker recalled, talking about Prince Philip in 1999. 'He needed something to do. But he was there with the Queen; that was the thing; he was like a bloody great pillar.' Back in London, the news had been relayed to Prime Minister Winston Churchill four hours previously. Operation Hyde Park Corner, with coded plans for the death of the King, was already in full swing. Churchill's private secretary, Jock Colville, recalled that when he went to Churchill's bedroom, he was sitting alone with tears in his eyes staring into space. 'I had not realised how much the King meant to him,' he said. 'I tried to cheer him up by saying how well he would get on with the new Queen, but all he could say was that he did not know her and that she was only a child.'

A child she was not. The mourning clothes which had been packed so carefully had gone on ahead with the official luggage, and the new Queen was forced to wear a floral frock and white sandals instead of her black dress, which she was not happy about, as she wanted to show proper respect for her father. She requested no photographs be taken as she left the lodge for London, but there were a couple of photographers already gathered outside.

'We stood silently outside the lodge,' one recalled, 'as the cars drove away in a cloud of dust, not one of us taking a shot at that historic moment. Seeing the young girl as Queen of Great Britain as she drove away, I felt her sadness, as she just raised her hand to us as we stood there silent, our cameras on the ground.'

When the Queen arrived back in London on 7 February, she found a nation in mourning. Flags were at half mast, cinemas and theatres were closed and sports fixtures cancelled. The diplomat Sir Evelyn

Prince Philip (ennobled the Duke of Edinburgh on his marriage) and Princess Elizabeth during their honeymoon at Broadlands in 1947.

Adopting an identical pose sixty years later in 2007. The Queen is wearing the same sapphire and diamond chrysanthemum brooch and pearl necklace.

The Duke and Duchess of York with baby Elizabeth on 29 April 1926,
a week after her birth.

The future Duke of Edinburgh with his parents Princess Alice and Prince Andrew of Greece in the same year.

Princess Alice of Greece and her son Philip, aged three, photographed
in 1924, by which time they were living in France.

Princess Elizabeth in February 1931, aged five, with her mother,
the Duchess of York.

Princess Elizabeth, her father King George VI and her sister Princess
Margaret, photographed in July 1946, a year before her wedding.

King George VI, Princess Elizabeth, Princess Margaret, the Queen and
Prince Philip at the wedding of Patricia Mountbatten in October 1946.

Princess Elizabeth and Prince Philip with children Charles and Anne in the garden of Clarence House, 1951.

Seven-month-old Prince Andrew is the centre of attention as the family enjoy their annual holiday at Balmoral Castle in September 1960.

Prince Philip in 1965 sharing a joke with famous comedian Jimmy Edwards
at a polo match. Philip enjoyed the waggish company of show-business
friends and would support their charity events.

Shuckburgh described the poignant scene as they walked down the steps of the aircraft. 'There was a touching picture of [the Queen] walking down the steps from the aircraft with the Privy Council lined up to greet her. One could just see the backs of their poor old heads: Winston, Attlee, AE [Eden], Woolton and so on. The twentieth-century version of Melbourne galloping to Kensington Palace, falling on his knees before Victoria in her nightdress.'

Philip had waited his turn to exit the plane. He knew that his role as head of the household had changed for ever. Furthermore, his hopes for a continuing career in the Royal Navy were dashed. Although the death of the King at such an early age could not have been foreseen, the Queen's whole life had prepared her for the change of circumstances. Not so Philip, who described his feelings years later: 'Within the house, whatever we did, it was together. I suppose I naturally filled that position. People used to come to me and ask me what to do. In 1952 the whole thing changed, very, very considerably.'

As the sovereign, the Queen had duties from which Philip was excluded. She had her weekly meetings with the prime minister. Every day she was sent red boxes full of papers – Cabinet minutes, Foreign Office telegrams, documents, briefs and drafts – none of which were shown to Philip. 'It was bloody difficult for him,' said Mike Parker. 'In the navy, he was in command of his own ship – literally. At Clarence House, it was very much his show. When we got to Buckingham Palace, all that changed.'

In his new role as consort, Philip sought the guidance of Prince Bernhard of the Netherlands, who as the husband of Queen Juliana had fifteen years' experience as consort, four of them since she took the throne. Bernhard was one of the founders of the World Wildlife Fund and its president before Philip took on that role. Bernhard gave him the benefit of his advice: 'You are new at this thing and you probably don't realise what you are up against. Practically everything you do will be a subject of criticism. You can't ignore it because some of it may be justified. And even if it isn't it may be politic to heed it. But don't let it get you down. In this job, you need a skin like an elephant.'

The move from Clarence House to Buckingham Palace was insisted upon by Winston Churchill. This was an enormous wrench for Philip, who had put so much time and effort in the refurbishment of Clarence House, the only home he had ever been able to call his own. For the Queen, she was quite simply going back to the place where she had lived for much of her life, so she felt at ease there. The palace was staffed with courtiers who answered only to the monarch. 'Philip was constantly being squashed, snubbed, ticked off, rapped over the knuckles,' according to Mike Parker. 'It was intolerable. The problem was simply that Philip had energy, ideas, get-up-and-go, and that didn't suit the Establishment, not one bit.' The same thing went for Windsor Castle, which became the week-end retreat of the royal family.

Another major blow to Philip that year came when it was decided that their children and their children's children should bear the name Windsor, after the Queen's family, not his name, Mountbatten. Philip was not just furious, he was deeply wounded. It was emasculating. It was cruel. 'I am the only man in the country not allowed to give his name to his children,' he protested.

'It hurt him, it really hurt him,' Countess Mountbatten recalled. 'He had given up everything – and now this, the final insult. It was a terrible blow. It upset him very deeply and left him feeling unsettled and unhappy for a long while. Of course, I don't blame the Queen.' It was of course Churchill, encouraged by Tommy Lascelles, who had decided on this, and together they forced the Queen's hand. She was too young and inexperienced to stand up for what she wanted for her husband, which was the name Mountbatten-Windsor.

Frustration, irritation and disappointment were daily occurrences for Philip, but outside the palace, he soon found roles to which he could apply his energies. The Queen made him Ranger of Windsor Great Park, in effect estate manager. He subsequently took an overseeing role at all the royal estates and greatly improved their efficiency. He was also made chairman of the Coronation Commission, which included the Duke of Norfolk, Winston Churchill, Clement Attlee and the Archbishop of Canterbury. The commission would consider every aspect of the Coronation, including the question of whether to permit the ceremony to be televised. Meanwhile, the Royal Mint had to issue new coins bearing the Queen's head, and Philip was made president of the committee to advise on the design of new coins and medals.

With the help of Mike Parker, who had become his private secretary, Prince Philip set about the reorganisation of Buckingham Palace, much to the consternation of the old guard. It was a struggle, but slowly he set about modernising things. He initiated a footman training programme. 'The old boys here hadn't had anything quite like it before,' he said. 'They expected the footmen just to keep on coming.'

He set up an organisation and methods review and he worked his way around every one of the palace's 600 rooms – discovering a deep underground wine cellar in the process that went on for 'miles and miles', with vintages and menus that dated back to Victorian times. He set in hand the redecoration of the private apartments on the second floor, installing a kitchen so that food did not have to be delivered along miles of draughty corridors. It was a massive and important job, albeit largely an unseen one, but it was clear that if he wanted to have an influence on how they lived their lives it would have to be done in ways such as this, as his public role was always going to be secondary to the Queen's.

Two days before the Coronation on Tuesday 2 June 1953, those who had not secured seats in the platforms along the processional route began to camp out on the streets to get a standing place. Eventually, half a million people would line the route in the lashing rain and wind. In typical British spirit, the crowd shared cups of tea with the occasional nip of brandy. 'A raincoat city' was how the *Daily Mail* described it as an estimated 10,000 people camped on the pavements that stretched from Marble Arch to Hyde Park Corner, many in what they described as their 'tent homes'. 'Children played hide and seek around the trees and tents and families from all over Great Britain and the Commonwealth joined in community singing. Everyone was having a wonderful time,' the newspaper reported.

Back at Buckingham Palace, Prince Philip had been told that Everest had been conquered when word reached Britain just before dawn that the Union Jack had been planted on the summit of the 29,002ft mountain by two members of the 1953 British Mount Everest expedition, led by Colonel John Hunt. New Zealander Edmund Hillary and his guide Tenzing Norgay reached the summit on Friday 29 May 1953. The conquest of Everest was probably the last major news item to be delivered to the world by runner and the encoded message to *The Times* was received and understood in London in time for the news to be released on the morning of the Coronation. 'The Queen and the Duke of Edinburgh and other members of the royal family were delighted,' the *Daily Mail* wrote. 'She sent her congratulations to the expedition.' Eileen Parker recalled pithily: 'My husband and Prince Philip were more interested in watching that than going to the ceremony.'

Although the war had ended eight years previously, there was still some rationing in place for sugar, meat and many other types of food, with confectionery rationing having ended earlier in the year. Because of this, the mood in Britain at the time of the Coronation was still gloomy as austerity continued to play a part in everyone's life, so the news of the conquest of the great mountain combined with the Coronation itself was a symbol of hope and the dawn of a new era. It was almost as if the new Queen was some sort of priest-ess who was going to make everything right again.

'Now with Elizabeth as our guiding star, and given a respite from monstrous calamity,' the *Daily Mail* commented, 'there is every prospect that this island and its sister countries will go for-ward into a future better even than the best of the past.' It was an awesome responsibility even for a woman of her will and determi-nation. Without Philip at her side, she would have been daunted by the expectations that lay ahead of her, but he could make her laugh and take a more prosaic view about the challenges and just get on with it.

'All our hopes rested with this one woman and how she was going to change everything,' said Lady Jane Rayne, one of Elizabeth's maids of honour. 'The war had changed an awful lot of things,' Lady Anne Glenconner, another of the Queen's maids of honour at the Coronation observed, 'but for the Coronation, we really went back to before the war, you know. Everything started again as though the war hadn't been.'

Indeed, at this point, the couple were adored in very much the same way as the Prince and Princess of Wales were thirty years later. Thousands of people would turn out to cheer them on foreign tours and they were talked about and written about as characters from a fairy tale. 'In the first years of the Queen's reign, the level of adulation – you wouldn't believe it,' Prince Philip said years later. 'You really wouldn't. It could have been corroding. It would have been very easy to play to the gallery, but I took a conscious decision not to do that. Safer not to be too popular. You can't fall too far.'

Philip's role in the Coronation was to kneel before his wife, taking the ancient oath of fealty: 'I Philip, Duke of Edinburgh, do become your liege man of life and limb and of earthly worship; and faith and truth will I bear unto you, to live and die, against all manner of folks. So help me God.' He then had to stand and kiss her cheek and back away. At the rehearsal, possibly feeling a bit emasculated, he did not play his part with any conviction. In fact, he mumbled the words at high speed, missed the Queen's cheek and retired backwards fast. The Queen told him off: 'Don't be silly, Philip. Come back here and do it properly.'

Of course, he performed seriously on the day, but his touch on the crown was a little heavy-handed and the Queen had to fleetingly adjust it. But the incident in the rehearsal illustrated just how committed the Queen was to doing things right at all times; she understood it was an important part of her role, and that she had a duty to fulfil.

But for the Queen, it was important to get it right for another reason. 'The Queen is a person of very deep faith,' said Michael Mann, former Dean of Windsor. 'She looked on the Coronation in the way in which the Coronation is intended.'

'The Coronation was a deeply moving spiritual experience for her,' her cousin Margaret Rhodes said, 'especially the part which wasn't filmed – when she stood bareheaded wearing only a white linen shift as the Archbishop of Canterbury marked the sign of the cross on her with the words, "As Solomon was anointed by Zadok the priest, so be thou anointed, blessed and consecrated as Queen over the people thy God hath given thee to govern."'

'And this feeling of being set aside to a particular task for the whole of her life was something that the Coronation set upon her like a seal,' Michael Mann confirmed.

Cecil Beaton, who had been commissioned to take the official photographs, gave one of the best and most vivid descriptions of the day as he entered the abbey:

Gold sticks [gentleman at arms of the Queen's bodyguard] stationed around the cloisters showed us on our way. They were already frozen blue. One of them asked me if I had heard the good news that Hunt had climbed Everest. The iced wind blew in circles round the winding staircase that took me to the rafters and I felt much sympathy for Hunt.

The guests, the peeresses en bloc – in their dark red velvet and foam white, dew spangled with diamonds. The minor royalties and the foreign royalties and representatives of states. The mother of the Duke of Edinburgh, a contrast to the grandeur, in the ash grey draperies of a nun ... That great old relic, Winston Churchill, lurches forward on unsteady feet, a fluttering mass of white ribbons at his shoulder and white feathers in the hat in his hand. Then the most dramatic and spectacular, at the head of her retinue of white, lily-like ladies, the Queen.

Beaton described her 'sugar pink cheeks and tightly curled hair and her demeanour of simplicity and humility', adding, 'as she walks she allows her heavy skirt to swing backwards and forwards in a beautiful rhythmic effect'.

Rain had fallen solidly throughout most of the ceremony, soaking everyone outside, especially those in uniform who were unable to take any shelter. The Golden Coach was waiting in Dean's Yard to take the Queen back to Buckingham Palace. But there was profound relief when the great ceremony was over and had gone without a noticeable hitch.

Then as now, both the Queen and Philip enjoy it when things go slightly wrong as their lives are so regimented. They were treated to one such moment in the procession back from the abbey when one of the attendants walking beside the Gold Coach started to head off in the wrong direction towards Hyde Park. John Taylor, the footman walking next to him, noticed straight away and signalled to the Queen, who told the Duke, who yelled out of the window at Taylor, 'Where does that man think he is going? Get him back!' Nothing had been left to chance, so the Duke had a walkie-talkie next to him on the upholstered seat of the coach so he could coordinate their arrival down to the second, but even he couldn't get to the footman, so a lot of discreet signalling went on.

Back at the palace, the newly crowned Queen and her consort's first concern was with their children. Four-year-old Prince Charles had watched part of the ceremony with his grandmother, while Princess Anne had been left behind. Lady Jane Rayne remembered how at one stage Charles picked up the crown, which was just lying on a nearby table, and put it on his head. 'I don't think, as he picked it up, that he could see how heavy it was and he sort of staggered to put it on his head and he couldn't even walk with it, it was so heavy. But he did look rather sweet and everybody laughed and it broke the tension.'

Then there were long sessions with Cecil Beaton, who had to get the official pictures done as soon as possible for the thousands of publications waiting for them. Prince Philip became at his most officious and tried to take control, which was very much unappreciated. 'He told me to smile at one point,' Anne Glenconner recalled. 'I could see that Cecil Beaton was getting very, very irritated because he is a professional photographer and the Duke of Edinburgh was telling him what to do.'

It may have been a high point of Beaton's career, but despite the tensions he still had time to make some pithy observations: 'The Queen looked extremely minute under her robes and crown, her nose and hands chilled and her eyes tired. The Duke of Edinburgh stood by making wry jokes, his lips pursed in a smile that put the fear of God into me. I believe he doesn't like or approve of me ... Perhaps he was disappointed that his friend Baron was not doing the job today: whatever the reason he was adopting a rather ragging attitude to the proceedings.'

The rain continued to pour down, but still the crowds roared and the Queen and Prince Philip reappeared on the balcony half a dozen times. After their final appearance at midnight, the crowd, which was by then a solid mass all the way to Trafalgar Square, started singing 'Auld Lang Syne'. 'The Queen led us out and we gazed at this extraordinary throng of people stretching for miles down the Mall,' Lady Glenconner recalled. 'You couldn't put a pin between the people and it was just a sort of roar of love for her.'

Eight days later it was Prince Philip's birthday, and Mike Parker threw a cocktail party at his home in Launceston Place in his honour. Prince Philip's sisters were still in London and were also invited. Margarita and Theodora (Dolla) were heavily built while Sophie, the youngest, was tall and slender. She had been married twice and her second husband was Prince George of Hanover. They all loved being with their younger brother in informal surroundings and chatted all evening, sharing private jokes in German.

Prince Philip adored his sisters, but spent much of the evening explaining to Prince Alfonso of Hohenlohe-Langenburg how the glass blower had managed to trap a bubble of air in the stem of his champagne glass. Philip felt completely at ease with the international set of glamorous rich playboys and Alfonso, who later married the fifteen-year-old Fiat heiress Ira von Fürstenberg, was one of those whose company he enjoyed.

Rather as with the Thursday Club, it made a change from the stuffy post-war British establishment who so mistrusted him. It upset him that he was treated as an outsider by them, but he knew that with the Queen he would be able to share challenges together. And with two children to raise on top of their public duties, they had plenty to keep them fully occupied as they moved into the next stage of their lives together.

Chapter 6

PARENTHOOD

Almost exactly a year after their wedding, the 21-year-old Princess Elizabeth gave birth to a boy. The Westminster Abbey bells rang out and a 41-gun salute was fired in his honour by the King's Troop Royal Artillery. The fountains in Trafalgar Square were floodlit blue and almost 4000 people flocked to Buckingham Palace to watch the comings and goings of the medical team.

The birth, at 9.14pm on a foggy night on 14 November 1948, had not been an easy one. The official bulletin, pinned to the gates of Buckingham Palace, announced that 'Her Royal Highness and her son are doing well'. It was later revealed he was born by Caesarean section, but such was the prudery of the age that this was never officially disclosed. Even her friends were not informed. Breast feeding was not spoken of and pregnancy, especially a royal pregnancy, was a condition that polite society feigned to ignore.

In another indication of the contemporary attitudes, Philip did not attend his wife during her confinement. When her labour started, Mike Parker remembers the royal family gathered in the equerry's room to await news of the birth. The King was stretched out by the fire and the prince was pacing the floor. Eventually Parker took him off for a game of squash. 'Well, time stretched a bit and he was getting restless,' Parker recalled. When the King's private secretary Tommy Lascelles bought the good news, Philip bounded upstairs into the Buhl Room, which had been converted into an operating theatre. He then held his first born, still wearing his sporting flannels and open-necked shirt.

His wife was drugged after the operation and did not come to for some minutes more. But as soon as she did, Philip presented her with a bouquet of red roses and carnations, thoughtfully provided for the occasion by Parker. Elizabeth would later say that her husband's face was the last she saw before she slipped under the anaesthetic and the first she saw when she came around again.

Prince Philip's mother Alice had recently moved to the island of Tinos in Greece in a house without a telephone, so he was obliged to send her a telegram with the news. She was thrilled and wrote to him at once: 'I think of you so much with a sweet baby of your own, of your joy and the interest you will take in all his little doings. How fascinating nature is, but how one has to pay for it in the anxious trying hours of the confinement.'

The princess had taken a far more pragmatic approach to her pregnancy ('After all, that's what we are made for,' she said), but she was beguiled by what she had produced. 'I still find it difficult to believe I have a baby of my own,' she remarked. In the long human tradition, she set about searching for family resemblances in his features. His hands attracted her attention. They were, she said, rather large 'but fine with long fingers'. Philip, always matter-of-fact to the point of seeming indifference, declared that he looked like a plum pudding.

The boy was christened Charles Philip Arthur George in the Music Room of Buckingham Palace. His godparents were George VI; his great-grandmother, Queen Mary; his aunt, Princess

Margaret; his paternal great-grandmother, Victoria, Marchioness of Milford Haven; his great-uncle, David Bowes-Lyon; Earl Mountbatten's daughter, Lady Brabourne; and his great-uncles, Prince George of Greece and King Haakon of Norway. Alice did not attend, but received all the news of her new grandson's progress from her younger sister Louise. She said the baby was like Philip, but Marina thought he was more like Lilibet. 'I am so happy for Philip,' she wrote, 'for he adores children and also small babies. He carries it [the baby] about himself quite professionally to the nurse's amusement.'

Elizabeth breast-fed her young son and Charles spent the first month of his life in a round wicker basket in the dressing room adjoining his mother's bedroom. She then contracted measles and the doctors advised she and the baby stay apart. He was taken away from his mother and handed into the care of Nanny Helen Lightbody and the nursery maid, Mabel Anderson. Charles spent much of his first months in the country estate, Windlesham Manor, his parents had rented. Two world wars had delivered a hammer blow to the cosy, upper-class world of servants and nurseries. The royal family, however, had weathered this development largely unchanged and Charles soon fell into the routine that had been so much part of Elizabeth's own childhood. He was taken to see his mother every morning at nine, just as she had been taken to see her parents. And in the evenings, engagements permitting, she would join him in the nursery. But that was just about the extent of it. They lived largely separate lives. 'To my knowledge, she never bathed the children,' Mrs Parker said. 'Nanny did all that.'

Once she had ascended the throne, her children's upbringing, as her own had been, was left in the care of the nursery staff. It was therefore to his nannies that Charles, who soon revealed himself to be a shy and sensitive child, turned for the affection he needed. It was Nanny Lightbody – Charles called her Nana – who got him up in the morning and dressed him, just as Allah had dressed Elizabeth. She also slept in the same room as him and comforted him when he woke during the night.

Much of his early life was lived 'behind the green baize door ... Mummy a remote and glamorous figure who came to kiss you good-night, smelling of lavender and dressed for dinner.' Prince Charles worshipped his mother, but from afar. The habits the princess had acquired in her own childhood were proving hard to break and, undemonstrative by nature, she always found it difficult to hug or kiss her son, preferring to leave such important tactile displays of emotion to the nannies.

Charles wasn't an only child for long, however, and by the time he was twenty-one months old, he had a baby sister for company. Princess Anne was born ten minutes before noon on Wednesday 15 August 1950 in her parents' newly refurbished marital home, Clarence House. Two years earlier, King George VI had decided that any children born to his eldest daughter would be known as 'Prince' or 'Princess'. A special decree published in the *London Gazette* in November 1948 stated: 'The children of Princess Elizabeth and the Duke of Edinburgh are to enjoy the style and titular dignity of Prince or Princess before their Christian names.' Had this decree not been issued, the infant would have been known simply as Lady Anne Mountbatten and would not have become a princess until her mother acceded to the throne.

Philip adored his baby daughter. 'It's the sweetest girl,' he told everyone who would listen after her birth. 'With quite a definite nose for one so young,' photographer Cecil Beaton added.

Philip's elder sister Princess Margarita of Hohenlohe-Langenburg was chosen as a godparent, as was his mother, Princess Andrew of Greece, and Lord Mountbatten; from Princess Elizabeth's side, her mother and the Rev Andrew Elphinstone were chosen. For the first and last time, Philip's side outnumbered Elizabeth's, by three to two, indicating his status as head of the family. The ceremony took place in the Music Room at Buckingham Palace on 21 October 1950 – by coincidence, and appropriately for Philip's career, it was the anniversary of the Battle of Trafalgar, one of the greatest naval battles in history.

Philip was the most attentive of fathers. He had been promoted to the rank of lieutenant-commander in the Royal Navy on the day Anne was born and given command of his own ship, the frigate HMS *Magpie*, so it was an even more special day for him. He helped choose her names – Anne Elizabeth Alice Louise – and had registered her with the Westminster Food Office. He was presented with the ration book, number MAPM/36, which the little princess, like the rest of the population in the austere post-war years, still required to obtain her allowance of meat, eggs, butter, bread, sugar, milk and, for a growing child, a weekly bottle each of orange juice and cod liver oil.

As we have seen in the previous chapter, Elizabeth and Philip's royal commitments and his naval career were their main priorities, so that when they toured Canada in 1951, the two young children remained at home. Princess Elizabeth became even more distant as a mother when King George VI died and she became monarch. Godfrey Talbot, the BBC's court correspondent at the time, recalled: 'She had been trained since the cradle by her father that duty came before everything, including her family. She reluctantly had to abandon her family and they virtually didn't see their parents for months on end. It was very upsetting and bewildering for [them].'

In 1953, the new Queen and her consort left on a long-delayed tour of the Commonwealth. They were away for six months. Like her mother before her, Elizabeth cried at the parting. And as her mother had discovered after her six-month trip to Australia in 1927, the long absence had exacted its inevitable toll. When they were eventually reunited, the Queen recalled, her children 'were terribly polite. I don't think they really knew who we were.'

In Philip's case that was even more understandable. He had managed to spend Charles's first Christmas with his wife and son, but that would prove to be the last time for a few years that they managed to be together for what are usually considered times for family celebration. In 1949, Charles's mother chose to leave her son at Sandringham with their grandparents and went to join her husband in Malta where he was serving in the Royal Navy.

Philip not only had his career to consider but, as we have seen, he tried to maintain something of a bachelor lifestyle as well, yet he could not escape his royal duties either. Naturally irascible, the demands of fatherhood served only to heighten his irritation and he had little time to devote to his son as he struggled to find a role for himself in these frustrating circumstances. Nor did he show any inclination to be a hands-on, nappy-changing kind of father. Charles, as everyone noted, was an 'exceptionally sweet-natured little boy' who was always thoughtful of others and the world around him. George VI, in his dying days, remarked: 'Charles is too sweet, stumping around the room.'

He was neither aggressive nor sporting, however. His little sister soon came to dominate him physically. Nor was he mechanically minded like his father. He suffered from knock knees like both his grandfather, George VI, and great-grandfather, George V. He had flat feet and had to wear a special pair of orthopaedic shoes. He was prone to chest complaints and suffered from a constant succession of coughs and throat ailments.

Perhaps unsurprisingly, these things did not overly impress his father. 'A resilient character such as Philip, toughened by the slings and arrows of life, who sees being tough as a necessity for survival, wants to toughen up his son – and his son is very sensitive,' Countess Mountbatten observed. 'It hasn't been easy for either of them.'

Philip believed in corporal punishment and Charles was summarily spanked if he was rude or obstreperous, a discipline that was quite normal at the time. Philip usually left the administration of such discipline to the nannies. His remarks, however, could be more wounding.

'He could be incredibly cutting, not only to his children, but to other people,' Mrs Parker recalled. 'He always had to fight for himself from the very beginning. The Queen adored him but she didn't rough it. He did rough it and I've heard him say some awful remarks.' According to her, Nanny Lightbody also had her reservations: 'She never said she didn't like him but I don't think she saw eye to eye with him one bit.'

'He just can't resist coming out with these personal remarks,' said Lady Kennard, a childhood friend of both the Queen and Prince Philip. 'He's at his worst with Charles, but he could be quite sarcastic with Anne, too.'

Philip's way of teaching his son to swim was to jump into the Buckingham Palace pool and loudly order the often-terrified Charles in after him. One Saturday morning, Charles was 'slightly chesty', so Nanny Lightbody did not want to let him into the water, but Philip insisted. The little boy ended up with a bad cold. Nana was furious. 'I was very cross with his father,' she said later, 'but the trouble is I can only say so much.' Philip, still the naval officer at heart, did not tolerate his decisions being questioned.

There were occasions when his manner would soften. He believed in encouraging his children 'to master at least one thing, because as soon as a child feels self-confidence in one area, it spills over into all others'. And Mabel Anderson publicly insisted: 'He was a marvellous father. When the children were younger he always set aside time to read to them or help them put together those little model toys.'

There were nonetheless moments when his exasperation got the upper hand. He tried to teach his son to sail, without noticeable success. Charles was often seasick and did not respond well to the hearty disciplines of life onboard. He later recalled: 'I remember one disastrous day when we went racing and my father was, as usual, shouting. We wound the winch harder and the sail split in half with a sickening crack. Father was not pleased.' The difference in their personalities opened a gulf between father and son. 'I didn't listen to advice from my father until I was in my late teens,' Charles said.

He was more at ease in the company of his grandmother, who now bore the title Queen Elizabeth, the Queen Mother. As a mother herself, she had been warm and loving but frequently distracted. Being a grandmother, however, suited her and she brought more affection to the role than Queen Mary had ever been capable of. In her dying days, the old Queen unbent a little, allowing her great-grandson to play with her collection of jade objects, a pleasure she had sternly denied her granddaughters, Elizabeth and Margaret. But, despite the mellowing sadness of old age (she lived to see her husband and three of her sons die and another exiled), she never lost her intimidating air of haughty majesty, even with her own family.

The Queen Mother, by contrast, was gentle and welcoming. She remembered her grandson as 'a very gentle boy with a very kind heart, which I think is the essence of everything'. The feeling was reciprocated. On her eightieth birthday, Charles said: 'Ever since I can remember, my grandmother has been the most wonderful example of fun, laughter, infinite security and, above all else, exquisite taste. For me, she has always been one of those extraordinarily rare people whose touch can turn everything into gold – whether it be putting people at their ease, turning something dull into something amusing, bringing happiness and comfort to people in her presence, or making any house she lives in a unique haven of cosiness and character.'

Charles and Anne's other grandmother was Philip's mother,

Princess Alice, who had now founded a nursing order of Greek Orthodox nuns and wore a nun's habit (which did not inhibit her chain-smoking consumption of noxious untipped Greek cigarettes or strong, caffeine-loaded coffee or her taste for sherry). She made occasional visits to England from her retreat in Greece and took delight in Charles's company, though he found her a rather alarming figure.

'She was very severe,' Eileen Parker remembered. 'She always sat bolt upright and had an almost overpowering personality. The room filled with smoke when she was around.' She spoke broken English in a thick, guttural accent and, because of her deafness, she was hard to make conversation with. 'She had to be near you so that she could look at you and lip read what you were saying,' Mrs Parker remembered. 'The Queen Mother was completely different. Very natural; she had the gift of putting you at your ease and making you feel as if you were the only person in the room.'

One thing Charles did share with his father was an interest in cooking and what went on in the palace kitchens and he was forever popping in to help the chefs weigh out the ingredients, fetching the pots, to give warning when the saucepans and kettles were coming to the boil. Not all his culinary efforts were successful, however. He was once sent to the palace storeroom by a chef named Aubrey – and dropped the tray loaded with butter, baking powder, two dozen eggs and sultanas on the floor on the way back. Not surprisingly, his presence did not always meet with the approval of the kitchen staff, who would complain that he got in the way.

His attempts at making ice lollies were equally fraught. Mabel Anderson kept turning up the temperature of the nursery fridge because his sibling's milk was getting too cold. Charles kept turning it down again because his lollies wouldn't freeze. Whether it was the milk or the lollies that came out right depended on who had last been at the fridge.

He enjoyed ballroom and Scottish dancing and was taught, as his mother had been, by Miss Vacani, who came to the palace to give him lessons with other children belonging to members of the household. But he found it difficult to mix and would cling to Nanny Lightbody and would watch as Anne 'would go off with the other children'. And while Charles was often too shy to talk, 'Anne talked non-stop'. When he was nervous, Mrs Parker noted, his mouth would twitch to one side in the manner later seized on by comic impersonators.

It had quickly become apparent that Princess Anne was growing up very differently. She once observed that she should have been a boy or, as she says, she would have 'probably been regarded as a tomboy'. There are those who are close to the royal family who believe that not only should she have been born a boy, but that she should also have been the eldest. Philip was one who held that view.

Single-minded, sporty and brave, Anne is unimpressed by rank or title, is unafraid of controversy and cares little for the opinion of others. And if she can be disconcertingly 'royal' when the mood takes her ('I'm not your "love", I'm your Royal Highness,' she once admonished an over-familiar photographer), she is someone who has no qualms or reservations about letting her hair down and mucking in when the occasion so demands. In other words, she is very much her father's daughter – in a way that Charles could never be his father's son.

'He always had more fun with Anne,' Eileen Parker observed. 'Charles is more like the Queen, while Anne is very like Prince Philip.' As Philip himself would later admit: 'Perhaps I did spoil her at times.'

'Anne would boss Charles; she would take command of things,' recalled Mrs Parker. 'If she saw a toy she wanted, she would grab it. She also grabbed everything that Charles wanted – and everything he had she wanted.'

Charles had a blue pedal car he was particularly fond of. He was often unceremoniously bundled out of it by his more aggressive sister. It was the same with the tricycle they shared. If Charles was riding it, Anne was sure to want it. 'There were terrible scenes,' said Mrs Parker, who used to entertain the royal siblings at her home in Kensington's Launceston Place. 'Nanny Lightbody would say, "Now stop this!"'

There was no stopping Anne, however. When their father presented them each with a pair of boxing gloves and tried to instruct them in the art of self-defence, they set about each other with such fury that he had to take them away again.

Once, when they were staying at Balmoral, Lady Adeane, the wife of the Queen's private secretary, gave them a paper bag full of mushrooms she had just picked. A row quickly ensued over who was going to present them to their mother. They started tugging at the bag, which burst open, spilling its contents over the gravel drive – at which point Anne, who had just returned from a riding lesson, set about her brother with her riding crop. Charles burst into tears just as the Queen opened the door. In exasperation, she shouted: 'Why can't you behave yourselves!' and boxed them both around the ears.

As the princess admitted: 'We fought like cats and dogs.' And 'no' was not a word she readily responded to. 'When she got really worked up, she would start throwing things at him,' Mrs Parker said. 'She was very strong-willed, a real menace.'

She was forever ignoring her nanny's instructions not to take too many toys out, but would instead empty the entire cupboard onto the floor and, in those days of coal fires in every room, make herself 'filthy in the process'. If she didn't get her way 'she had the most frightful fit of temper, lying on the floor and kicking with sheer temper'.

Charles was surprisingly nice to his boisterous little sister ('perhaps too nice,' Mrs Parker observed), always inviting her to join in his games, taking a concerned and conciliatory attitude towards her excesses. And for all their squabbles, the two got on reasonably well together, as they had to. For, like their mother and her sister before them, Charles and Anne spent more of their infancy in the company of adults – servants, courtiers, family members – than they did with children of their own age and it was to each other that they turned for playful companionship. That happened to suit Charles, who did not mix easily.

But if Anne was more than her brother's equal, it was Charles who commanded the greatest attention, no matter what their father might have thought about his abilities. He was born to be king and that fact was subtly drummed into him and his sister from their earliest memory. By her own account, she 'always accepted the role of being second in everything from quite an early age. You adopt that position as part of your experience. You start off in life very much a tail-end Charlie, at the back of the line.' And however much she might kick and scream, there, by genetic accident and the law of primogeniture, she was destined to remain.

She would be grateful for that in years to come. She developed a healthy view of her position in the royal hierarchy. 'I'm the Queen's daughter and as a daughter I get less involved than the boys,' she said. That allowed her to develop her own interests, in her own way, without the pressures of a centre-stage royal role that so inhibited Charles. 'I'm me, I'm a person, I'm an individual, and I think it's better for everybody that I shouldn't pretend to be anything that I'm not,' she once remarked.

There was no place for her, though, at the great occasion of the Coronation of her mother. She was too young to witness that pivotal transition not just from one reign to the next, but from one era to another. Anne, not quite three, remained at Buckingham Palace, suffering 'the normal sisterly fury at being left behind'. There was a party for all the children in the Madame Vacani dancing class. They watched the ceremony on a flickering black-and-white television set.

Anne's memories of the day itself are inevitably vague. What she does remember was being taken out onto the balcony afterwards with the rest of the family and being told to 'wave to the people'. It was a public lesson in the demands that came with being a princess. There was no escape from being royal. As she would later say, 'The idea of opting out is a non-starter.'

'The pattern of my life from birth until I went to boarding school, at the age of thirteen, was living in London during the week and at Windsor at the weekends,' she said. 'The holidays were divided between Christmas and the New Year at Sandringham, Easter at Windsor and most of the summer holidays at Balmoral.'

She settled into the time-honoured routine of country life. Schoolwork would occasionally intrude and, to help improve their French, a tutor, a certain Mlle de Roujoux, was employed. But football seemed to play as important part in the curriculum as irregular verbs. 'The Queen is always goalkeeper and Prince Philip, Princess Margaret and the children join in,' Mlle de Roujoux recalled. 'Charles and Anne were real little devils and never stopped playing tricks on me. The last words they shouted at me as I left for the train back home were "Cafe au lait, au lit", which I had taught them and which they had found most amusing. It means, "coffee with milk in bed".'

Anne has no complaints about the way she and Charles were treated as children, even though their parents were not around as much as they would have liked. She thrived in the freedom they had. While to modern eyes this distance looks odd, at the time it was nothing unusual – the fictional world of Enid Blyton's Famous Five or Arthur Ransome's Swallows and Amazons shows how often parents were relatively distant figures in children's lives. Most wealthy parents left their children with nannies and governesses, and they seldom travelled with their children until the advent of cheap flights. 'They were supportive and never really quibbled about what you wanted to do,' Anne said. 'There were occasional comments about was that really a good idea?'

'We may not have been too demanding, in the sense we understood what the limitations were,' she recalled recently. 'But I don't think that any of us for a second thought that she [the Queen] didn't care for us in the same way as any other mother did. In the early fifties, when I was growing up, there were still lots of people working and living in the countryside. Information was passed from parents to children, knowledge was absorbed rather than taught. My "knowledge" of ponies, horses and riding was largely acquired that way, by absorption.'

Interestingly, it was her father who really encouraged her riding. When he saw just how good she was – and how much better than her brother – he contacted Sir John Miller, the then head of the Royal Mews at Buckingham Palace and told him to 'get on with it'. Charles was still at the end of a leading rein when Anne was off jumping and galloping before she had properly learned how to trot. Philip had no reservations about letting his daughter expose herself to the dangers inherent in equestrian sport. 'It was almost as if he treated her as a son,' one observer recalled.

He also found the time to introduce his daughter to sailing on the waters of Loch Muick near Balmoral, with considerably more success than he'd had with Charles, and Anne soon became a proficient yachtswoman, as she still is today.

He would also take the children camping on the windblown Highland hills. They would cook over a fire and spend the night in sleeping bags in a bothy built in Victoria's day as a picnic hut. Again, it was Anne rather than her altogether more delicate brother who derived the greater pleasure from these Spartan escapades. But that, given their physical differences, was inevitable. Charles was a poor athlete; Anne became a first-class tennis and lacrosse player and, most notably, an Olympic three-day event rider.

The contrast was reflected in their relationships with their parents. Charles gravitated to his mother, who provided him with a sympathetic ear; Anne was close to Philip. Charles sometimes gave the impression of being 'terrified' of his father, who had little understanding of his son's fears and inhibitions and was inclined to laugh at them. He laughed at Anne too, but she could deal with that, cheerfully braving his ridicule, saying anything she wanted to him, and laughing back at him and with him, as she did when they were playing a game involving car number plates.

To keep his children amused on long car journeys, Philip would call out the registrations of passing vehicles and ask them to make a sentence out of the letters. One car had the number plate 'PMD'.

'That's easy,' Anne said. "Philip's my dad!"'

She paints her childhood as an enviable outdoor 1950s lifestyle, surrounded by family and animals. 'We grew up singing on the way to and from barbecues,' she recalls. 'Mostly First World War songs – we have quite a repertoire of those. The Queen is a very competent singer. I think we were very lucky as a family to be able to do so much together. We all appreciated that time.'

The question of education is always an important one for parents, and the Queen and Prince Philip were no different in that compared to anyone else, though their options were obviously constrained by convention and issues of security, as they looked to do what they felt was best for their children. With Charles, because his shyness carried through into his studies, the Queen understood that he was likely to get more embarrassment than encouragement from working as one of a group (looking back today, he is certain that her assessment was right), and she consequently decided that he should have lessons alone when he began his education.

Miss Catherine Peebles, who was promptly named Mispy (from Miss P), set up a schoolroom at Buckingham Palace, but instead of inviting other children to join him in his studies, he was taught on his own. Even Anne was not allowed in when he was working. Miss Peebles discovered that she had to deal with a vague child or, perhaps more accurately, a child who still had only a vague relationship to the external world. He was a 'plodder' who was good at art but took rather a long time learning to read, found it hard to concentrate on written subjects, and was incapable of understanding the 'language' of mathematics.

Like his mother before him, Charles was taken on educational visits to the museums and, of greater interest, to Madame Tussaud's waxworks, where he gazed at the effigies of the parents he saw less of than he would have wished. To ensure that these outings went off with the minimum of disruption, the Queen's press secretary, the later knighted Richard Colville, sent a letter to the editors of the Fleet Street newspapers asking them to allow him to enjoy himself without the embarrassment of constant publicity.

It was a vain appeal. Attitudes towards the royal family had changed since the days when his mother could go for open carriage rides around London waving politely to the people. In the still ordered society of the 1930s, royalty was treated with respectful deference. Twenty years later, public interest in this grand family had sharpened. Royal watching was becoming a national sport. The popular newspapers had started pandering to their readers' interests and wanted to provide them with as much coverage as they could – though by today's standards, they were still very restrained.

However, the Queen and Prince Philip were determined to give Charles as normal a childhood as they could, and in a break from royal tradition decided to abandon the system of private tutoring. In 1955, the Palace announced that he would be going to Hill House, a pre-prep school five minutes' drive from Buckingham Palace in Knightsbridge. This, they believed, was the best way to equip him for his future role, and the Queen was encouraged wholeheartedly by her husband. When he went there for the first time, an army of photographers and reporters descended.

'The Queen and I want Charles to go to school with other boys of his generation and learn to live with other children, and to absorb from childhood the discipline imposed by education with others,' Philip explained. The academic side was deemed to be of secondary importance, as he told his son: 'Look, I'm only going to bother if you're permanently bottom. I really couldn't care less where you are. Just stay in the middle, that's all I ask.'

The middle was where Charles stayed for the whole of his school life, except for mathematics where he was permanently rooted near the bottom. That did not particularly concern his father. It was his character that he was interested in and while it was the Queen who authorised this experiment in royal education, it was Philip who had the deciding say in which schools he would attend and, unsurprisingly, he would choose the schools that he himself had attended when Charles reached the age to go boarding.

Hill House was only a day school and every evening he retreated to the security of the palace. At the age of eight, however, the boy who, as one of his biographers observed, 'had never been shopping ... never been on a bus ... had never been lost in a crowd ... had never had to fend for himself' was marched out of this supportive environment to follow in his father's footsteps, first to Cheam, then up to the remote coastal plain of Morayshire to Gordonstoun. He found the transition excruciatingly painful.

Far more sensitive than his father, Charles was miserable and homesick. It was the start of his long march in his father's always too large footsteps. He was only eight years old and he felt the family separation very deeply. Unlike his father at the same age, he was used to the security of the matriarchal palace society of nannies, nursery maids and his grandmother, but suddenly he was on his own, one of twelve lowly new boys in a school of one hundred pupils. Philip shone in this kind of environment; Charles crumbled.

His first few days as a boarder at Cheam, he would later recall, were the most miserable of his life and his mother recalled how he 'shuddered' with apprehension as he journeyed there for his first day. 'He dreaded going away to school,' Mabel Anderson recalled.

Heartbroken, he would write to Mispy every day. He used to cry into his letters and say, 'I miss you.' The governess was equally distressed by the absence of the little boy she had come to love. She stayed on to teach Anne and later Andrew, but her real interest was always Charles, and they corresponded regularly for the rest of her life. (She died in the impersonal vastness of Buckingham Palace in 1968. After she retired to her rooms one Friday night, no one missed her and her body was not found until forty-eight hours later. Charles, his family remembered, was 'inconsolable' when he was told the news.)

He eventually settled in as best he could at Cheam, but he did not have a particularly happy time there. He was too diffident, too shy to make friends easily or to stand out and up for himself in the rough and tumbles. He still carried his puppy fat and during one game of rugby was upset to hear the shout directed at him from somewhere below, 'Oh, get *off* me, Fatty!'

The education of Princess Anne was not as constitutionally important or sensitive, and neither the Queen nor Prince Philip took much interest in Anne's academic progress. Before she was sent away to Benenden, a girls' boarding school in Kent, like her brother she had been educated privately at Buckingham Palace under the tutelage of Miss Peebles. The schoolroom was in the old nursery wing, and the Queen's rooms were close by on the floor directly below, yet Anne does not recall her mother paying even one visit to her classroom to see how she was progressing.

It was left to Princess Margaret to monitor her niece's work, and she did so with enthusiasm, going into the schoolroom to speak with the governess and even conducting oral examinations of her own. It was the foundation of a relationship between aunt and niece that matured into an adult friendship that few outside the family circle knew about.

Being educated in the Buckingham Palace schoolroom with a few carefully selected friends was an idealised, hugely privileged style of education, and in any previous generation it would have continued to its conclusion. Philip had other ideas. As with Charles, he wanted Anne to experience life on the other side of the palace walls. It was, he argued, a vital preparation for dealing with the exigencies of the modern world. Benenden, a traditional establishment for 'young ladies', was duly chosen and at the age of thirteen Anne became, not the first princess (that honour belongs to her cousin, Princess Alexandra), but the only daughter of a reigning sovereign ever to be sent away to school. Anne's own memories of Benenden were pleasant ones. 'I enjoyed my time at school, and no doubt my riding experiences helped,' she wrote.

Charles could not say the same when he went to Gordonstoun. Philip had thrived there, but it did not suit his son. The hearty outdoor life, if never as Spartan as legend made out (there were always hot showers to go with the cold, and the early-morning runs were little more than fifty-yard trots up the road and then never when it was raining), was still tougher than he would have wished. 'I hated the institution, just as I hated leaving home,' he would later say. 'I did not enjoy school as much as I might have, but this was because I am happier at home than anywhere else.'

'I had a dream,' he once recalled, 'that I was going to escape and hide in the forest, in a place where no one could find me, so

I wouldn't have to go back to school.' A housemaster of that time described the school thus: 'Good for the very clever, good for the laird's idiot son, but not so good for the average boy.' And in matters academic and athletic, Charles was never other than average. He only managed to pass O level mathematics at the third attempt. His history was something of a struggle (on one well-reported occasion his tutor, Robin Birley, shouted at him in front of the whole class, 'Come on, Charles, you can do better than this – after all, this is the history of your family we're dealing with!'). He was disappointing at rugby and cricket.

Where he did excel was in music and acting. He was taught to play the cello by an old German woman who had been at the school since Philip's day. And his ability on the stage was quickly noted by Dr Eric Anderson, who would go on to become headmaster of Eton. Anderson cast him in the role of Macbeth and he turned in a memorable performance. However, Prince Charles sees it in an altogether different light and still talks about the humiliating day his parents came to the school to see him perform and his father burst out laughing.

'I had to lie on a huge fur rug and have a nightmare,' Prince Charles remembers. 'My parents came and watched along with other parents. I lay there and thrashed about and all I could hear was my father and ha ha ha. I went to him afterwards and said, "Why did you laugh?" and he said "It sounds like the Goons."'

In 1994, Charles revealed to his official biographer, Jonathan Dimbleby, that he felt 'emotionally estranged' from his parents and all his life he had yearned for a different kind of affection that they had been 'unable or unwilling to offer'. His revelations hurt his parents, but all Prince Philip would say on the record is that they did their best. And according to Lady Kennard, their best wasn't so bad. She maintained Philip was a 'wonderful parent. He played with his children, he read them stories, he took them fishing, he was very involved.'

The Queen Mother, aware of her grandson's introverted nature, had argued that he would be better served at Eton College, on the other side of the Thames from Windsor Castle, and with 600 years' experience of accommodating the wide interests of its pupils. A number of the Queen's advisers agreed with her, but Philip was not to be swayed and Gordonstoun it was. 'In effect the decision meant an attempt to mould him in his father's image, to which . . . he did not naturally approximate,' royal expert Dermot Morrah wrote.

His difficulties at the school did not prevent him becoming Guardian, as Gordonstoun's head boy is called, as his father had been. The whole point of Charles's education, as Prince Philip saw it, was to train him to accept responsibility, a responsibility that was his by birthright and one which was not to be evaded.

For Charles, there was no escaping his destiny. 'I didn't suddenly wake up in my pram one day and say, "Yippee,"' he said, referring to the prospect of his kingship. 'It just dawns on you slowly that people are interested . . . and slowly you get the idea that you have a certain duty and responsibility. It's one of those things you grow up in.'

He was surrounded by reminders of who he was and what lay ahead. His mother's face was on the stamps he stuck on the letters to Mispy and on the coins he bought his chocolate with in his schools' tuckshops – a fact that his schoolmates were not slow to point out. Brought up among the sons of the privileged, he was always more privileged, and a personal protection officer accompanied him to Gordonstoun. Whereas everyone else had to see each term at Gordonstoun through without the benefit of a break (there was no half-term holiday at the school when he was there), he was allowed out to join his parents on various state occasions.

He was spared the anxiety of choosing a career – he was going to Cambridge. Then, and despite his seasickness, he was going into the navy. Everything was laid out for him. His great uncle, Earl Mountbatten, spelt it out: 'Trinity College like his grandfather;

Dartmouth like his father and grandfather; and then to sea in the Royal Navy, ending up with a command of his own.' A suitable marriage would follow. In 1987, in a cry of frustration, he declared: 'You can't understand what it's like to have your whole life mapped out for you a year in advance. It's so awful to be programmed. I know what I'll be doing next week, next month, even next year. At times I get so fed up with the whole idea.'

As a youth he had to bear it even if he couldn't grin. And no matter how definite the plan, it provided no protection against the bruisings he received along the way. Rather the contrary. When he was at Cheam, he watched his mother on television announce that she was going to make him Prince of Wales. 'I remember being acutely embarrassed,' he recalled. 'I think for a little boy of nine it was rather bewildering. All the others turned and looked at me in amazement.'

He was faced with similar moments throughout his schooldays. His photograph was often in the newspapers, and if the accompanying stories owed more to imagination than fact that was no consolation to Charles as he struggled and usually failed to live up to the image the press were determined to create for him. When faced with situations over which he had no control, however, he would withdraw deep into himself. Fearful of confrontation, desperate to avoid ridicule, he constructed a wall of regal reserve to protect the sensitivity which had been his most notable characteristic as a child.

On one occasion, one of the senior boys had the bright idea of making a tape recording of Prince Charles snoring. Waiting until he was asleep, several boys crept to the open window of Charles's dormitory and lowered the microphone by an extension cable to just above his head. It was easy as Charles's bed was next to one of the windows, which were always kept open. The plan worked like a charm and a little later that night the excited plotters listened to the loud snores of their future king on the tape recorder.

It was bullying of the cruellest kind and, although the tape was confiscated, the Charles-baiting went on without respite. Furthermore, he was always being told about his father's wild exploits when he had been at the school. Without a doubt, Philip had 'been one of the lads' and was often referred to as a 'good man' or a 'good shade', as the Gordonstoun terminology has it. To other pupils, it seemed as if he was always trying hard to live up to his father's great reputation, not by misbehaving or having adventures, but striving energetically to excel at everything he did. He has been doing so ever since.

Chapter 7

PHILIP AND ALBERT

With the Queen now settled on the throne, Prince Philip needed to secure for himself a proper role, and he had to fight to ensure that his own needs and position weren't entirely overlooked, as the courtiers' focus was unsurprisingly on his wife. For Philip, it was a difficult transition, and one in which he would have to learn to make his own way. As we have seen, he spoke to Prince Bernhard of the Netherlands about it, but there was also one other very important role model he could look to in the past: Queen Victoria's husband, Prince Albert – the last man to have been in a similar position to him. And what he saw, when he looked, made him realise that he wasn't getting treated as well.

Prince Philip's family name before he became Philip Mountbatten was Schleswig-Holstein-Sonderburg-Glücksburg, a name handed down from his Danish great-grandfather, but the German connections in his family tree were the cause of some gossip among the establishment in the early post-war years. Indeed, this may have been one of the reasons why he was initially treated so poorly by some who worked in the palace.

It is a fact that all four of Prince Philip's sisters married aristocratic Germans, of whom two were active in the 1930s in Hitler's Nazi party. None of the sisters was invited to the wedding of Philip and the Queen, largely because of these links to our wartime foes. But if that was the case, it was also true that Philip's mother Alice risked her life to save persecuted Jews in Athens during the war, for which she was awarded Israel's highest award for a foreigner. In 1994, Philip and his sister Sophie went to Jerusalem to receive the award posthumously on behalf of their mother.

For his own part, one of the greatest influences in Philip's life was Kurt Hahn, a German Jew who founded Salem school and later Gordonstoun. Hahn had to flee Germany to escape persecution from the Nazis. There is a world of distinction between being German and being a Nazi, but in those difficult times some chose not to make that point. Indeed, as we will see later, these spurious allegations would never entirely go away.

The fact is that, in common with the British royal family, Philip has German blood on his mother's side and many German relatives. This background still has an impact, even in some minor ways: for example, they retain the German custom of opening their presents on Christmas Eve rather than Christmas morning, following the tradition that Prince Albert maintained.

His mother's family name was Battenberg and her father was Prince Louis of Battenberg, a German who joined the Royal Navy aged fourteen and rose to the rank of First Sea Lord by 1912. Although he was married to Queen Victoria's granddaughter Victoria of Hesse, Louis was forced to resign in 1914 because of anti-German sentiment brought on by the war, and he subsequently anglicised the family name to Mountbatten. For the same reason, in 1917 King George V abandoned the German-sounding family name Saxe-Coburg-Gotha and changed it to Windsor, after the castle.

The royal family had taken the dynastic name of Saxe-Coburg-Gotha when Queen Victoria married her first cousin, Albert. By contrast, Philip was forced to abandon his family name for his children in favour of Windsor. His reported reaction was to exclaim: 'I am the only man in the country not allowed to give his name to his children. I'm nothing but a bloody amoeba.' But, under a declaration made in Privy Council in 1960, the name Mountbatten-Windsor was applied to male-line descendants of the Queen and Prince Philip when a surname was required.

It wasn't the only way in which Albert's official status appeared greater than Philip's. Queen Victoria's husband was formally titled 'HRH Prince Albert of Saxe-Coburg and Gotha, Duke of Saxony' for seventeen years until he was awarded the formal title of 'The Prince Consort' by Queen Victoria in 1857. He is the only husband of a British Queen to have held it. The Duke of Edinburgh is a prince of the United Kingdom but he is not Prince Consort. Yet Clarence House has announced it is likely that when Prince Charles becomes sovereign, his wife, the Duchess of Cornwall, will have the title 'HRH the Princess Consort'. It may seem a small point to some, this matter of titles, but to a proud man such as Philip it did appear to diminish him in some way. There are no specific duties for the consort that have been laid down by Parliament or established by custom, nor is any power conferred by the title. As Prince Philip himself said: 'Constitutionally I don't exist.'

Philip says he read several biographies of Prince Albert to see what he could learn from his experience. He also admits his interest in science, and in originating the Prince Philip Designers Prize, was inspired by what his predecessor did in setting up the Great Exhibition. He considers Albert an original thinker and says: 'All original thinkers have a certain quality you can probably recognise.'

There are parallels to be drawn between Prince Albert and Prince Philip. They were both of German ancestry and by all accounts both were very good looking as young men. Queen Victoria wrote: 'Albert is extremely handsome ... his eyes are large and blue and he has a beautiful nose and very sweet mouth with fine teeth.' In both cases, it seems to have been love at first sight when their future wives first set eyes upon them.

Each also had an influential, empire-building uncle working to support them: in Albert's case, it was King Leopold of the Belgians, and in Philip's, Lord Louis Mountbatten. When Albert married in 1840, Queen Victoria was already on the throne and took precedence over him. In Albert's own words: 'I am very happy and contented; but the difficulty in filling my place with the proper dignity is that I am only the husband, not the master in the house.' It was a situation very similar to that in which Philip found himself when his family had to move from Clarence House to Buckingham Palace after the accession.

There were, however, significant differences between Prince Philip's role as consort and that of Prince Albert, who involved himself in affairs of state soon after his marriage. Albert read the government papers delivered daily to the Queen in red boxes. He gave her advice, which she welcomed, and became her private secretary and closest adviser. Only months after his marriage, Albert wrote: 'Victoria allows me to take much part in foreign affairs and I think I have already done some good.'

By contrast, and to some extent reflecting the changing role of the monarchy in politics since Albert's time, Philip does not see the contents of the red boxes and, indeed, has never wished to do so, which has allowed him the freedom to speak his mind, as he so often does.

Albert's meddling in political matters, as some saw it, made him unpopular with the majority in Parliament. He was not granted a peerage or other title after the marriage and was voted a smaller annuity than previous consorts, £30,000 instead of the usual £50,000 – still an enormous sum in today's money, and when compared with Philip's civil list allowance. As time went by, Albert's influence behind the throne increased substantially. He had access to all Victoria's papers, drafted her correspondence and was present when she met her ministers. The Clerk of the Privy Council, Charles Greville, wrote of him: 'He is King to all intents and purposes.'

Albert described his position in a letter he wrote to the Duke of Wellington, saying: 'As natural head of the Queen's family, superintendent of her household, manager of her private affairs, sole confidential adviser in politics . . . he is besides the husband of the Queen, the tutor of the royal children, the private secretary of the Sovereign and her permanent minister.' In short, he saw for himself a much larger role than could ever be possible nowadays for Prince Philip, but as an active man the Duke of Edinburgh needed to find an outlet for his energies, as his predecessor had done.

Albert was only twenty years old when he married Queen Victoria; yet within a few years he had modernised the royal finances, set up a model farm at Windsor, increased the revenues of the Duchy of Cornwall and improved the other royal estates. On the Isle of Wight, Osborne House, an Italianate villa, was constructed largely to Albert's design as a holiday home for their growing family. He was also instrumental in securing Balmoral as a royal residence, buying the estate sight unseen in 1848, and in 1853 commissioned the building of the existing castle.

Active with progressive ideas in many fields, including the abolition of slavery, the ending of child labour and the reforming of university education, Albert had a special interest in science and technological progress in the manufacturing industry, in which Britain was the world leader.

Perhaps Albert's most famous project was the Great Exhibition of 1851, held in the 'Crystal Palace' in London's Hyde Park. It was organised by the Society of Arts, of which Albert was president, and owed most of its success to his efforts to promote it. Albert had to fight for every stage of the project. Opponents prophesied that foreign rogues and revolutionists would overrun England, subvert the morals of the people and destroy their faith. Albert thought such talk absurd and believed, quite rightly, that British manufacturing would benefit from the exhibition as a showcase for all they could do.

The Queen opened the exhibition on 1 May 1851, and it proved a huge success. It generated a surplus of £180,000, which was used to purchase land in South Kensington on which to establish educational and cultural institutions, including the Natural History Museum, Science Museum, Imperial College London and what would later be named the Royal Albert Hall and the Victoria and Albert Museum. The area became known as 'Albertopolis' at the time. His impact and name lives on in the hundreds of roads, streets and squares and other places named after him.

Prince Philip has certainly seen an opportunity for himself to do something similar in the way he promotes key activities. He has for many years taken a special interest in and done much to further the interests of British science and engineering, including setting up the Queen Elizabeth Prize for Engineering.

He used the Great Exhibition as a starting point for the address he gave to the British Association for the Advancement of Science, of which he had accepted the presidency in 1951. Not content with reading the short speech that had been prepared for him, he decided to deliver an ambitious and far-reaching address that was a summary of the progress of science over the previous century from Darwin to nuclear fission. At the time, Philip was still a serving officer in the Royal Navy and enjoying his first proper command of the frigate *Magpie*. He prepared for his speech for weeks, with his cabin a mass of reference books and papers. His audience on the day of the address was one of the largest gatherings of scientists ever seen in Britain, with some 4000 in attendance.

He opened the speech with a quote from the address that Prince Albert had made to the same association in Aberdeen in 1859. After an hour, he concluded with the words: 'It is clearly our duty as citizens to see that science is used for the benefit of mankind. For of what use is science if man does not survive?' His speech was warmly received by the scientists and was well reviewed in the press. Prince Albert had not been quite so fortunate in all his interventions. He had supported the theory of evolution by natural selection, based on Charles Darwin's book *On the Origin of Species*, which the church would not accept. He had even put forward Darwin's name for a knighthood, but it was rejected after opposition from the bishops.

But that was not all Philip did. By 1953, he had already taken on two major projects with great success. He had been made chairman of the Coronation Commission and had overseen every detail of the ceremony. Leaving nothing to chance, he even stood on the balcony at Buckingham Palace to find the best angle from which the Queen could watch the fly-past after the ceremony without getting a crick in her neck while still wearing her heavy crown.

At the suggestion of King George VI, Philip became chairman of the National Playing Fields Association (NPFA) in 1949. He set about raising the equivalent of many millions of pounds in today's money to open new playing fields across the country. He enlisted the help of Frank Sinatra and Bob Hope to make charitable appearances and so successful were his endeavours that, four years later, new playing fields were still being opened at the rate of 200 a year. He remained president of the NPFA for sixty-four years until Prince William took over in 2013.

Like Albert, Prince Philip involved himself in the modernisation of the royal estates. After her accession, the Queen made him Ranger of Windsor Great Park, a job for which Philip had to immerse himself in a course of estate management. He turned the farms at Sandringham and Windsor into profitable concerns, as well as supplying the royal households with food. At Balmoral, a herd of Highland cattle was put on the land and a forestry programme was introduced. Despite opposition from the stuffy officials at Buckingham Palace, Philip introduced many changes following a much-maligned time and motion study. An intercom system was installed so that if the Queen wanted a cup of tea or Philip a sandwich, it no longer took four footmen to pass the order on to the kitchen.

Between 1959 and 2011, he chaired the judging panel for the Prince Philip Designers Prize, which rewarded the innovation and creativity of designers and engineers shaping daily life. Winners have included product designer Sir James Dyson, of vacuum cleaner fame, architect Lord Foster, designer of the Gherkin in the City of London, and Andrew Ritchie, inventor of the Brompton folding bicycle.

Although Prince Philip ended his active naval career in July 1951, he remained very closely connected to the armed forces. In 1952, he was appointed Admiral of the Sea Cadet Corps, Colonel-in-Chief of the Army Cadet Force and Air Commodore-in-Chief of the Air Training Corps. The following year he was promoted to Admiral of the Fleet and appointed Field Marshal and Marshal of the Royal Air Force. For his ninetieth birthday, the Queen gave him the title Lord High Admiral.

He has been patron of some 800 organisations focused on the environment, science and industry, sport, education technology and design. He has served as chancellor of the universities of Cambridge, Edinburgh, Salford and Wales, but despite all of this work, he once said: 'I am not a graduate of any university. I am not a humanist or a scientist, and oddly enough I don't regret it. I owe my allegiance to another of the world's few really great fraternities, the fraternity of the sea.'

However, of all Prince Philip's many interests and achievements, the Duke of Edinburgh's Award scheme is the best known across the globe. Set up in 1956, it has helped more than 6 million young people to believe in themselves. It was originally administered by Sir John Hunt, who had led the first successful climb of Mount Everest. The scheme was based on the principles of physical fitness and community spirit laid down by Kurt Hahn and has become the world's leading youth achievement award. Bronze, silver and gold awards are earned through volunteering, physical activities, life skills and expeditions.

But, if pressed to say which of his many duties is the most important to him, it is likely that his duty as consort to the Queen would be named first. To support and protect her as sovereign, to accompany her to official ceremonies such as the State Opening of Parliament, to be at her side at state dinners and foreign tours, has been the central part of his life. At the Coronation in 1953, Prince Philip knelt before the Queen and swore to be her 'liege man of life and limb', and that pledge is something he has never forgotten. It was only in August 2017, at the age of ninety-six, that he finally stepped back from royal duties to enjoy life at his own pace.

Victoria was already Queen when she married Prince Albert on 10 February 1840 in the Chapel Royal at St James's Palace. In her diary entry for that day she wrote: 'The Ceremony was very imposing, and fine and simple, and I think ought to make an ever-lasting impression on everyone who promises at the Altar to keep what he or she promises. Dearest Albert repeated everything very distinctly. I felt so happy when the ring was put on, and by my precious Albert.'

In an age where dynastic marriages were often loveless affairs, and it was taken for granted that princes and kings had mistresses, Albert proved to be the exception. There has never been any sug-gestion that he was not true to his wedding vows until his untimely death at the age of forty-two. Albert's horror of infidelity could be

traced back to his childhood, when he witnessed at five years old
the departure of his beloved mother, who, having been mistreated
by his father, embarked on an affair and was banished from the
household for ever. A sincere and devout man, if he made vows,
he honoured them. It is also clear he was a man of passion, and he
and Victoria often sent each other erotic works of art as presents;
she was enthralled by her intimacy with him, which produced nine
children.

With Philip, however, the story has not been quite so straightforward, perhaps not helped by his membership of the Thursday Club
and his life as a sailor. Throughout their long marriage, rumours of
his alleged affairs have been rife. Biographers and royal chroniclers
have failed to prove the stories that have circulated since the 1940s
and no one has come up with convincing evidence to support the
allegations.

Even before his engagement, Prince Philip's love life had come
under scrutiny. In 1945, Philip was twenty-four and very good
looking; a tall, slim, blond Adonis. He was on active duty in the
balmy trade winds of the Pacific with Mike Parker, the Australian
fellow naval officer who later became Philip's equerry. According
to Parker, who went on shore leave with Philip: 'Philip was actually
quite reserved. He didn't give away a lot. There have been books and
articles galore saying he played the field. I don't believe it. People say
we were screwing around like nobody's business. Well, we weren't.'

Parker did admit in an interview with a biographer of Prince
Philip that there were always 'armfuls of girls'. He later said: 'Jesus,
I wish I'd never used that phrase. What I meant was this: we were
young, we had fun, we had a few drinks, we might have gone dancing, but that was it. In Australia, Philip came to meet my family, my
sisters and their friends. There were girls galore, but there was no
one special. Believe me. I guarantee it.' There is, of course, no reason
why Prince Philip should not have had girlfriends at that time.

Why Parker thought it necessary to defend his friend's actions when he was not even engaged is not clear, but the subject kept on being raised with him. Years later, Parker said: 'Philip has been one hundred per cent faithful to the Queen. No ifs, no buts. Take it from me, I know.' However, as Parker was Philip's best friend and secretary, some have chosen to take any statement made by him on behalf of Philip with extreme caution.

Once the Queen and Prince Philip were married, the period over which the biggest questions arise in many people's minds came in 1956, when Philip left the Queen at home with the children and embarked on a world tour on the royal yacht *Britannia*, with the object of visiting some of the smaller far-flung outposts of the Commonwealth, as well as opening the Melbourne Olympics on 22 November that year. The tour lasted just over four months. Questions were raised at the time in the press as to why Philip had left his family in London for so long, and there were rumours of wild parties during the voyage. *Britannia* had a crew of 220 men and twenty officers. Also on board were Mike Parker and an aide-de-camp to Philip. It is hardly credible that anything could have taken place without the knowledge of at least some of those on board.

Perhaps led on by baseless gossip, Joan Graham, the London-based Mayfair correspondent of the *Baltimore Sun*, ran the story in 1957 that London was rife with rumours that the Duke of Edinburgh had more than a passing interest in an unnamed woman whom he met on a regular basis in the West End apartment of a society photographer (presumably his friend Baron Nahum). 'Report Queen, Duke in Rift Over Party Girl' ran the headline. The story was soon picked up by the international press. The rumours were further fuelled by the fact that Mike Parker had chosen this moment to tender his resignation. It was taken as a sign that he had to go because he had been leading Philip astray, but in fact he felt he had to resign because his wife had filed a petition for divorce from him.

According to Parker, 'The Duke was incandescent. He was very, very angry. And deeply hurt.' In a break from the rule that the Palace never comments on rumour, the Queen authorised an official and complete denial. 'It is quite untrue that there is any rift between the Queen and the Duke,' said Commander Richard Colville, the royal press secretary.

In a letter from February 1958, Princess Margaret touched on the controversy when writing to her American friend Sharman Douglas, whose father had been the US ambassador in London in the late 1940s: 'I see the fine old press in your country tried to make out the Queen wasn't getting on with my b-in-l [brother-in-law]. So of course, the stinking Press here repeated it all sheep-like, like the nasty cowards they are. However, all is well and he's terribly well and full of fascinating stories of his journeys and it's very nice indeed to have him home again. The children are thrilled.'

At the end of the tour, the Queen flew out to Lisbon to join Philip for a state visit to Portugal. During the long voyage, Philip had grown a full naval beard, which he shaved off before boarding the Queen's plane. He found the entire party on the plane, including the Queen, wearing false ginger whiskers. When the royal couple emerged to meet 150 reporters on the tarmac, they were smiling happily. *Time* magazine reported that this was 'an all's well signal that spread to the four corners of the earth'.

Whether the unnamed showgirl referred to in the *Baltimore Sun* was Pat Kirkwood, a beautiful musical comedy star, is unknown. However, there were persistent rumours in the press that Philip was having an affair with her as early as 1948, when the Queen was pregnant with Prince Charles. Kirkwood, then the highest paid star on the London stage, was the girlfriend of society photographer and Philip's fellow Thursday Club member Baron.

One evening after a performance of the musical *Starlight Roof* at the London Hippodrome, Baron took Philip and an equerry to meet

Pat in her dressing room. The foursome then went out to dinner at Les Ambassadeurs Club in Hamilton Place run by John Mills, a Polish ex-wrestler. After dinner, they went at Philip's request to the Milroy Club for some music and dancing. According to Kirkwood, Philip would not let her sit down and danced to whatever the band played. Later they went to Baron's flat for scrambled eggs. Philip's conduct had not gone unnoticed at the Milroy and rumours of an affair with Pat spread.

According to Kirkwood, they only met again when she was presented to Philip at command performances in the theatre. She later said: 'I wish Philip had never come uninvited into my dressing room that night. I have had to live with the consequences for the rest of my life.' The rumours persisted for years.

After her death in 2007, Pat's fourth and last husband said: 'I have in my possession correspondence which passed between my wife and His Royal Highness the Duke of Edinburgh which leaves no room for doubt that the allegations so often made regarding a relationship between them are entirely without foundation. It was my wife's express wish that these letters should be handed in the fullness of time to the Duke's official biographer in order that the truth may be finally established. Until that time, they will not be released for publication.' Even this comment, however, does not explain why she and Philip should have been corresponding with each other at all.

Another name with whom Prince Philip was romantically linked is Hélène Cordet, formerly Hélène Foufounis. She became friends with him when she was six and he was three and they spent holidays together at her parents' villa in Le Touquet. Hélène became well known on television as the hostess of the BBC variety show *Café Continental* and as founder of The Saddle Room, London's first discotheque. Hélène had two children while separated from her first husband, but declined at the time to name the father.

When Philip elected to become godfather to both children, some assumed that he must be their father. Matters weren't resolved when she allowed the paternity of her children to remain a mystery. Even in her memoir, *Born Bewildered*, published in 1961, years later, she does not name the father. Many years later, her son Max, who became a professor of economics, was finally provoked into issuing a public statement utterly denying this.

Over the years, the rumour mill produced several other names of those they claimed he'd had an affair with, including the Countess of Westmorland, the wife of the Queen's Master of the Horse; the novelist Daphne du Maurier, wife of the Comptroller of the Royal Household 'Boy' Browning; the actresses Merle Oberon and Anna Massey; the TV personality Katie Boyle; the Duchess of York's mother, Susan Barrantes; the Duchess of Abercorn, wife of the Lord Steward of the Royal Household; Philip's cousin, Princess Alexandra; and his carriage-driving companion, Lady Romsey.

The satirical magazine *Private Eye* even linked Prince Philip with Stephen Ward, the society osteopath at the centre of the Profumo affair which rocked the Conservative government in 1963. Ward, a fellow member of the Thursday Club, was notorious for throwing wild parties at which 'The Man in the Mask' served drinks wearing only a skimpy apron. *Private Eye* took to referring to Prince Philip as 'The Naked Waiter', but in the investigation by Lord Justice Denning into the Profumo affair he described Ward as an unreliable witness.

Of all Prince Philip's respected biographers, only Sarah Bradford is adamant that Philip has had affairs. 'There is no doubt in my mind at all,' she told Gyles Brandreth. 'The Duke of Edinburgh has had affairs – yes, full-blown affairs and more than one. Not with Pat Kirkwood or Merle Oberon or any of those people. You're quite right, all that was nonsense, complete nonsense. I don't think there was ever anything in any of that. But he has affairs. And the

Queen accepts it. I think she thinks that's how men are. He's never been one for chasing actresses. His interest is quite different. The women he goes for are always younger than him, usually beautiful and highly aristocratic . . . Philip and Sacha Abercorn certainly had an affair. Without a doubt.' Sacha Abercorn denied that they did.

Because the rumours persisted until late in his life, when Prince Philip told Princess Diana that her wayward behaviour was destroying the essence of everything that he and the Queen had dedicated their life to preserving, and that her actions were also damaging her children's inheritance, she decided that she was going to do her utmost to discover about his alleged affairs as a revenge for what she saw as his disloyalty. According to her, after much careful detective work, she came to believe he had illegitimate children, as the rumours suggested, and that they had been financially cared for in perpetuity, though their identity was never going to be allowed to come to light.

So prevalent did the stories become that he was even asked directly about them himself. When a female journalist quizzed him about the rumours of extra-marital infidelities, Philip said: 'Have you ever stopped to think that for the past forty years I have never moved anywhere without a policeman accompanying me? So how the hell could I get away with anything like that?'

There is no doubt that Prince Philip enjoys the company of pretty women, preferably years younger than he is. I have seen him myself gliding around the dance floor at the Royal Yacht Squadron Ball during Cowes week with Penny Romsey. Neither of them gave a damn who saw them or what anyone might have said. Philip was with his yachting cronies and no one seemed to take any notice. Philip, an excellent dancer in the old-fashioned style, was completely in rhythm with the beautiful Penny Romsey as they moved around the floor.

He is undoubtedly close to Penny. In 1996, at the height of what was dubbed 'the war of the Waleses', a snooping radio ham Neville Hawkins taped a mobile phone call made by Philip to a 'plummy voiced' woman in which they discussed the bitter marriage battle between Charles and Diana, with Prince Philip likening it to a soap opera. It turned out to be Penny, but at one point she handed the phone to her husband, rather breaking any illusion of some clandestine contact between them. She is around at many Windsor weekends and often acts as the eyes and ears of both Prince Philip and the Queen as to what is going on in the outside world. Ever since 1975, when she was first introduced to Prince Charles, she has always been popular with the royal family. It was her lively mind, as well as her beauty, that turned this former meat trader's daughter into a central figure at the heart of royal life.

Friends of Philip knew, as a man who always had an eye for a pretty woman but who also gets bored easily, he was certain to find her intelligent and amusing company irresistible. He taught her the rudiments of carriage driving, at which she excelled, and now, at an age when the Duke is unable to do much carriage driving, he has found another reason for them to spend time together – painting in watercolours. Philip has always liked to flirt and make suggestive remarks, and the Queen is the first one to make jokes about his lascivious nature.

If all of these stories were to be heard in a trial for divorce, there is certainly not enough evidence of both desire or opportunity on Philip's part to permit a judge to reach a definite conclusion on this score. What the Queen feels about it all, we will never know. She would never let on that she might have been hurt when the rumours of her husband's supposed dalliances reached her ears. Or perhaps they never did. It is quite possible she would have been the last one to ever know and, even if she did, she could have buried her head in the sand and pretended it wasn't happening. It was lucky for him that the Queen has what many would consider an old-fashioned view of marriage and always advocated accepting a husband for what he is. In her early thirties she once remarked: 'There's nothing worse than to fence a man in and stop him from doing what he wants.'

With her approval, Philip has managed to get through his life doing just that. Her serene acceptance of the man has kept the marriage alive, and within the home she has always deferred to him. She has always been wise enough to appreciate his phenomenal energy and let him get on with things. He, in turn, has been her greatest support and has always protected her. And their partnership was about to produce another new arrival.

Chapter 8

BRINGING UP
ANDREW AND EDWARD

The Queen and Prince Philip had been married for twelve-and-a-half years when Andrew came along on the afternoon of 19 February 1960, becoming the first child to be born to a reigning British monarch in 103 years. The pregnancy was unplanned, coming on the eve of a Canadian tour which was scheduled to cover 16,000 miles in six weeks. It was not a practical journey for a woman in the early stages of pregnancy, but the Queen refused any advice to change her plans. She was, she insisted, in the best of health and had found her other two confinements relatively uncomplicated. However, the strain of the intervening years had taken their toll and the hormonal changes the Queen experienced made her very tired, but she refused to give in and rest. Stubborn to the last, she came home from the tour at the beginning of August exhausted and was immediately ordered to bed by her gynaecologist Lord Evans. Five days later, she had recovered sufficiently to journey to Balmoral for the rest of the summer.

The announcement of the 7lb 3oz infant prince's arrival was

greeted with the usual British fervour reserved for royal births. There was much rejoicing among the crowd in the Mall, who were deafened by a fly-past of thirty-six Hunter jets over Buckingham Palace as well as the traditional twenty-one-gun salute. As with her two previous births, Prince Philip remained in his study as the baby was being delivered; his wife had made it perfectly plain she didn't want him hanging around, let alone being by her side for the birth. The whole idea was loathsome to her and she was far happier to be in the care of her medical team headed by Lord Evans, John Peel – later Sir John, who had spent the night in a nearby room – and midwife Sister Rowe.

Lord Evans was the first to tell Philip that his anxious hours of waiting were finally over and as soon as he heard the news he ran out of his study, taking the stairs two at a time, and burst into the bedroom of the Belgian Suite, so named in honour of King Leopold of the Belgians, situated on the ground floor of Buckingham Palace next door to the swimming pool. He took his new-born son from the nurse and held him in his arms. 'It's a boy!' he shouted excitedly to the nursery staff.

There was more good news for him on the vexed question of the baby prince's name. A few days before Andrew's birth, a decree was issued by Buckingham Palace declaring that from henceforth the Queen's children would use the surname Mountbatten-Windsor. Under a declaration made in the Privy Council, the name Mountbatten-Windsor applies to male-line descendants of the Queen without royal styles and titles. It was a combination of Philip's adopted name of Mountbatten and hers of Windsor. So, when Andrew Albert Christian Edward was christened in the Music Room of Buckingham Palace, on 8 April 1960, he became the first royal child to hold the new family name from the moment of his birth. After having complained about the exclusion of his name when Charles and Anne had been born, it was a mark that his own status had been enhanced.

Andrew was also the first recent royal child not to have any official christening photographs. Instead, his father snapped away with his own Hasselblad as the godparents (or sponsors as they are known in royal circles) stood around the silver lily font. The late Duke of Gloucester, Princess Alexandra, Lord Elphinstone, the Earl of Euston and Lady Kennard were the honoured friends and relatives chosen.

Both Prince Philip and the Queen were aware that Charles and Anne had suffered unnecessarily from over-zealous media attention during their formative years and decided to best way of avoiding a repetition of the situation was to keep the baby, who was second in line to the throne, away from public places. Instead of going to the park, his nanny would restrict walks to the gardens of Buckingham Palace or Windsor Castle, a discreet distance from any public highway. That way the palace could control the amount of coverage the baby received. Like any parents, they were learning from their previous experiences, and trying to ensure they could provide the best environment for their child.

The first photographs to be released of Prince Andrew were those taken by Cecil Beaton, when the baby was already one month old. As always, Beaton's diaries give a revealing and acerbic account of the event. He thought the Queen's bright red dress was 'better than most of hers', but he 'felt that the odds were ganging up against me ... I clicked like mad at anything that seemed even passable. But the weight of the Palace crushed me. The opposition of this hearty naval type must be contended with, and due deference to the Queen. She seemed affable enough but showed no signs of real interest in anything ... Not one word of conversation – only a little well-bred amusement at the way I gave my instructions in a stream of asides.' Philip, 'in that maddening Royal way', kept on making suggestions, including that Beaton should climb a ladder to take the photos. Eventually, Philip decided to take his own pictures with his own camera.

Prince Philip behaved in the same dismissive way to Beaton's 1990s equivalent, Terry O'Neill, at the christening of Prince Andrew's younger daughter, Princess Eugenie, in December 1990. When Terry, who works very quickly with just one assistant, was snapping the christening group at Sandringham, Prince Philip kept saying, 'Come on! Come on! Haven't we done enough?' Then he added what is known as his photographer's phrase: 'If he hasn't got what he wants by now, he's an even worse photographer than I thought!'

After that time, there was a lack of news about the royal baby and, because of the lack of photographic evidence to the contrary, whispers began that there might be something wrong with the baby. People were noting how Andrew had been kept away from public gaze much more than was the case with Charles or Anne. Eventually, it was left to the foreign press to make the first move and a French newspaper ran a story claiming that the baby was malformed. Prince Philip was furious, the Queen upset and Buckingham Palace defeated in its aim to keep things private. Then as now, the Palace are reluctant to give way to media pressure, but they saw little sense in keeping Andrew hidden any longer. So, at sixteen months old, he made his public debut on the Buckingham Palace balcony for the Queen's birthday parade. When the crowd spotted the baby dressed in his best embroidered romper suit bobbing up and down in his mother's arms, a huge cheer went up. This was what they had waited to see.

Nanny Mabel Anderson was thirty-four when Prince Andrew was born and she ran the nursery in the traditional royal manner: unchallenged, unopposed and almost as a private fiefdom. She had the assistance of an under-nanny, June Waller, who helped her in much the same way as she herself had helped Helen Lightbody with Charles and Anne, and a nursery footman. Royal nannies do not have to clean, cook or do the laundry. Their job is to purely see to the children's wellbeing and run the nursery, which Mabel did perfectly. She set up an unswerving routine, like so much of their structured royal lives. Mabel was the central pivot around which everything revolved for Andrew. His parents were almost strangers by comparison.

By now, the Queen had been on her throne for eight years, and compared with the austerity years when Charles and Anne were younger and the Queen seldom had the time to see them during the day, she was now able to find more time for Andrew. Where previously she might have sometimes popped into the ballroom where they had their weekly dancing lessons with Madame Vacani, now, with Andrew, it was different. She had more time available, and so was able to schedule time with him into her diary in a way that had not been possible before.

'Leave him with me, Mabel,' she would say some mornings, and Andrew would be left with his mother, playing on the floor of her study while she worked at her desk. Perhaps because he was older, perhaps because he had finally found the right niche for himself, but Philip also found fatherhood the third time around more enjoyable. He liked doing things with Andrew, who was an endless source of entertainment. With a brother almost twelve years older and a sister nine years older, he could have been spoilt, as he was very much the youngest member of the family, but he was encouraged to be self-reliant.

Andrew recalls his parents divided their responsibilities towards him half and half: 'Compassion comes from the Queen,' he said. 'And the duty and discipline and duty comes from him [Philip]. I think our mother probably put a bit more effort to make sure there was time for us as children, bearing in mind she was Queen when we came along. We used to see her in the afternoons and in the evenings the usual standard bath time sort of routine. And Father would usually read us a story or we would read to him – the *Just So Stories* – all sorts of things like that.'

Philip would also tell his children stories he had invented himself. However, his appearance in the nursery filled Mabel with apprehension, as it had Nanny Lightbody before her. It was usually a prelude to tears, as Andrew often became over-excited when playing with his father, leaving his nanny to sort out the mess – though not before once collecting a black eye in the rough and tumble.

With Charles and Anne away at boarding school, Andrew and later Edward should have been able to enjoy the individual attention of their parents, but the reins of monarchy were always pulling. When the Queen and Prince Philip did join their children for tea in the nursery, they never arrived unannounced and the staff always knew when one of them was coming. Mabel would fuss around making sure everything was in place and the children were clean and tidy. Sometimes, on Mabel's day off or when she went to her evening pottery classes, the Queen would babysit the two children.

It was still very formal, however, and she would bring her own page and footman who would serve her supper in front of the nursery television. If the children awoke she would soothe them back to sleep. She relished those private moments with her children and in later years admitted she felt guilty about not spending more time with them. Although there was no escaping from the merry-go-round of royal duties, the Queen and Prince Philip would never go out to dinner without saying goodnight to their children. If they were going out to an official function, such as a film premier, nanny would take them out into the corridor so they could wave goodbye. Before she got into the car wearing her tiara and a long dress, the Queen would always look up to the nursery floor and see their anxious faces pressed against the glass and give them a wave, while Philip would blow a kiss.

The Queen and Philip's theories about bringing up children had been tempered by experience. As Philip explained: 'It's no good saying do this, do that, don't do this, don't do that. It's very easy when children want to do something to say no immediately. I think it's quite important not to give an unequivocal answer at once. Much better to think it over. Then if you eventually say no I think they really accept it.'

When the Queen wasn't around, Philip took charge of the children, but he became easily distracted and often let them wander off. One weekend, when he was five, Andrew took advantage of this and made his way to the Royal Mews at Windsor while his father was out carriage driving. The coachmen and grooms who worked there had little time for the prince, having often seen him aim sly kicks at the dogs and taunting the helpless guardsmen. Sensing their studied indifference and trying to attract attention, the prince started beating the ground with a large stick. No one took any notice, so Andrew doubled his efforts and beat the ground even harder, taking a sideways swipe at the legs of the horses.

When he refused to stop, two grooms picked him up, threw him into the dung heap and shovelled manure all over him. The prince was too shocked to cry, but the impact of his humiliation hit him and, when he managed to extract himself from the foul-smelling mess, he ran as fast as he could up the hill to the castle saying: 'I'll tell my mummy on you! I'll tell my mummy.' No one knows if he ever did but there were no repercussions.

Nor were there on another occasion when his taunting so annoyed a young footman that he took a swipe at Andrew that deposited him on the floor and left him with a black eye. Fearing for his job, the footman confessed what had happened and offered his resignation. When the Queen came to hear of it, she refused to accept it. She said her son had obviously deserved it and the footman was on no account to be punished for Andrew's bad behaviour.

By that time, of course, Andrew had a younger brother to keep him company. Prince Edward was born on the evening of Tuesday

10 March 1964 and there at the bedside, holding the Queen's hand, was the Duke of Edinburgh. It was the first time he had been present at the birth of one of his children and he was there at the express invitation of his wife.

The Queen was thirty-seven. She had not found giving birth easy, but sixteen years had passed since Charles was born and fashions had changed in the interim, even in matters as primary as obstetrics. Now the accent was more on the relationship between mother and baby and how that could be enhanced, both physically and emotionally, by the mother being aware of what was happening – and how important it was to involve the father in the process.

As a keen reader of women's magazines which had been devoting an increasing number of their pages to articles expounding these theories, she had become fascinated by this new approach. It struck a timely chord. The Queen's life had always been subject to the advice of others. Even in matters as intimate as how they were delivered of their own children, the royal family had been subjected to checks and scrutiny. Prince Philip had been barred from the birth of Charles, Anne and Andrew. The idea of having him there with her would have been almost incomprehensible to most people, if not distasteful in an age so decorous that it forbade the publication of any photographs of the Queen in her pregnancy and never officially acknowledged that she had delivered her first-born by Caesarean section. But this time, she decreed, Philip would attend the birth – the first time in modern history that any royal father had been allowed in to see his progeny born.

More sensitive than his abrasive public image suggests, Philip took a concerned interest in the proceedings, and when the spirits of others started to wane, his cheerful banter revived them. As with Andrew, the baby was born in the bathroom of the Belgian Suite, which had once again been converted into a delivery room. During the Queen's confinement, black drapes were hung over the floor-to-ceiling French windows which look out over the terrace to the palace gardens and the lake.

Attending the Queen that day were five doctors – her surgeon-gynaecologist Sir John Peel, who had been present at the birth of her three elder children; her new family doctor, Dr Ronald Bodley Scott; Sir John Weir, eighty-two, who had been one of her physicians since 1952; John Brudenell, a consultant at King's College Hospital; and Dr Vernon Hall, dean of the Medical School at King's College Hospital – and two midwives: Sister Annette Wilson and Sister Helen Rowe.

Also there was Betty Parsons, whose relaxation techniques and no-nonsense advice had helped thousands of women to deal with the concerns and fears of childbirth. Betty paid attention to breathing and, in one of her most famous exercises, would extol both the expectant mothers and the many fathers-to-be who attended her anti-natal classes to pant like a dog. Relations were not of the smoothest between Parsons and the doctors, who, most conventional in their methods as befitting their eminent positions, had little empathy with Betty's newer, 'alternative' approach. The Queen, however, had enjoyed her training sessions with the former midwife and insisted that she be there at the birth. Philip, too, was supportive. He had drawn the line at attending her pre-natal classes – it was hardly the Duke of Edinburgh's style – but when Betty had arrived at the palace the morning the Queen went into labour, it was Philip who had quickly ushered her into the delivery room before the doctors could lock her out.

By this stage, though, the doctors were too involved in looking after their patient to worry about Betty. The baby was not due for another week and only the previous morning the Queen had been out walking in the palace grounds with her corgis and Andrew, seemingly on course for a full-term pregnancy. But the contractions had started early the following day and by the evening she was in full labour.

The delivery was slower than they might have hoped for. It was at this point that Philip's good humour proved so valuable. 'It's a solemn thought that only a week ago, General de Gaulle was having a bath in this room,' he remarked when he walked into the bathroom and saw all the glum faces. It was said in a jocular way, which helped ease the tension that had been building up among the doctors and the nurses attending their sovereign.

Despite the involvement of Parsons, the Queen did not have what today would be called a 'natural' childbirth, though by the standards of the time it was regarded as very straightforward and the Queen did not suffer a lot of pain. The birth, however, was 'a bit slow', which was why Philip's asides were appreciated. Finally, at 8.20pm, to the relief of all involved, the Queen was delivered of a 'small but healthy' boy.

Although it was the first time he had attended the birth of one of his children, Philip would later declare: 'People want their first child very much when they marry. They want the second child almost as much. If a third comes along they accept it as natural, but they haven't gone out of their way to get it. When the fourth child comes along, in most cases it is unintentional.' He was clearly not going to get too sentimental.

His wife took a keener view of the process. As a young girl, she had declared that, when she grew up, she wanted to marry a farmer, live in the country and have lots of animals. Above all, she wanted four children – two boys and two girls. She had married a sailor, not a farmer, but her other wishes had been fulfilled. So why not a second daughter to go with the two sons she now had? So convinced was she that she was going to have a daughter that she had not bothered to think of boys' names during her pregnancy – only girls' names had been discussed.

This was one matter, though, over which even a sovereign had no say and, much to the Queen's surprise, if not that of her doctors, who throughout had taken the more pragmatic medical view, the baby was a boy. Philip telephoned the news to the Queen Mother at Clarence House, then interrupted Prince Charles doing his prep at Gordonstoun and finally spoke to Princess Anne at school at Benenden in Kent.

Sir John Weir called him 'a bonny baby', while Dr Vernon Hall said he was 'a very serious looking boy'. He added: 'Everything went well – no problems.'

By comparison with his siblings, he was a small child, weighing only 5lb 7oz, and was finally named Edward Anthony Richard Louis after his godfathers Lord Snowdon, Richard, Duke of Gloucester and Prince Louis of Hesse, prefixed by the old royal name of his great-great-grandfather, Edward VII. His parents had taken a long time in the selection and his names were not officially announced until twenty-four hours short of the forty-two-day deadline which, if it is exceeded, can result in a fine (though not in this case, for the sovereign, as the embodiment of the law, is above the law). He was christened wearing the robe of Honiton lace that had been made in 1841 for Queen Victoria's eldest child, Victoria, who married the German emperor and whose son, Kaiser Wilhelm II, led his nation into war with Britain.

What the Queen called 'my second family' was now complete. Being older, Philip was less demanding of Andrew and Edward than he had been with Charles, while the Queen had acquired the confidence of experience that enabled her to adopt a more relaxed and hands-on approach to motherhood. It showed with Andrew, but it showed even more with Edward. Andrew would always be his mother's favourite, but Edward was also allowed to crawl around on the floor of her study while she worked on her state papers. Indeed, so intent was she to spend more time with her children that she brought her weekly meetings with her prime ministers forward by half an hour so she would be free to bathe Edward and put him to bed herself. Many working mothers have to adapt their diaries to accommodate children, and the Queen was doing just that so she could give as much attention as possible to both her family and her royal duties.

After the press rumours about Andrew, she also took the precaution of giving her subjects an early sight of the latest addition to her family and made a great show of bringing Edward out onto the Buckingham Palace balcony after Trooping the Colour in June, holding him aloft for the crowds below to see and cheer. As Philip observed: 'We try to keep our children out of the public eye so that they can grow up as normally as possible. But if you are really going to have a monarchy, you have got to have a family and the family has got to be in the public eye.'

There was a limit to how far the Queen and her consort were prepared to go, however, down this path. Change is rarely in monarchy's best interest. There is security in sameness; it is a bulwark against the agitations of social upheaval, and the 1960s were a very perturbing time indeed for the *ancien regime*. Outside the palace walls, a veritable social revolution was taking place, and by 1964 it was well underway. In Britain, Sir Alec Douglas-Home, the hereditary 14th Earl of Home, was swept from power by Harold Wilson and a Labour government dedicated to tearing down the old class barriers and building a modern, forward-looking society in their stead. In such a world, where Wilson was emphasising the 'white heat of technology', the monarchy was always going to appear out of date.

Change wasn't evident only in the UK. In the United States, still traumatised by the assassination of President John Kennedy, his successor, Lyndon B. Johnson, was signing the Civil Rights Act, the most sweeping civil rights law in American history, which he said would 'close the springs of racial hatred'. In South Africa, a young lawyer named Nelson Mandela was sentenced to life for treason for plotting to overthrow the all-white government. In India, Jawaharlal Nehru, prime minister since the country became independent from Britain in 1947, thereby stripping the Queen's father, George VI, of his title of Emperor, died. In the Soviet Union, Nikita Khrushchev was ousted in a coup by hardliners led by Leonard Brezhnev.

It wasn't just in high-level politics that there were so many signs of change. Entertainment was becoming more central to people's lives, thanks to the proliferation of television. So when Richard Burton married Elizabeth Taylor, the actors' wedding was given almost as much attention as any royal occasion. For the first time in almost a century, the royal family was being publicly made fun of on television's satirical *That Was The Week That Was,* produced by Ned Sherrin and presented by David Frost. The approach to raising their family could not be immune to all these changes.

Furthermore, the western world was gripped by the mass hysteria of that most light-hearted of phenomena: Beatlemania. Even Prince Philip was touched by it. The Beatles, he said, are 'entirely helpful. I really could not care less how much noise people make singing and dancing. I would much rather they make any noise they like singing and dancing. What I object to is people fighting and stealing. It seems to me that these blokes are helping people to enjoy themselves and that is far better than the other thing.'

The gap between the four long-haired pop stars from Liverpool and the Greek-born prince was nevertheless a yawning one. When the group performed for the Queen at the Royal Variety Show, John Lennon looked up at the Royal Box and invited the poor to clap – and the rich to rattle their jewellery. The 'impromptu' remark had in fact been carefully rehearsed in the dressing room beforehand. Several expletives were contained in the original version, which gave crude expression to Lennon's less than reverential opinion of the British establishment that the royal family personified. The Beatles' manager, Brian Epstein, never sure what the iconoclastic genius would do next, was in a tail-spin of worry lest at the last moment Lennon threw caution and career to the wind and delivered the unsanitised version. He did not, of course, preferring cheeky impudence to crude impertinence.

Lennon was not alone, though, in questioning the value of the royal family at that time. At a luncheon of the Foreign Press Association thirteen days before Edward was born, Prince Philip was asked: 'Do you think that the monarchy has found its proper place in the Britain of the sixties?'

Philip replied: 'Here we are in the sixties. What am I supposed to say? Perhaps you would enlarge on the question.'

The questioner did: 'One sometimes hears criticism in the press that the monarchy has not found its place, although it is, of course, playing a useful role in this country, but has still not found the right approach to the problems of Britain today.'

Philip answered: 'What you are implying is that we are rather old-fashioned. Well, it may easily be true; I don't know.'

He continued: 'One of the things about the monarchy and its place – and one of the great weaknesses in a sense – is that it has to be all things to all people. Of course, it cannot do this when it comes to being all things to all people who are traditionalists and all things to all people who are iconoclasts. We therefore find ourselves in a position of compromise, and we might be kicked by both sides. The only thing is that if you are very cunning you get as far away from the extremists as you possibly can because they kick harder.'

He concluded, warming to his theme: 'I entirely agree that we are old-fashioned; the monarchy is an old-fashioned institution.' And that was the way it was going to stay. The Queen's radical decision to have her husband by her side during the birth notwithstanding, the great ship of royalty continued its majestic course with barely a sideways glance at the foam of change churning up around it. 'I am a traditionalist,' the Queen bluntly declared, and the habits of her Court reflected that.

The royal family, as well as being an institution that functions best in calm conditions, is also a business. Philip has called it 'The Firm', and it employed a full-time staff of several hundred people – cooks, chamber maids, ladies' maids, coachmen, footmen, valets, butlers and nannies. Hierarchical and tradition-bound, they were dutiful, loyal and clung steadfastly to the old ways, and the palace continued to be run in the most paternalistic manner. But the Queen, for all her riches, was forever looking for ways of making small savings, in the endearing if incorrect belief that by counting the pennies the pounds of royal expenditure would somehow manage to look after themselves. So, for example, Edward slept in the same cream-painted cot his brothers and sister had used, and played with the same toys.

Being part of The Firm meant that other conventions had to continue in their timeless way. Philip may have attended Edward's birth, but this was no New Man in the making, and two days later and without thinking too much about it, if he thought about it at all, he flew to Athens to attend the funeral of his cousin, King Paul of the Hellenes. He saw it as his royal duty to be there, and that putting on the public display of mourning was more important than remaining at the bedside of his wife, doing his private duty. As so often in the royal marriage, the competing demands of the public and private roles were on display, and the public role won out. The Queen, the doctors assured him, was doing well and she was comfortable in her room. She had a television set and a view of her gardens to keep her interest and she was well looked after by the palace staff, as was his young son.

The moment Edward was born, the royal child-rearing machinery had clicked into gear. The Queen would indeed spend more time with Edward than she did with her elder children, and his childhood was marked by an informality which would have been out of place in Charles and Anne's day. When it came to his formal education, the Queen, Prince Philip and Sir Martin Charteris, the Provost of Eton at the time, discussed what would be best for their youngest son's future. They called in James Edwards, headmaster of Heatherdown School, where Andrew was already a pupil, to get his opinion. They had decided on this school for him, rather than Cheam as before, because it was closer to Windsor Castle and many of the Queen's family and friends had sent their children there.

Edwards was not in favour of the idea of Gordonstoun and told the Queen so. She listened, but in the end Prince Philip won through again and the Queen agreed he should go to Gordonstoun, but not before first joining his brother at Heatherdown. Philip may have been an affectionate father, but he did not agree with indulging children. He remained a devout disciple of Kurt Hahn's guiding principle: character first, intelligence second, knowledge third. For Andrew, who was not intellectual, perhaps that order was correct. He was not timid like his elder brother and perhaps Eton would have polished off Andrew's rough corners and given him a better scholastic education, which would certainly have helped him. Instead, he appeared uncertain if he wanted to be a prince or one of the lads, and his inability to solve that dilemma would become something of a handicap. He never became head boy or guardian as his father and elder and younger brothers did.

'Edward got on with everybody; he was easy to teach and very well behaved,' Edwards recalled. 'His elder brother was much more extrovert. There are some children who naturally get dirty and some who naturally stay clean. You can sit a child in a chair spotless and five minutes later he is dirty. Why? Don't ask me. You can get another child who can spend an hour playing in the woods and he comes out looking like a bandbox, and Edward was one of those children.'

By now the Queen was a more confident parent than she had been when Charles was born, and she had developed a rare understanding of people and personalities gained from her years on the throne, which she now applied to her own children. 'Some parents who gave their children to nannies hardly know their children at all, but the Queen knew hers,' Edwards confirmed. 'She's very on the ball and she's one of the best raconteurs I've ever met – terribly funny.' He added: 'Prince Philip appeared, but not as much as the Queen. She determined and controlled their early schooling. I discussed their school reports with her rather than him.'

The Queen did not pick up her children from school on their days out, but she always took them back. 'She used to drive herself in her green Vauxhall station wagon with her detective Perkins beside her,' Edwards said. 'She would always come into my study and have a chat about anything and everything. When she talked about the children, she was totally aware of their shortcomings and was extremely patient.

'One thing she absolutely insisted on, however, was good manners, and it showed. The Queen never let them down. She came to every single school sports day, play and carol service that we had. And over nine years that is good. She only missed one and that was when Edward was playing the part of Saul in *The Boy David* and she was on tour in Australia on a state [*sic*] visit. So the Queen Mother came instead.'

It was at Heatherdown that Edward began to develop his enthusiasm for the theatre, and he secured a starring performance as Mole in *Toad of Toad Hall*. Nicholas Tate was Toad, Andrew Wills was Badger and Alexander Cameron was Rat (while David Cameron, his younger brother, was one of the rabbits). As Edwards recalled, it was a show that had it all: 'I remember Andrew Wills as Badger and his younger brother was sitting on the aisle in the third row. He was about nine and he laughed so much he fell off his chair and lay in the aisle absolutely convulsed! The Queen's face was a picture as she looked at this boy rolling about! I was very worried because in one of the songs when they [the weasels] come to invade Toad Hall, they all had flails attached to their wrists by leather thongs. They were waving these clubs about right on the front of the stage with the Queen in the front row, and I thought *please don't break!* They were absolutely lethal.'

Around the time Edward left the school in the summer of 1977, he wasn't the only one moving on. For the Queen and Prince Philip, they were about to become grandparents for the first time as the Silver Jubilee got underway; his eldest brother, now the Prince of Wales, was beginning to develop his own career and charitable interests; his aunt would soon be caught up in divorce. And while people would be singing 'God Save the Queen', it wasn't always the version that the royal family would appreciate. This truly was a period of change for the royal marriage.

Chapter 9

WATCHING
THE FAMILY GROW

I n November 1972, the Queen and Duke of Edinburgh celebrated
their silver wedding anniversary. At a speech at the Guildhall in
London, the Queen uttered those words which have made it into the
Oxford Dictionary of Quotations: 'I think everybody really will
concede that on this, of all days, I should begin my speech with the
words, "My husband and I".'

She went on to say: 'A marriage begins by joining man and wife
together, but this relationship between two people, however deep
at the time, needs to develop and mature with the passing years . . .
When the bishop was asked what he thought about sin he replied
with simple conviction that he was against it. If I am asked today
what I think about family life after twenty-five years I can answer
with equal simplicity and conviction. I am for it.'

For most people, family is the most important thing in their
lives. It is what keeps them together and it is what keeps civilisation
together. Life revolves around significant family events – education,
career, marriage, children and grandchildren. Family life is also

central to the monarchy, as Prince Philip explained. 'If you have a monarchy, you have got to have a family and the family has got to be in the public eye.'

But as at first one, then all but one, of the marriages of the Queen and Prince Philip's children came to their bitter ends, the methods by which they were raised appeared to be woefully inadequate training for dealing with the demands and pressures of the modern age.

Princess Margaret's doomed marriage to man-about-town photographer Tony Armstrong-Jones in 1960 set a precedent. After numerous rows and affairs and two children, they divorced in 1978 – the first royal divorce since Henry VIII split from Anne of Cleves in 1540.

The divorces of the Queen's children were not because they didn't have a loving and united family life. Despite the demands of their parents' position, they all always had family time together – Christmas at Sandringham, holidays at Balmoral and Windsor – but to a very large extent they were left to their own devices or to other people to educate and bring them up. Their career opportunities were limited and for some of them were mapped out in advance. They either went into the forces or they did charity work or, in most cases, both.

Trade has never worked for the immediate royal family as, whether they liked it or not, they were automatically separated by their heritage from the rest of the world. A royal prince or princess must act like one and not be seen to exploit their status for commercial gain, and this distinction has caused Prince Andrew some awkward moments. For the senior branch of the family, the isolation is reinforced by a protocol so rigid that even her children must bow or curtsey to the Queen.

This problem with commercial activities became even clearer in 2001, when Prince Edward's wife Sophie was duped by the 'fake sheikh' Mazher Mahmood – an undercover reporter for the now-defunct *News of the World* – into revealing all kinds of indiscretions about the royal family. She was terrified of the repercussions when, in order to promote her company R-JH, she was recorded mocking the then prime minister, calling him President Blair, and referring to his wife Cherie as 'horrid, absolutely horrid'. She also described the Queen as the 'old dear'.

Both the Queen and Philip stood by her, but insisted she withdrew from her business life and that Edward gave up work at his film company, Ardent Productions. Prince Philip had wanted Edward to learn accountancy, or at the very least take a management training course, but it was not what Edward had wanted. To even suggest it was something of a radical step; for the son of a reigning sovereign to be directly involved in business was a new and worrying notion to some. Commerce had always been an anathema to the royal family. It was partly a snobbish thing; the British upper classes, bought up to regard land as the only honourable measure of wealth, traditionally looked down on 'trade'. That was not going to influence Philip's judgement. He had always been impatient and, on occasion, rudely dismissive of the establishment's prejudices as patronising and old-fashioned.

But direct involvement also went against the grain of the impartiality so vital to the good name of the royal family, and even Philip had to take that into consideration. It is why they prefer to play the role of 'ambassador' for all British industry, rather than be a salesman for any one company. As Philip acknowledged: 'Any member of the family who has been anywhere near a commercial activity is always criticised because it is going to give them an unfair advantage.'

Only Princess Anne managed to break free from the royal conventions to bring up her children in a relaxed and truly normal way, and she could do that only by turning her back on her royal inheritance. She was the first of the Queen's children to marry.

In keeping with royal tradition, the Queen offered her husband, commoner Mark Phillips, an earldom on their wedding day, but he declined, meaning that the couple's children were the first grandchildren of the sovereign to have no title. Princess Anne had said she would prefer a quiet wedding, but in deference to her mother she eventually agreed to Westminster Abbey, the traditional venue for royal weddings.

The ceremony on 14 November 1973, a showcase event for the royal family, was watched by an estimated 500 million television viewers around the world, and on the streets of London, crowds of people lined the streets to share in the celebrations, which had been declared a national holiday. Prince Philip walked his daughter up the aisle in much the same way he once did the Queen's sister at her wedding. The bridegroom was a likeable man, educated at Marlborough College and Sandhurst, and eventually became a captain in the army. He was an excellent horseman, which was very important for Princess Anne at the time, and the Queen and Philip had high hopes for the marriage. They also liked Mark's parents, Peter and Anne Phillips, who were the first in-laws to be integrated into the immediate royal family.

When her first grandchild, Peter, was born on 15 November 1977, the Queen was about to conduct an investiture in the ballroom at Buckingham Palace. The baby was born at 10.46am and the investiture scheduled to start at 11, but she was so overjoyed she delayed the ceremony for an unprecedented ten minutes, while she asked for a call to be put through to Prince Philip, who was in Germany at the time, so she could tell him the good news. He was equally delighted. He admired his forthright daughter and had always been close to her. He was convinced motherhood would soften her edges and give her another dimension to her life.

Four years later, on 15 May 1981, Anne gave birth to a daughter, Zara, meaning 'bright as the dawn', due to her somewhat prompt arrival into the world. As they grew up, the Queen loved having her grandchildren to stay with nanny Pat Moss, but she was firm with the discipline. She might have been a doting granny but she was a strict one too. 'She was always chastising them,' a rating on board the royal yacht *Britannia* recalled. 'I've seen her shake Zara as she was so naughty running up and down the main stairs on board the yacht and refusing to stop even when the Queen told her to do so.'

From the start, Anne refused to be influenced by public opinion or the opinion of her parents as to the way she brought up her children. That meant country pursuits and country schools. And so it was that the Queen and Prince Philip's first grandchild, the great-great-grandson of King George V, began his education, not with a governess in the peaceful atmosphere of the Buckingham Palace schoolroom, but in a local nursery school in Minchinhampton. 'I think the Queen found it all rather alarming,' said a former footman. 'But Anne wanted to do things her way and deal with the children herself.'

Her father understood. 'It's only too easy to think of education as a process of teaching young people about conventional academic subjects in schools,' he said. 'That is a very important aspect, but to give education this exclusive quality is to imply that young people need no other instruction or experience to prepare them for adult life.'

Despite her royal duties, including her increasing work with Save the Children (her chosen charity), Anne still found time to be with the children. It had been the idea of her private secretary, the late Peter Gibbs, to affiliate her with Save the Children, and the choice was nothing to do with her parents. It was the same with the way she brought up her children; they let her get on with motherhood and running her working life and were proud of her for doing so.

For Prince Charles, however, there was no such escape. He was a prisoner of his position and he had to find a suitable wife, with every move he made closely scrutinised by the press. He eventually did – in the gangling, teenage form of a local Norfolk girl, who also happened to be a family friend and the granddaughter of an earl. Lady Diana Spencer was young, she was a potential beauty and, most important of all, she was unsullied by any sort of scandal or romantic past, as most of Charles's previous girlfriends had been.

In November 1980, while Diana was visiting Sandringham as their guest, the press interest in her peaked and photographers surrounded the estate hoping to get a picture or at least a sighting. It bothered the Queen, who was both irritated and worried by the attention being caused by Diana's presence at the big house. She was uncomfortable with it but characteristically said nothing to Charles directly, but instead discussed it with Philip, who wrote their eldest son a carefully considered letter. Media pressure was creating an intolerable situation, said Philip, which meant that Charles must come to a rapid decision. Either he must offer Diana his hand or he must break off the relationship to avoid compromising her reputation.

'Read it!' Charles would furiously exclaim to friends in later years, whipping the letter out of his breast pocket. 'It was his attempt to say that he was forced into the marriage,' recalled one who saw the note. However, another who read it confided: 'It was actually very constructive and trying to be helpful. It certainly did not read as an ultimatum.'

On 24 February 1981, Prince Charles announced his engagement to the twenty-year-old Lady Diana Spencer. She was the youngest daughter of Viscount Althorp and his wife, Frances Shand Kydd, and the maternal granddaughter of Lady Fermoy, who was a friend and lady-in-waiting to the Queen Mother. Diana's father, later the 8th Earl Spencer, had served as an equerry to the Queen between 1952 and 1954 and to George VI for the two years before that. The family lived at Park House on the Sandringham estate and the Queen had known Diana fleetingly most of her life. Diana's elder sister Sarah had been a girlfriend of Prince Charles's and her other sister, Jane, was married to Robert Fellowes, the Queen's assistant and later her private secretary.

'She is one of us,' the Queen wrote to a friend. 'I am very fond of all three of the Spencer girls.' Whether or not she realised the troubles brewing with Diana during the months leading up to the wedding, she chose to ignore them.

It had started so well in Scotland the previous summer, when Diana had joined in with the after-dinner games, laughed at Prince Philip's jokes, got wet, fallen into bogs, said all the right things. The nineteen-year-old passed into their august royal circle with flying colours. She had now received a magnificent oval sapphire and diamond engagement ring and was dazzled by romantic ambition, having caught what she called 'the big fish'. But she had given little thought to what that actually meant for the future and hadn't really considered what being a member of the royal family entailed. Now she would be condemned to live with the consequences. She was given a police escort wherever she went, moved into Buckingham Palace's old nursery suite on the second floor and found that her freedom was gone.

The Queen was sympathetic to Diana's anxieties, but had no inkling that she was already suffering from the bulimia that was to plague her for years to come. As much as she wanted to help, the Queen had the affairs of state to deal with and many of her own problems. On 14 June 1981, she had been riding on her faithful horse Burmese at Trooping the Colour when six pistol cracks rang out. Sudden fear gripped onlookers – had the Queen been shot? Fortunately, they were blanks and the Queen was unharmed and, thanks to her excellent horsemanship, not unseated.

'It wasn't the shots that frightened her – but the cavalry,' the Queen said of her horse afterwards. 'If someone wants to get me it's too easy,' she added. It was a serious threat to her personal security and in the light of the forthcoming royal wedding, security in general and surveillance were stepped up.

Just over six weeks later, the Queen and Prince Philip threw a pre-wedding party at Buckingham Palace for Prince Charles and Lady Diana Spencer. It was the most lavish royal ball in over half a century, with a guest list that included just about every European royal, both major and minor, as well as America's first lady, Nancy Reagan, a raft of prime ministers and heads of the Commonwealth. There were footmen and maids in attendance on each floor and every room in the palace was full, such was the pressure for accommodation. From the Queen's point of view, the party was a showcase to entertain princes, kings and politicians. The wedding two days later was a state occasion and a showcase for the nation.

On the Prince of Wales's insistence, the wedding ceremony took place in St Paul's, not Westminster Abbey, because the cathedral could accommodate the three orchestras he wanted and the vast number of guests deemed necessary to be invited for such an event. Weddings are a declaration of hope for the future and this one was seen and shared in by more people than any in history.

That night the Queen and many of the important guests from the wedding attended a party at Claridge's Hotel in London's Brook Street given by party supremo Lady Elizabeth Anson. 'I arranged for video screens to be erected so the guests could see the ceremony replayed,' she recalled. 'The Queen sat next to Nancy Reagan and Princess Grace on a circular sofa, all glued to the screens. There was a wonderful atmosphere as people were elated by the day and we all fell about laughing when someone thought the man in Lester Lanin's band was the King of Tonga.'

By the time November came around, Diana was expecting a baby and the press frenzy reached a new peak. After she was photographed pregnant wearing her bikini on a beach on the private

Mountbatten estate in the Bahamas, the Queen was genuinely worried about Diana's ability to cope and instructed her press secretary to invite all the Fleet Street editors to Buckingham Palace for a meeting to ask them to rein back. In an unprecedented move, the Queen appealed to them personally. It worked, but not for long.

In April 1982, Prime Minister Margaret Thatcher announced Britain was at war when Argentina invaded the remote Falkland Islands in the South Atlantic in a dispute over sovereignty. A task force was sent to take back control of the islands by amphibious assault. Among the serving helicopter pilots onboard HMS *Invincible* was 22-year-old Prince Andrew. He had joined the Royal Navy in 1979, and had only recently completed his training. There were some in the government who felt he should not be sent into combat, and the Queen was concerned, not only as head of state but as a mother. However, Buckingham Palace issued a statement confirming she had no doubts that her son should take part and stay with his ship.

Within a few days of the victorious conclusion of the war, the Queen had further good news. On Monday 21 June at 9.03pm, Diana gave birth to a son, who was to be second in line to the throne. 'I am very pleased that we have another heir,' the Queen told injured Falklands servicemen with characteristic understatement. She was of course delighted and saw the birth as one of the few positive things in an otherwise difficult year. It was about to get much worse.

A couple of weeks later, Michael Fagan overcame the supposedly foolproof security system of Buckingham Palace and broke into the Queen's bedroom on 9 July. By unfortunate coincidence, all the Queen's family were out of London and her page, Paul Whybrew, was taking the corgis for their morning walk. The Queen's first reaction on waking and seeing a man at the foot of her bed was that it must be member of staff and she told them to get out. Fagan has told many versions of the story, but suffice to say the Queen bravely kept him talking while she tried to summon security with the panic button – but there was no response. Eventually her house-maid appeared and screamed with shock when she saw the intruder. The Queen, still in her nightdress, managed to lure Fagan out of her bedroom and into the pages' pantry, where her maid gave him a cigarette.

When Whybrew returned with the dogs, she signalled to him to go into the pantry, which he duly did, plying Fagan with whisky until security arrived. The Queen claims she was not unnerved as it was so surreal she didn't have time to be frightened. But she must have been rattled that such a thing could happen, although she has dined out on the story and imitated her maid's horrified reaction ever since.

What was particularly alarming was that someone could scale a wall of the palace, get through an open window, walk along a couple of corridors and enter the Queen's bedroom undetected. Prince Philip, who had been sleeping in the adjoining bedroom, had left the palace early and was furious when the story broke that the entire world should know their sleeping arrangements. He was, of course, incandescent with rage that such a thing should be allowed to happen and applauded the bravery of his wife in remaining calm and collected in the face of the intruder.

A week later, the Queen went to hospital, ostensibly to have a wisdom tooth removed, but conveniently at the same time as her long-serving police officer Commander Michael Trestrail, of whom she had been very fond, had to resign after it was revealed he was conducting an affair with a male prostitute.

As if all of that wasn't enough, on 20 July the IRA detonated 25lb of high explosive from a blue Austin car parked in the South Carriage Drive of Hyde Park just as the Household Cavalry Blues and Royals rode past. The blast killed three soldiers and injured a further twenty-three, but the horses took the worst of it and seven were killed or so badly injured they had to be destroyed. One of the horses, Sefton, had an eight-hour operation; survived his thirty-four injuries to become a national icon and symbol of the appalling tragedy. That night the watchman outside the Queen's door said he heard Her Majesty saying repeatedly: 'The horses, the poor horses . . .' Two hours after the first attack, there was a second blast underneath the bandstand where the regiment of the Royal Green Jackets were playing to a crowd of over a hundred onlookers. The final death toll was eleven and over fifty were injured.

Where royalty is concerned, the show must go on and on 4 August, with her smile fixed firmly in place, the Queen attended the christening of the heir presumptive in the Music Room of Buckingham Palace. Diana was not at her most supportive and resented the attention being focused on the Queen Mother, who was celebrating her eighty-second birthday. She said she felt 'excluded totally', and little William Arthur Philip Louis, sensing his mother's distress, cried throughout.

That significant family moment, with four generations of the royal family gathered together, highlighted the big changes that were occurring within the Queen's own family and their difficulties in adapting to the times. They were still expected to be royal and behave like royalty, and at the same time people wanted them to be ordinary enough to have a drink in a pub. They were no longer cocooned by a deferential press, but exposed and, indeed, overexposed. In an interview with the *Observer* newspaper, Prince Philip tried to explain what it was like living above 'the shop' at Buckingham Palace. 'We didn't choose this house, we didn't build this house, we simply occupy it like a tortoise occupies a shell,' he said firmly. 'We go to state occasions all dressed up but we wouldn't dress up like that if the occasion were not a state occasion – the state occasions are part of the living theatre of the monarchy.

People expect us to be all things to all men and to all kinds at all times.'

After all the dramas of 1982, the next significant event in the royal couple's family life took place on 15 September 1984 at 4.20pm. The Queen was on her Balmoral break with the Duke of Edinburgh and members of her family when the Princess of Wales gave birth to her second child, another boy. His name was announced from the steps of the Lindo Wing of St Mary's Hospital in Paddington as Prince Henry Charles Albert David and he would be known as Harry. Diana had a difficult pregnancy, was tired and overwrought, and felt thoroughly miserable as she acknowledged she was not made for the production line. The Queen had been aware for a while that her daughter-in-law was finding it difficult to adapt to the pressures of her royal role, but assumed she would eventually find her feet. And, to outward appearances at least, that is what Diana seemed to be doing. She carried on performing her royal duties until July, to the admiration of people she met.

Four days before Christmas, Harry was christened in St George's Chapel, Windsor. Lord Snowdon, who took the official photographs, despite being divorced from Princess Margaret, had an almost impossible task. William was trying to get all the attention and kept tugging at the ancient Honiton lace christening robe his brother was wearing and protesting loudly when he was not allowed to hold the baby. Snowdon's assistant recalled his behaviour, feeling it to be spoilt: 'Every time he did something naughty they roared with laughter. No one admonished him and he was a thorough pest.'

The christening was shown in the Christmas broadcast that year, with rare footage of William chasing his cousin, Zara Phillips, round the legs of the Archbishop of Canterbury. In another sequence, Diana was seen trying to explain to William how many generations of royalty had worn the robe he had tried to tear to pieces. 'Great-Granny was christened in it,' she said. Charles quickly interjected: 'And I was christened in it.' He was trying to cover up for his wife's mistake, for the great-granny in question was the Queen Mother who, like Diana, was an earl's daughter and therefore had most definitely not worn the regal robe.

Weddings and christenings are the things that bind families together and in March 1986 Prince Andrew had become engaged to Sarah Ferguson, the lively daughter of Prince Charles's polo manager, Ronald Ferguson. 'I am delighted he's getting married,' Prince Philip said, when he and the Queen returned from their tour of Australia and New Zealand, 'but not because I think it will keep him out if trouble because, in fact he's never been in trouble, but because I think Sarah will be a great asset.'

Sarah was indeed a great asset to begin with. On the wedding day, the Queen chose a particularly stunning outfit designed by her Hartnell-trained couturier, Ian Thomas. It had prompted a rare compliment from Prince Philip, who came into her dressing room during one of the fittings. According to Thomas, she had blushed with pleasure – it was a great example of the ongoing strength of their love for each other, as they approached forty years of marriage.

She may not have felt quite so happy with Prince William's behaviour as a sailor-suited page at the wedding in Westminster Abbey. He jiggled and fiddled throughout the ceremony and the Queen kept glancing disapprovingly in his direction. She had been taught to sit still when she was far younger than the four-year-old Prince William – and to keep a straight back. As far as she could see, he had not been taught any royal discipline at all.

It was, however, an exceptionally joyful day. The Queen liked her new daughter-in-law and was delighted with the match. The feeling was mutual and Sarah often spoke of their 'special bond'. They both loved horses, dogs, country life and of course Prince Andrew – and to this day the Queen keeps in touch with her.

The joy and cheerfulness generated by the Duke and Duchess of York's wedding was gradually diminished as the eighties drew to end. First of all, Prince Edward dropped out of the Royal Marines in January 1987, much to the horror of his siblings, who thought they had persuaded him to stay and complete his training.

Prince Philip was extremely understanding; indeed, it was he, not the Queen, who was the more sympathetic to Edward's decision. The royal family had a long association with this most martial of services: Edward's grandfather George VI was Captain General of the Royal Marines, his father succeeded him and his great uncle Earl Mountbatten was Colonel Commandant up to the time he was murdered. Royal private secretaries and equerries were frequently drawn from those with a Marine background. Both Charles and Andrew had undergone commando training before they joined the Royal Navy and earned the right to wear the coveted green beret.

Edward had wanted to go one better than his brothers and make the Marines his full-time career – perhaps to prove that, in effect, he was better than them. Whatever the reason, Edward had his mind set on the Marines from the age of ten, so it was a huge surprise when he decided to quit. The Queen's initial shock quickly turned to icy-cold regal displeasure, while the Queen Mother couldn't understand it as she felt Edward's decision smacked of dereliction of duty. Given his well-earned reputation for irascibility, it was perhaps inevitable that many would surmise that Philip had been outraged by Edward's decision and that harsh words had been exchanged between the two; even that Edward had been reduced to tears by his father's anger. It was a potent image and it grew in the telling and retelling.

The truth was quite the opposite. Philip was in fact the most supportive of all the royal family. More worldly than his wife, he could analyse the problem in a rational, objective way, while the Queen saw it only in terms of family duty and royal reputation, which by her logic were one and the same. Adam Wise, Prince Edward's private secretary at the time, recalled: 'The first person he went to when he'd really had enough of the Marines was Prince Philip and he was extremely understanding about the whole thing. He was very reasonable and gave very sensible advice.' He added: 'Prince Philip did not get on his high horse at all and did not get cross about the fact that his son was rejecting the Royal Marines of which he was Captain General.'

The counsel Philip gave was straightforward and practical. As he informed the Marines' Commandant General Sir Michael Wilkins in a private and confidential letter, which later appeared on the front page of the *Sun*, the family had made every effort to make Edward change his mind, 'but we all made clear that the final decision was his and his alone'.

Philip, infuriated by trivialities, was showing himself to be clear-headed at a time of major crisis. In a significant public gesture, father and son were photographed walking together side by side to church at Sandringham the following Sunday. He understood his son's decision, which he considered a brave one, and supported him fully. Edward had explained to him he felt he was never going to be able to fit in as neatly as he had hoped: 'I was always going to have a policeman there. I could never go out with the rest of the lads into the town as everyone knew who I was. I didn't see the way really it was going to work.'

James Edwards, his former headmaster, received a letter from the prince two days after his resignation. 'It was a long letter thanking me for my concern and explaining why he had done what he had done. He said Prince Philip had been extremely supportive and because of that, he felt he could make the right decision. I think he had had a rough time and had been bullied and teased about gayness until he couldn't take it any more. Physically he did not have a problem as he was very tough despite his angelic looks.'

Edwards explained that the prince's detective Andrew Merrylees was away on a recce of New Zealand at the time and perhaps if he had been around Edward might have stuck it out at least until the end of his course.

Prince Philip and the Queen may not always agree, and clearly did not in this case, but as James Edwards said: 'They are a tight unit. Cross one and you've crossed them both.'

For all their superficial differences, Philip had a better relationship with Prince Edward than with Charles or Andrew, based on respect on Edward's part and equally genuine affection on Philip's. He is not a demonstrative man, but in private he will affectionately put his arm around his son's shoulder – he calls him Ed – and give him a kiss. Before his marriage in 1999, Edward always kept one book on his bedside table at Buckingham Palace. It was his journal of the Duke of Edinburgh's Award, its handwritten pages bearing testimony to the years he spent achieving his three awards. The book is a diary of his youth, written in many different hands by those who taught him and those he came to respect. It is a symbolic reminder of the empathy between the prince and his father, whose name the scheme bears.

Indeed, his father and the award have been two of the most notable influences in his life. It was Philip, for instance, not the Queen, who came to see Edward receive his degree on graduation day from Cambridge. 'Prince Philip can freeze or melt an atmosphere depending on his mood,' says friend and former director of the Duke of Edinburgh's Award, Sir Michael Hobbs. 'If he is irritable or unhappy about something he will make no attempt to hide it.'

'Prince Philip's attitude to life was formed by a very tough upbringing,' observed Hobbs. 'He meets discomfort head on and isn't worried by it. He is much less overtly compassionate as a result. He keeps it well hidden.'

Like the duke on a good day, Edward can move smoothly through a room, sipping a drink, smiling at the appropriate moment, making a humorous remark, before seamlessly moving on. It is an acquired skill, one that did not come easily, and is something the Queen has always found difficult.

That Edward should study his father is perfectly natural. That Philip should take such an interest in this son is perhaps more unexpected. Philip's relationship with his youngest child is conducted on a level of easily familiarity that he has never managed with his eldest. The distance between Philip and Charles remains quite extraordinary. For extended periods, their only contact was via memo, while his relationship with Edward is conducted on a much more informal, friendly level.

He is also very fond of the Countess of Wessex, who married Edward after a seven-year courtship in 1999. During that period, the Queen took the unusual step of inviting Sophie Rhys-Jones to live at Buckingham Palace so she could familiarise herself with the protocol and rituals of the royal family. Some churchmen criticised the Queen for allowing an unmarried couple to live together, but she felt it was of vital importance after the failure of her children's other marriages that Sophie knew exactly what she was letting herself in for. It showed how they had gained in understanding of the pressures faced by outsiders joining the royal family, and that the best preparation for what would follow was to give them direct experience of it.

In the popular imagination, the royal family are in daily consultation. In fact, they live surprisingly separate lives. They seldom get together during the week, even if they happen to be under the same roof at Buckingham Palace. The Queen often has her dinner alone in her private apartment, which she serves herself from a hotplate. Philip, meanwhile, until recently, if he returned late from an engagement, could be dining on the floor below with his private secretary. At the same time, Edward, before his marriage to Sophie, could have been having a snack by himself in his rooms. It would never have occurred to any of them to pick up the internal telephone to organise an impromptu family supper.

If Edward's resignation from the Marines had brought some criticism, the way he followed it up brought much more. That summer he produced the charity TV show *It's a Royal Knockout*, in which members of his family dressed in period costume as captains of four teams in a celebrity tournament at Alton Towers theme park. It was undignified, loud and, to make things worse, Edward was in a truculent mood and lost his temper and flounced out of the ensuing press conference after they made it clear what they thought of it all. It was such a disaster it is still talked of today as one of the greatest PR gaffes the royal family have made.

For the Queen and Prince Philip, who were celebrating their fortieth wedding anniversary, and the Queen Mother, who was about to celebrate her eighty-seventh birthday, it was a sorry episode. The Queen Mother was incensed and told Andrew, Edward and Anne (who each captained a team, along with the Duchess of York) that she had spent years building the reputation of the monarchy with the King only to have them try to destroy it in one evening. Her underlying fear was that everything her daughter had strived to build since the beginning of her reign by hard work and duty could so easily be erased by the behaviour of her own grandchildren and the vigilant press attention they attracted.

As the Queen's confidant the Right Reverend Michael Mann, former Dean of Windsor, explained: 'For the best reasons in the world, younger members of the royal family wanted to make the monarchy more approachable. I think the supreme example of that was when they all participated in *It's a Knockout*. It was making it a soap opera.'

In 1988, the Queen and Prince Philip were overjoyed when Sarah and Andrew had their first child – and their fifth grandchild. She was named Princess Beatrice after Queen Victoria's youngest daughter. The Queen was at Balmoral as usual, but four days after the birth Sarah made the effort to travel to Scotland so the Queen and Philip could see the baby before Andrew returned to his ship in the Philippines. Having grandchildren of her own made the Queen more aware of the kind of world they would one day inherit.

Philip and Andrew have never been close and Philip often couldn't resist taking a verbal swipe at his middle son whenever the opportunity arose. But in those early days he got along well with Sarah, though that was soon to change when their marriage fell into difficulties, something that came about relatively quickly after they had a second daughter, Princess Eugenie, who was born on 23 March 1990. By March 1992, they announced their separation and suddenly the Duke of Edinburgh's attitude changed. Unsentimental and dispassionate, he only ever spoke badly about one of his children's partners and that was Sarah.

In the end, he just couldn't be in the same room as her, and if she came in one door he would leave by another. When the couple finally divorced in 1996, he refused to allow her in any of the royal residences if he was there, and that has applied to this day. He simply felt she had let down the Queen and the institution of the monarchy by her indulgent behaviour and was no longer to be tolerated. However, Andrew has not only chosen not to remarry, but remains on close terms with his ex-wife, despite the disapproval of the Queen and Philip.

Philip felt differently about Anne. She was a similar sort of personality to him, and she had separated from Captain Mark Phillips in 1989 before they finally divorced in April 1992. By the end of the year, she had remarried Timothy Laurence, who had been the Queen's equerry between 1986 and 1989. When a cache of her love letters from him was offered for sale to one of the Murdoch newspapers, Philip just shrugged and said let them get on with it. In the end the newspaper didn't publish them. He was hopeful she would find happiness with her second husband, but to this day continues to worry about her.

It was not in the Queen's nature to become a participant in other people's troubles, especially those of her own children. She found it hard enough dealing with her own and, like her mother, preferred to overlook a problem rather than confront it, in the belief that if she ignored it long enough it would go away. But even more significant than the problems in the marriages of Princess Anne and Prince Andrew were the growing problems in the marriage of Prince Charles and Princess Diana, as this had a direct bearing on the future of the monarchy.

The Queen's response was to listen to what those in the younger generation had to say, and by that stage she had much to listen to: Diana's tearful accounts of the state of her marriage; Princess Anne's horror over love letters addressed to her being stolen from Buckingham Palace and offered for sale; Prince Charles's despair at Diana and his reunion with Camilla Parker Bowles. The Queen, aware of the broader picture, did just what she always did and counselled patience. She told Diana what she told her own children: 'Just wait and see what happens.'

She was about to find out that things could get very much worse.

Chapter 10

TRIALS AND TRIBULATIONS

Throughout their seventy-year marriage, the Queen and Prince Philip have carried out their duties according to their own beliefs about how to uphold the institution of the monarchy. Together they have met nearly all the great leaders of the age, some good, some bad and some utterly deranged, and together they have visited most of the world's countries. But nothing, including bereavement, death and disaster, could have prepared them for the troubles which overwhelmed the royal family in what she would term the Annus Horribilis of 1992. Early in her reign, the Queen had faced some challenging times as she struggled to cope with her new role as monarch, but these were small by comparison.

During her first Commonwealth tour of Australia in 1954, the Queen was welcomed with great warmth and enthusiasm. With her handsome and cheerful husband at her side, they were the picture of a truly romantic couple and heralded a brighter and more successful future. But, despite the success of the trip, there were times when it became overwhelming. She came from a very sheltered background and she remained painfully shy. She was still only twenty-eight, in a distant land, and her children and her family were half a world away. She had been Queen for only two years and the responsibility still terrified and confused her.

She was head of a great and venerable institution and, by her way of thinking, it would have been an egotistical abjuration of a sacred obligation to surrender to self-doubt. But with Philip by her side, she felt she would always be able to cope. He made her see the funny side of situations, and he was often the only person she could talk to in a superficial vein about what they had seen and done; she didn't have to be on her guard with him, worrying in case she might say the wrong thing, or create the wrong impression that would provoke a minor controversy. He gave her some much-needed courage when she was meeting the hundreds of people who were waiting for her. Sometimes he could be brusque, sometimes he made what became known as his gaffes – but they were often his way of relieving the tension. What was important was that he always managed to make her laugh as they faced the tedium, pitfalls and difficulties of royal duties together. In short, they learned how to work together to overcome the normal type of obstacles and challenges that life in the public eye threw up, but this sort of experience – honed through the following decades – was not going to be sufficient in 1992.

For all that their lives were extremely comfortable, there were also some major and very personal issues to deal with early on. The troubles had started immediately after the Coronation, when the British press picked up on Princess Margaret brushing an imaginary bit of fluff off Group Captain Peter Townsend's uniform. This tiny but intimate gesture was noticed, and people immediately recognised the significance of it. Townsend had been an RAF pilot during the war, before moving to work in the royal household in 1944. What made the whole thing more significant was that Townsend had recently divorced his wife, and in those days that was deemed to be beyond the pale in polite society – especially when a member of the royal family was involved.

The Queen's closest friend was always her sister. She loved the mercurial, whisky-drinking, cigarette-smoking beauty whose life held such promise. She would tolerate in Margo, as she called her, things she wouldn't consider in anyone else and, together with the Queen Mother, they formed a tight, impenetrable trio. They sometimes conversed in French (the Queen's French is better than Philip's, despite his cosmopolitan background) and they had no need to leave their own enclosed, privileged circle. If they could, they lunched together, dined together, holidayed together and spoke to each other on the telephone at least once a day. If the Queen Mother thought anyone in the family was shirking, she would tell her daughter to remind them of their duty or 'devoir' as she called it. Sometimes in a loud stage whisper she would say 'devoir', and the Queen knew exactly what she meant.

Prince Philip was wary of the trio. The popular conception is that Margaret and Philip never particularly liked one another. That is not true, but when she was younger Margaret said she found him 'cold'. He made a play of his disapproval of her and subjected her to his constant sarcastic teasing, but she became used to him and would not allow him to upset her. Eventually her wit triumphed over his and they became sparring equals, if not the closest friends, and her only comment on him was that she liked him. He was there for her when she needed him as an impassive and often wise counsellor, who was not swayed by the snobbery or restrictions of those rather pretentious times. Philip had been an outsider, Townsend was made an outsider and Margaret became an outsider by her own volition.

As far as the Townsend affair was concerned, Philip kept out of it as much as possible, only listening to what he was told and then trying to make light of it. He recognised that his duty lay with his wife and trying to keep her on an even keel when dealing with the dramas caused by her sister and Townsend's love. In November 1952, Townsend had told both him and the Queen that he and Margaret were madly in love and wanted to marry, for which he had to obtain her consent. He had just obtained his divorce, but chose not to inform the Queen Mother of his intentions regarding her daughter for another three months. Philip's advice to his wife was to keep as quiet as possible, unless there was something constructive they could do. Eventually she suggested that they wait while she went on her Commonwealth tour in 1953, perhaps hoping things would blow over and thus avoiding any sort of repetition of the scandal with Edward VIII and Mrs Simpson.

When the Queen Mother was eventually told, she was upset, although she put on a brave front. She discussed it with her daughter and wrote to Tommy Lascelles, now her daughter's private secretary. 'I would like to talk to you soon, please,' she wrote to Lascelles. 'I have nobody I can talk to about such dreadful things.' When she finally spoke to him she wept, which was understandable: her husband was gone, her elder daughter was Queen and her younger daughter looked as if she might bring disrepute on the new reign they were trying so hard to put in place. She believed that only heartache could come out of such a liaison and she felt that if the King had still been alive it would not have happened. They had both had such high hopes for their younger daughter, believing that she would find a suitably distinguished husband. We will never know, but the King might have intervened to stop the affair sooner than the Queen Mother, who was inclined to ignore tricky situations and hope they would go away, in very much the same way her daughter did with the Princess of Wales forty years later.

In his autobiography, *Time and Chance*, Townsend eloquently describes the tension and drama which led up to the end of the affair. The press were essentially on the side of the lovers, but complained that, after two years since their relationship became public, they should make up their minds. The Queen was portrayed as being on the side of the Church as its Supreme Governor, and the establishment figures of the day, which included the Privy Council, were described as antagonistic and unhelpful. They could not prevent the marriage, but they could influence Parliament, to whom the veto, when relinquished by the sovereign, then passed. 'She would have nothing left – except me,' Townsend wrote. 'It was too much to ask of her, too much for her to give. We should be left with nothing, but our devotion to face the world.'

The dénouement of the whole affair came to a head in October 1955. 'We felt mute and numbed at the centre of this maelstrom,' Townsend wrote as Princess Margaret drove to Windsor Castle to join her mother, the Queen and the Duke of Edinburgh for lunch. All that was said or what happened has never been disclosed, but facing up to the gravity of the situation, they discussed the princess's situation together for once. It cannot have been easy, and when the Queen Mother said her daughter 'hadn't even thought where they were going to live', Prince Philip was incensed at the triviality of the statement and replied with heavy sarcasm, 'It is still possible, even nowadays, to buy a house.' The Queen Mother was so annoyed by him she 'left the room angrily, slamming the door'. Later that day, Margaret rang Townsend 'in great distress'. She did not say what had passed between her and her sister and brother-in-law, 'but doubtless the stern truth was dawning on her,' he observed.

Prince Philip had largely kept his silence during the discussions, but he was there to lend a private ear to the Queen when she needed his support, which of course she did. She was just too close and emotionally involved to decide between her wish for her sister's happiness and the need for the royal family to do the right thing.

On Monday 31 October 1955, Margaret and Townsend met for the last time at Clarence House. Their love story ended with words crafted by Townsend on a rough piece of paper. This became the princess's statement later broadcast to the world. When she read out what Townsend had written, she quietly and sadly agreed: 'I have decided not to marry Group Captain Townsend,' she began, when the statement was issued that evening at 7pm, and continued: 'I have reached this decision entirely alone, and in doing so I have been strengthened by the unfailing support and devotion of Group Captain Townsend.'

Although he may not have been close to her, if proof of his loyalty to his sister-in-law was needed, four years later Prince Philip walked Princess Margaret down the aisle on her wedding day. It was the first royal wedding to be fully televised and the Duke of Edinburgh accompanied Margaret from Buckingham Palace to Westminster Abbey in the Glass Coach. Before they left he kept hurrying Margaret as, being a naval man, he hated the thought of being late, even by a couple of minutes. As a fanfare of trumpets heralded her arrival at the abbey, Prince Philip turned to her and whispered, 'Don't know who's more nervous, you or me,' adding: 'Am I holding on to you or are you holding on to me?'

'I am holding on to you,' the princess whispered in reply. Her husband-to-be, Antony Armstrong-Jones, couldn't have been more different from Peter Townsend, as he was a photographer. But at that moment at least he appeared to make her happy, and the Queen was pleased her sister had found what she thought was a more suitable kind of love. She remained the Queen's adored sister and was very much a royal princess, never letting anyone forget it if they did not treat her with due respect.

During the difficult years leading up to the separation and eventual divorce of the Prince and Princess of Wales, it was Margaret's turn to support her sister. By that time, she could feel pleased by the professional success of her own children, Viscount Linley and Lady Sarah Chatto. Linley had set up as a furniture maker, and in

1993 would marry Serena Stanhope, while Sarah became a painter and married a year later than her brother. For the first time in years, Margaret felt that perhaps her life had been a fulfilling one.

As a young woman, she always felt that the Queen was so good and perfect while she was very much the opposite, doomed to an unhappy marriage and a succession of unsuitable romances. Then she found a new kind of confidence and, for the first time in her life, she felt able to give the Queen advice, rather than the other way around. The ironic poignancy of this reversal of their situations was not lost on the Queen or Prince Philip. This was not how anyone could ever have seen things turning out, with Margaret at ease with herself and her children happily settled, while the Queen and Philip were faced with a parent's failure in their own family.

Margaret had no sympathy for the Princess of Wales, despite the similarity of their predicaments. Once supportive of the princess, she became almost as vocal as Prince Philip in her condemnation. She felt Diana had let the Queen down. And if there was a touch of hypocrisy in her reaction – and Margaret's life was hardly a shining example – there was no doubting the sincerity of her devotion to her sister. But if that was a comfort, it was not a solution. There was no escaping the fact that the early 1990s were joyless times for the Queen. At a time of life when she should have been enjoying the fruits of a lifetime's dutiful labour, she was facing the gravest crisis of her reign.

Prince Philip tried to talk to Prince Charles about his marital difficulties and the effect they were having on the institution he was born to head. It was meant as fatherly advice, but because of the distant nature of their relationship, the two found it uncomfortable to exchange confidences and their conversations usually ended with Charles looking at his watch and making an excuse to leave the room. Thwarted in his own efforts to introduce some sense into an increasingly senseless situation, Philip asked his wife to bring her

considerable authority to bear. The Queen consistently refused to do
this, much to Philip's exasperation. Often so intimidating to those
outside her own family who overstepped the mark, the Queen was
unwilling to confront those within it.

Left to her own devices, she would have let the situation drift.
The Queen Mother had made a habit of contracting a diplomatic
illness whenever she came under stress (she contracted pneumonia
on her honeymoon and spent the week of the abdication crisis in bed
with flu). Her daughter's natural inclination was to ignore the situation and hope it would go away. It was a policy that had hitherto
served her well. What was more, the Queen Mother had warned
her against becoming too involved in the problems of her offspring
and their families. When the Queen had turned to her hoping for
sympathy, she got none. On one occasion when they were discussing the children's problems, the Queen Mother looked up from her
game of patience. 'Darling,' she said. 'I don't know why you care
any more. It's another generation ... just let them get on with it.'
She then dealt herself another hand.

But the truth was that the Queen was alarmed by her daughter-
in-law. She was not scared of Diana as a person, but she was deeply
suspicious of Diana's Hollywood glamour and the way she used it
to manipulate public opinion. Although she regarded Diana as hard
working, she doubted if she had any real sense of commitment to
the institution which had elevated her to public prominence in the
first place. Diana dismissed the monarchy as 'old-fashioned' and
behind the times, while to the Queen those were its very strengths.
The monarchy is hierarchical and the Queen, as its head, was mis-
trustful of the way Diana ignored the parameters of her position.

When troubles overwhelm the Queen, she has a habit of switch-
ing off and going for a walk with her dogs. Sometimes she will
even feed them under the table at lunchtime to avoid a disconcerting question. Prince Philip calls this displacement activity 'her dog

mechanism'. It is the equivalent of the Queen Mother's games of cards and everyone in the family has experienced it. It took the Duke of York three weeks to fight his way past the dogs to tell his mother that his marriage was in trouble. The meeting was brief and painful. Andrew muttered words like 'mutual incompatibility' and Sarah apologised for her behaviour, which she agreed had been a long way short of what was both expected and required. The floodgates were bursting, yet the Queen still clung to the delusion that time would heal the breach. Sarah wrote of that moment: 'She asked me to reconsider, to be strong, to go forward.' According to the duchess: 'The Queen looked sadder than I have ever seen her.'

The Queen might have been sad, but Prince Philip was not. He was, according to a member of the household, 'incandescent' with anger. There was an element of personal animosity in this. There had been several occasions when Sarah had come to Andrew's defence when he was being berated by his father for some perceived weakness or other and, as the Queen has noted, Philip is not a man who likes to be contradicted. However, it was her public deportment rather than any private disagreements which most annoyed the prince. An outsider himself who had to learn to adapt to the exigencies of royal life, he was able to take an objective view of its requirements and regarded his daughter-in-law's behaviour as selfish and reprehensible. He kept up the refrain: 'If she wants out she can get out.' He felt he same about Diana but wisely held back from expressing his views in public.

On 19 March 1992, a statement from the Palace broke with normal protocol and expressed the Queen's personal unhappiness over the matter.

'In view of the media speculation which the Queen finds especially undesirable during the general election campaign, Her Majesty is issuing the following statement: "Last week, lawyers acting for the Duchess of York initiated discussions about a formal separation for the Duke and Duchess. These discussions are not yet completed and nothing will be said until they are. The Queen hopes that the media will spare the Duke and Duchess of York and their children any intrusion."'

Then, the following month, Princess Anne and Captain Mark Phillips were finally divorced. If all of that was bad, worse was to come as, in June 1992, the *Sunday Times* began to serialise Andrew Morton's book *Diana: Her True Story*. The Queen and Philip were at Windsor that weekend and were stunned by what they read. They were aware of how unhappy their daughter in-law was, but they never thought for one moment she would resort to airing her dirty linen in such a public way. Their whole royal life was based on obligation, discretion and duty. Prince Philip had tried to help and had written to Diana saying he wished 'to do my utmost to help you and Charles to the best of my ability. But I am quite ready to concede that I have no talent as a marriage counsellor!' It was to no avail; it was too little too late.

The tension was there for all to see when Diana attended Royal Ascot with the rest of the family as the second instalment of Morton's revelations was rolling off the press. Prince Philip snubbed Diana in full view of all the top-hatted people in the royal enclosure. But at least she was there – the Duchess of York was in social Siberia.

With all three of the Queen's children's marriages in trouble, it seemed things could not get worse – but they did. That summer, there was nothing even her loyal husband could do when photographs of Sarah, topless in the South of France having her toes sucked by her financial adviser John Bryan, appeared in the *Daily Mirror*. She was staying at Balmoral with the family when that fatal nail was driven into the coffin of what was left of her reputation. The Queen was 'furious', as the duchess recalled. She was cold and abrupt as she berated her semi-detached daughter-in-law for exposing the monarchy to such ridicule. Prince Philip was even more direct, likening her to Edwina Mountbatten, whose morals had long been a source of embarrassment to the royal family. He said to her: 'You should get to a nunnery – or a madhouse.'

There was still more to come. On 20 November – their forty-fifth wedding anniversary – Windsor Castle was engulfed by flames. Prince Philip was in Argentina at the time on a private visit and could not be contacted immediately. The fire was started by a restorer's lamp which set a curtain alight. It quickly spread through the Queen's private chapel and devoured St George's Hall. Prince Andrew organised the rescue of many of the ancient works of art, but great parts of the building itself were consumed in the blaze. The Queen Mother was lunching at Clarence House when she received the news and as soon as she could leave her guests was driven to Windsor to be with the Queen, who had already arrived from London. Mother and daughter stayed at Royal Lodge that weekend and alone together they could talk over the unhappiness that had recently been thrown at them. The Queen later thanked her mother, saying: 'It made all the difference to my sanity after that terrible day.'

The castle is Crown property and the fire damaged part of the state apartments, not the Queen's private rooms. Like other Crown or national properties, Windsor Castle is covered by government indemnity and, not surprisingly, Prime Minister John Major immediately announced that the government would pay for the restoration, as it was the state's loss, rather than a private one. The decision was greeted with a maelstrom of protest, with even the normally supportive *Daily Mail* asking: 'Why should the populace, many of whom have had to make huge sacrifices during the bitter recession, pay the total bill for Windsor Castle, when the Queen pays no taxes, contributes next to nothing?'

Within a week, John Major announced plans that had been in preparation since the summer, and agreed with the Queen and Prince Charles. The civil list, by which all senior members of the royal family were paid a combined salary of £900,000 to cover the costs of their royal duties, would cease, except for the Queen, Prince Philip and the Queen Mother; the rest of the royal family would now be paid for by the Queen. Furthermore, for the first time, she would pay tax on her income from April 1993.

None of this, however, dealt with the immediate issue of paying for the repairs, and so it was eventually agreed in the following spring that the Queen would open the State Rooms of Buckingham Palace to the public during the summer from then on. It was hoped that the £37 million cost of repairs would therefore not need any contribution from the public purse.

Four days after the fire, the Queen made a remarkable speech at a luncheon at the Guildhall to mark the fortieth anniversary of her accession earlier in the year. She had flu and a temperature of 101, but she refused to cancel. Her voice hoarse and deep, she stood up to speak: 'Nineteen ninety-two is not a year on which I shall look back with undiluted pleasure. In the words of one of my more sympathetic correspondents, it has turned out to be an "Annus Horribilis" [her correspondent was Sir Edward Ford, the former assistant private secretary to King George VI and then to the Queen].'

She continued by saying:

This generosity and whole-hearted kindness of the Corporation of the City to Prince Philip and me would be welcome at any time, but at this particular moment, in the aftermath of Friday's tragic fire at Windsor, it is especially so . . . It is possible to have too much of a good thing. A well-meaning bishop was obviously doing his best when he told Queen Victoria, 'Ma'am, we cannot pray too often, nor too fervently, for the royal family.'

The Queen's reply was: 'Too fervently, no; too often, yes.' I, like Queen Victoria, have always been a believer in that old maxim 'moderation in all things'.

I sometimes wonder how future generations will judge the events of this tumultuous year. I dare say that history will take a slightly more moderate view than that of some contemporary commentators. Distance is well-known to lend enchantment, even to the less attractive views. After all, it has the inestimable advantage of hindsight . . .

There can be no doubt, of course, that criticism is good for people and institutions that are part of public life. No institution – City, monarchy, whatever – should expect to be free from the scrutiny of those who give it their loyalty and support, not to mention those who don't. But we are all part of the same fabric of our national society and that scrutiny, by one part of another, can be just as effective if it is made with a touch of gentleness, good humour and understanding . . .

Forty years is quite a long time. I am glad to have had the chance to witness, and to take part in, many dramatic changes in life in this country. But I am glad to say that the magnificent standard of hospitality given on so many occasions to the Sovereign by the Lord Mayor of London has not changed at all. It is an outward symbol of one other unchanging factor which I value above all – the loyalty given to me and to my family by so many people in this country, and the Commonwealth, throughout my reign.

The Queen's lunchtime audience was touched and responded with a standing ovation. The speech not only paved the way for the government's announcement about the Queen's taxes and the royal family's incomes, it would soon be followed by another important family development.

On 9 December, John Major stood up in the House of Commons and said: 'It is announced from Buckingham Palace that, with regret, the Prince and Princess of Wales have decided to separate . . . This decision has been reached amicably, and they will continue to participate fully in the upbringing of their children . . . The Queen and Duke of Edinburgh, though saddened, understand and sympathise with the difficulties that have led to this decision.'

The Queen was at Wood Farm on the Sandringham Estate with only a handful of staff in attendance when the announcement was made. She did not watch the prime minister on television. Instead, she did what she always did when she was agitated: she took her dogs for a walk through the wintry woods and ploughed fields of Norfolk. When she returned to the back door, a member of staff approached the solitary figure of the sovereign, who was dressed in wellington boots and a loden coat and headscarf. He said how very sorry he was to hear the news. The Queen replied: 'I think you will find it is all for the best.'

The separation did not go smoothly. On the fortieth anniversary of her Coronation, the Queen awoke to find that the morning newspapers were dominated not by happy remembrances but by the report of a speech Diana had given the night before to the charity Turning Point, in which she had talked of the 'depression and loneliness' felt by so many women as they battled against post-natal depression and violence at home. Philip was incensed at what he saw as a deliberate (and highly successful) attempt to upstage the Queen. It was happening too often, he argued, and on his prompting the Queen dispatched her private secretary, Sir Robert Fellowes, to inform the princess that her royal schedule was to be cut back. Diana responded to that rap across her knuckles by announcing her retirement from public life, thereby turning rebuke to advantage and securing another sheaf of headlines of the kind Philip had been so anxious to avoid.

Philip has always enjoyed a pivotal role in the Queen's life. The Queen is the monarch – but it is Philip who always has the final say in family matters. And now his attitude towards his two daughters-in-law became as brutal as it was simple. It was this: Diana and Sarah wanted out of the royal family, so as far as he was concerned they could get out – and stay out. He let them both know exactly what he thought, in letters (he penned dozens to both Diana and Sarah, outlining his point of view in language both blunt and pertinent) and, on occasion, face to face.

It was Philip who had Sarah banned from all the royal homes, including at Christmas time. Despite the Queen's affection for Prince Andrew's ex-wife, she would not go her against her husband's wishes on the matter and has never done so. She tried to persuade Philip to change his mind and allow Sarah to spend part of each summer's holiday at Balmoral, but he would not budge. In domestic situations such as these, however, the Queen was not above a little underhand subterfuge, and when Philip left Scotland for a few days she would telephone the duchess and say, 'Here's your chance – come up now.'

It did not take long for Philip to find out that Sarah had been there, of course. He was not unduly angry – after seventy years of marriage, the Queen and her husband have settled into a state of benevolent compromise on most issues. He simply repeated what he had said before, which was that she had taken the decision to walk out on the royal family, so out she should stay.

His initial attitude to Diana was more ambivalent. Or it was for a while, and then he changed his mind. And that added to the pressure under which the Queen found herself. Like the Queen, he recognised the prominent role in the royal family that Diana had carved out for herself, but he did not like it. This most fiery of men has always been careful to follow tradition and defer to his sovereign on all matters outside the household, even though she happened to be his wife. 'His constant job is looking after the Queen,' said his friend and former private secretary, Mike Parker. 'He told me his job first, second and last was never to let her down.'

It was inevitable, given his belief in the duty of consort to his wife, that he would find himself at odds with the woman who put her personal happiness before the job of being consort to her husband. When the Queen expressed her sympathy with Diana's predicament, Philip was incensed. As always, he articulated himself forcefully. He accused his wife of 'procrastinating' on the question of whether Charles and Diana should divorce. Perhaps unsurprisingly, Princess Anne took her father's side, as did Prince Edward.

The Queen's sympathy for Diana's position was finally put to the sword by the *Panorama* interview which was broadcast on 20 November 1995. Watched by an audience of 15 million in Britain alone, Diana chose the vehicle of television to declare that there were three people in her marriage. She said she wanted to be Queen of People's Hearts and she inferred her husband was unfit to be King. 'Because I know the character,' she said. 'I would think the top job, as I call it, would bring enormous limitations to him and I don't know whether he could adapt to that.'

It was their forty-eighth wedding anniversary and that night the Queen carried on as if nothing had happened. Accompanied by Prince Philip, she attended the Royal Variety Performance at the Dominion Theatre in London starring Cliff Richard, Des O'Connor and Elaine Paige. True to her character of forgiveness, the Queen still retained a smidgen of sympathy for her troubled daughter-in-law and, despite Prince Philip's misgivings, informed Diana the invitation to spend Christmas with the royal family at Sandringham still held firm.

Diana was not sure what to do and kept changing her mind. When she finally telephoned the Queen to tell her that she would not, after all, be spending Christmas at Sandringham, it was the final straw. This was the moment that Philip took charge. According to one eyewitness, he went 'ballistic'. Just the mention of Diana's name was enough to send him into a tirade. Princess Margaret joined the chorus, and so did the Princess Royal.

In any other marriage, it would have been the husband whom one would expect to deal with a situation of this kind. But the royal family is an institution unique unto itself – and the Prince of Wales, like his mother, is not very good at dealing with difficult or unpleasant issues. By default, therefore, it was left to the Queen to face up to the matter and deal with it as best she could. There was no other course open to her, Philip pointed out most firmly. A divorce was the only solution to this untenable mess. And as sovereign, it was within the Queen's authority to make that clear.

Philip almost had to guide her pen hand across the paper, but at last it was done, and on the morning of Monday 18 December, the letters were hand-delivered to the Prince and Princess of Wales demanding they seek a divorce. Diana was taken aback by the firmness of the Queen's tone. But it was no longer a matter for her to decide. In giving the *Panorama* interview, Diana had taken the future out of her own hands. The Queen had reached breaking point and divorce, as painful in its details as its inevitability, was the only option left.

The Queen and Prince Philip's next concern was for their grandchildren, Princes William and Harry. For William it was particularly difficult as he was only two months into his first 'half', as Eton call their terms, when his mother gave her infamous interview. He was thirteen years old and every poignant moment of his parents' messy life was being played out in daily reports in the press. His parents did what they could, but they too were limited in what they could achieve. Charles, for all his heartfelt concern for his son's predicament, had always found it difficult to confront problems, while Diana's influence was now being seriously undermined by the courtiers she both disliked and feared. Her private secretary, Patrick Jephson, noted: 'It was no secret that towards the end of her life, reactionary elements in the establishment were questioning her desirability as a mentor in the art of kingship.'

The one person who could help, who had to help, was the Queen. She knew only too well what pressures William was facing. She told her advisers that she feared he might crack up like his mother had. But her natural inclination was to let the situation ride in the hope that somehow the problem would melt away. Once again, it was down to Prince Philip to intervene and he pointed out vocally that it was not going to happen and the problem was not going to go away. He insisted the situation that Diana had created had to be confronted – and with Charles too wrapped up in his own concerns, the Queen had to step in to encourage and help their grandson.

On Sundays, all the Eton boys are allowed out into the town. For William it involved a short walk along the high street and across the bridge to Windsor with his detective Graham Cracker at his side. He started joining the Queen and Duke of Edinburgh for lunch. Afterwards, Prince Philip would make a discreet exit and leave the Queen and her grandson together in the Oak Drawing Room overlooking the quadrangle. They talked in a way they could never have done before. One of her great sadnesses was that, until the separation, she had hardly seen him. Now at last she was able to do so on a regular basis and form a proper relationship.

In this quiet intimacy, the Queen was able to impress upon William that the institution of the monarchy was something to be upheld and respected, and worth preserving. It was his birthright, after all, as much as hers. Many years later, William admitted the two of them agreed they had a 'shared understanding of what's needed'. But this all came about because, once again, the Duke of Edinburgh had stepped in and saved the day.

Chapter 11

THE DEATH OF DIANA

For any older couple, the death of their grandchildren's mother is a moment of grief, but also a time when the impact on the whole family can be devastating. When you have to deal with the situation with the whole world watching on, and commenting on your actions, it becomes even more challenging. Twenty years ago, the death of Diana plunged the royal family into chaos. It drew millions onto the streets, exposed the divisions within British society and unleashed an outpouring of public anger against the monarchy that threatened its stability. If in life Diana had been troublesome and difficult, in death she proved a force beyond control, which drove the Queen and Prince Philip to despair as they saw everything they had worked so hard for come close to being destroyed.

The royal family, holidaying in their Highland fastness at Balmoral that summer, had no inkling of the crisis about to overwhelm them when they received the news that Diana had been killed in a car crash in Paris. The call came through from the embassy in the French capital at 3.30 on the Sunday morning of 31 August 1997, and their first reaction was simply one of dazed bewilderment.

The Queen and Philip were stunned and shocked. Both in their seventies, they were aware of the problems Diana's relationship with Dodi Fayed was causing, but they never expected it to spiral out of control in such a dramatic way. They had recognised the potential in their daughter-in-law in their different ways and saw her loss for the terrible waste it was. Now they were about to find out just how potent a symbol Diana had become.

Initially, the Queen had been woken by her page at 2am to be told that the princess had been involved in a fatal crash. The first information coming in from Paris was that Dodi Fayed was dead but that Diana had miraculously survived. Pulling on her old-fashioned dressing gown, she had immediately gone out into the corridor, where she met Charles coming out of his own bedroom three doors away on the first floor of the castle.

By then the whole castle had been stirred from its slumbers. Sir Robin Janvrin, the Queen's deputy private secretary who was in attendance that weekend, had taken up his position in the equerries' room on the ground floor and was liaising with the embassy in Paris. Footmen and staff had been roused and the Balmoral switchboard, through which all calls are made, was fully manned.

Prince Charles went into his sitting room, which is next to the Queen's dressing room, to take the calls now coming in, some through the switchboard, others on his mobile telephone, which vibrates instead of ringing. The Queen ordered tea, which was brought up from the kitchen downstairs in a silver teapot and then ignored, as mother and son, joined by Prince Philip, paced up and down, anxiously asking each other what was to be done.

Their first concern, however, was to discover just how badly injured Diana was. Not too badly, they were told – first reports were that she had walked away from the twisted wreckage of the Mercedes virtually unscathed. Prince Charles resolved to travel immediately to France to be at his ex-wife's side. It was as a flight was being arranged that Robin Janvrin took the call from Paris informing him that the princess was dead. He immediately rang up to Charles and said: 'Sir, I am very sorry to have to tell you that I've just had the ambassador on the phone. The princess died a short time ago.'

The Queen was bewildered and caught up by the mood of suspicion as to what had caused the accident. Her first comment, upon being told of Diana's death, was to say: 'Someone must have greased the brakes.' It was an extraordinary remark for the Queen to make and it astounded her staff when they came to hear of it, which most had by the time the dawn broke over Balmoral's wooded hills. What she was most probably referring to was the possibility, long mooted, that one of Harrods owner Mohamed Al-Fayed's many enemies had sworn to get him and had now contrived the killing of his eldest son and the princess he was urging Dodi to marry. The Queen, however, neither repeated nor offered any explanation for her comment, and in the absence of any clarification, her staff chose to see it as an indication of just how shaken she had been by the turbulence of Diana's life and sudden death.

Nor was she the only one. The whole royal apparatus was thrown into disorder by the news of the crash. Viewed through the opaque window of deference which protected the royal family from the scrutiny of outsiders, the royal household appears a dull but smoothly run business which compensates for its lack of imagination with the security of routine. Schedules are prepared months and sometimes years in advance, and there is not a day when the senior members of the family it serves do not know where they are supposed to be or what they are supposed to be doing, right up to and including the moment of death.

The courtiers who keep these gilded wheels turning reflect the system they serve. They are the only branch of government service in Britain appointed, not by competitive examination, but on personal whim, and its members tend to be of a type – stolid, reliable, upper class, brought up in the public-school ethos of team spirit, of 'playing the game' and letting convention do the thinking for them. It is an antiquated, undemocratic organisation based on patronage, and overall it works reasonably well. But it is heavily reliant on precedent and therefore makes no allowance for the unforeseen and the unexpected. That flaw – and it soon proved to be a disastrous one – was ruthlessly exposed by Diana's death. Before first light on that Sunday morning, the wheels of royal state were starting to rattle loose.

From the mid-eighties onwards, the royal family had been divided into two separate and sometimes antagonistic bureaucratic camps. While the Queen continued to rely on courtiers of the old school, Prince Charles surrounded himself with younger, less hidebound but also less experienced advisers. Given their divergent views as to what the style and role of the monarchy should be, and with each side working to its own set of priorities, conflict was frequent. In the turmoil following Diana's death, it was inevitable.

Despite or maybe because of her agitation, it had to be business as usual, the Queen decreed, and she asked that everyone should go to church at nearby Crathie that morning. The only people exempted from that royal command were Princes William and Harry. Given the enormity of what had happened, the Queen felt that it was up to them to decide whether they wanted to attend morning service – and face the inevitable battalions of press photographers converging on Balmoral. After a brief discussion between themselves, both boys said they would go.

It was a sorrow-torn period for Diana's sons. Yet it was noted by the staff that William and Harry showed remarkable resilience in the face of the tragedy. Both boys behaved very much as Diana might have predicted. Harry, always matter of fact, appeared to take the loss in his young stride, while William, on the verge of manhood

The Queen and the Duke of Edinburgh, the glamorous couple, at a state banquet in Lagos in February 1956.

Ten years after their wedding, in their seats for the world premiere of the film *Dunkirk* on 20 March 1958.

Prince Philip carriage-driving with Lady Penny Brabourne at
Windsor Horse Show.

Sharing a joke with his daughter-in-law Sophie, the Countess of Wessex, at
the Derby at Epsom on 4 June 2011. The Queen's horse Carlton Hall was
favourite but came third, with Pour Moi winning.

Prince Philip and his daughter-in-law, the late Diana, Princess of Wales, at a polo match at Smith's Lawn in the 1980s. They had a difficult relationship as Diana did not always appreciate his advice.

Prince Philip looking doubtfully at the Queen as she drinks a toast to the new century at the Millennium Dome in 2000. It was not an evening either of them enjoyed as they were forced into staged celebrations with the then prime minister Tony Blair.

The Queen with five-year-old Prince Harry and Michael Mann, Dean of Windsor, on Easter Day, April 1989. Mann established an excellent rapport with the Queen and Prince Philip and was much loved by them both.

Prince Harry and his grandfather, Prince Philip, at the Rugby World Cup final at Twickenham in 2015. Prince Philip enjoys being around his grandsons, especially at sporting events.

Prince Philip painting at an easel during the filming of the 1969 TV documentary *The Royal Family*. He is a talented artist and enjoys his hobby while being extremely knowledgeable about the subject.

The Queen riding with the Princess Royal in 2002. Age has not diminished her enthusiasm, and fifteen years later she takes every opportunity she can for a gentle hack. Despite safety issues she never wears a hat as it messes up her hair.

The Queen laughing at Prince Philip as he stands to attention at Windsor prior to the Queen's Company Grenadier Guards ceremonial review, 15 April 2003, a week before her seventy-seventh birthday.

On Prince Philip's ninetieth birthday, the Queen made her husband Lord High Admiral, the titular head of the Royal Navy. Here he lends a helping hand to the Queen after a service, in March 2015, commemorating British troops' thirteen-year involvement in Afghanistan.

The Queen and her racing manager John Warren cannot contain their delight as her horse Estimate wins the Gold Cup at Ascot in 2013 with jockey Ryan Moore and trainer Sir Michael Stoute.

Although Prince Philip is no fan of racing, he dutifully accompanies the Queen to Ascot and the Derby. He is seen here with the Queen and the Duke of York at the 2016 Derby. The Queen presented the trophy for the first time in her reign to the Aga Khan, whose horse Harzand won.

and very much aware of his royal destiny, made the demanding effort of keeping his emotions to himself.

It would be unwise and terribly unfair to read too much into the princes' apparent calm. There is no doubt that both were deeply affected by the death of a mother who had poured so much of her emotional energy into their welfare and made herself so central to their young lives. They have spoken of it since, but only recently have they admitted how angry they were that their mother was so viciously and suddenly taken from them. 'I can safely say that losing my mum at the age of twelve, and therefore shutting down all of my emotions, had a serious effect on not only my personal life, but my work as well,' Prince Harry said in April 2017.

'The shock is the biggest thing,' Prince William confessed at the same time. 'I still feel it twenty years later. People think shock can't last that long, but it does. It's such an unbelievably big moment and it never leaves you. You just learn to deal with it.'

At that time, however, they could see their mother's weaknesses as well as her strengths, and fifteen-year-old William had become increasingly concerned at the direction in which her life appeared to be heading. They had spent several days that summer with her in the South of France as guests of Mohamed Al-Fayed, who had pulled out all the stops. In his typically flamboyant style, he provided helicopters, yachts and speed boats and even opened a discotheque especially in an effort to impress them. It was all too lavish, too embarrassing, too over-the-top, too 'foreign' as they put it, for young men brought up to believe in the virtue of discreet understatement. Diana was lured by the glamour. Her sons, more royal than she realised, were not.

In her determination to ensure that they should enjoy as normal an upbringing as possible, Diana sometimes inadvertently led them in directions which went against their natural inclinations. William, for instance, much preferred the hills of Scotland to the beaches of the Riviera, shooting to waterskiing, the companionship of his school friends to the company of international playboys like Dodi Fayed, and he was starting to find the programme of entertainments his mother insisted on organising for him increasingly irksome. The prospect of spending the next few years in Mohamed's jet stream did not appeal in the least.

It did not appeal to the royal family either. An off-the-record call was made to the private office of Al-Fayed by Prince Edward, who explained to Mohamed's sidekick Mark Griffiths that there was concern over the ongoing Harrods sponsorship of the Royal Windsor Horse Show and it couldn't continue. Harrods was the main sponsor of the show and when Al-Fayed had taken over he had increased the sponsorship and included a carriage driving competition in which Prince Philip competed.

Al-Fayed was then in the power position and sat next to the Queen in the royal box and they presented the prizes to the winners together. The clear and undisguised message from the Palace was that this could no longer happen. Not now Diana was being photographed in the South of France cavorting with Al-Fayed's son. However, Prince Edward took great care to emphasise that the Diana issue had nothing to do with it, instead saying it was the other matters involving Al-Fayed at the time that might cause the royal family embarrassment. In particular, the 'cash for questions' scandal, in which he claimed to have paid various MPs to ask questions in Parliament on his behalf, even though they did not declare the income, was a cause for concern.

Diana fell into Dodi's arms after a dialogue was opened through the English National Ballet, of which she was patron, and Al-Fayed finally met the princess and befriended her. She liked him – or so she told me. She found his naughty sense of humour and Anglo-Saxon terminology amusing. She had been undecided as to where she would take her boys for their summer holidays when he suggested she avail herself of his St Tropez villa, with its secluded beach and state-of-the-art security. The rest just fell into Dodi's hands from there.

That all ended on the night of the accident. There was now no chance of an Al-Fayed–royal family link – so much so that instructions were sent to the morgue in London's Townmead Road that the two bodies were not to lie side by side when they were brought back from France for the coroner to examine. Dodi's body arrived first, having been transported by helicopter to Battersea heliport. While the body was examined, officials, police and Al-Fayed's team waited around nervously. There had been a directive issued to the police that the bodies were not even to be in the mortuary at the same time, so there was huge pressure on the coroner to complete Dodi's post mortem before Diana's body arrived. Finally, the hearse carrying Dodi turned slowly out of the gates of the mortuary just as the hearse with Diana turned in.

On that Sunday morning after church, Charles had flown to Paris aboard an aircraft of the Queen's flight, accompanied by Diana's sisters, Lady Sarah McCorquodale and Lady Jane Fellowes, Sir Robert's wife, and his press secretary Sandy Henney. Charles had ruled that it would be better if the princes did not accompany him on this mournful mission, and they remained at Balmoral in the care of the Queen and Prince Philip. They also had the company of their favourite cousin Peter Phillips, their father's old nanny Mabel Anderson, who was also staying at the castle, and Tiggy Legge-Bourke, Prince Charles's child helper that Diana so disliked.

In her forty-five years on the throne, the Queen had dealt with ten prime ministers, starting with Sir Winston Churchill. She had got on well with some, less well with others, and the new occupant of 10 Downing Street, Tony Blair, fell firmly into the latter category. 'Too much too quickly', was her unguarded summary of her current prime minister.

Blair had been at Northolt military airfield in West London to greet the plane bearing Diana's coffin, draped in a Royal Standard. On the Sunday, he had issued a statement which sounded more American than British in its wording. It read in part: 'We are a nation in a state of shock, in mourning, in grief ... She was a wonderful and warm human being.' But it was the soundbite in the last sentence that really caught the nation's attention: Diana, the prime minister declared, was 'the People's Princess'. That was the headline in most of the newspapers delivered to the castle on Monday morning and the phrase struck a resounding chord in the hearts and minds of millions who had never even met Diana. They knew little about her other than what they read in the newspapers they professed to disbelieve, yet had come to see her as one of their own.

The Queen was not amused, to put it mildly. She disliked the title 'People's Princess' and the implicit challenge it posed to her position as the Queen of all her people. A traditionalist to the core, she had quickly come to the conclusion that New Labour was no friend of the monarchy or the values she believes it embodies. She distrusted its plans for the reform of the House of Lords and its decision to accommodate homeless people in Admiralty Arch at the other end of the Mall to Buckingham Palace (she called that 'a publicity stunt'). After her regular Tuesday meetings at the palace with Blair, she would often emerge tut-tutting under her breath. On this morning and in the days to come, her irritation became more sharply focused on the belief that the government was trying to expropriate the princess for its own political ends.

It soon became abundantly clear, however, that it was the government and not the family she had once been a member of that knew best how to deal with Diana in death. In London and borne to power by the biggest electoral victory in Labour's history, the Blair administration could sense and see what the royal family, out of touch in rural Scotland, could not; they recognised the mass hysteria her demise had caused. Flowers were left in front of the gates of Buckingham Palace and on park lawns in front of Kensington Palace where she had lived. They grew into fields and then into vast savannahs. Trees and lamp-posts were ringed with candles. Notes, teddy bears, gifts, photographs and hand-written verses of poetry were pinned to railings. Churches which had stood virtually empty for years were filled with people on their knees praying for her soul. It was a spectacle that was both childish and moving, part Beatlemania, part national mourning and decidedly un-British. In its spontaneous desire to honour a woman who had died at the side of her playboy lover, a nation that had always prided itself on its self-control and its reserve threw off its restraints and allowed itself to be swept up in a frenzy of lamentation.

By contrast, the royal family demanded the right to be left to grieve for one of their own in privacy. It appeared they wanted to have it both ways. In the mind of the public at large, it was the royal family who had rejected Diana, isolated her, stripped her of her title as Her Royal Highness, leaving her a princess not in her own right but under sufferance and only for as long as she remained unmarried. But the further they had tried to push her into the shadows, the more potent her symbolic status had become. The royal family were dealing with a real person. The public were captivated by an emotional icon and in death Diana was posthumously crowned.

The family, gathered in the seclusion of Balmoral, simply did not understand what was taking place over 500 miles to the south. More damagingly, nor did their senior advisers – at least, not at first. The politics of the street was something they regarded with well-bred disdain. They ignored the ever-more frantic messages they were receiving from London and instead sought refuge in the battered redoubt of precedent.

The funeral, the Queen decided, should be a small, family affair at Windsor, followed by a burial in the graveyard at Frogmore, where successive generations of the royal family, with the exception of the reigning monarch and their consorts, are laid to final rest (since Queen Victoria's time, kings and queens have been buried at St George's Chapel, Windsor). The Queen's private secretary, Sir Robert Fellowes, agreed. The situation, however, was being torn from their grasp. In London, the crowds of mourners were perilously close to turning into a mob. Their wrath was palpable and growing. They wanted to know why no flag was flying at half-mast over Buckingham Palace, why no royal tributes to the princess had been forthcoming and, above all else, why the royal family had chosen to remain in Scotland instead of returning to the capital to join in the nation's mourning.

In fact, there was nothing unusual or pernicious in their decision to remain where they were. The royal family traditionally does its grieving in private and in a more devout age their wish to keep their sorrow to themselves would have been treated with quiet respect. There had been no complaints when the royal family had gone into retreat at Balmoral following the deaths of the Duke of Kent in 1942, of the Queen's glamorous cousin Prince William of Gloucester in 1972, or of Prince Charles's beloved great-uncle Earl Mountbatten of Burma in 1979. Like Diana, all had died violently: Kent and Gloucester in plane crashes, Mountbatten at the hands of the IRA.

But Diana was different. Her death had changed the rules to such an extent that even the royal family's attendance at Crathie church on the morning of her death had been criticised. How was it, the swelling army of critics were asking, that they could go to morning service, taking the bereaved Princes William and Harry with them, and show not a glimmer of grief? It was a cruel judgement which either missed or ignored the point that the Windsors are a religious family who find quiet solace in their faith, not in an Oprah Winfrey-style exhibition of public soul-wringing.

A public display of royal grief, however, was exactly what the millions converging on the capital were demanding, and the flag over Buckingham Palace became the symbol of what was now being perceived as the royal family's cold-hearted indifference. By time-honoured tradition, the only flag that flies over the palace is the Royal Standard and then only when the sovereign is in residence. It never flies at half-mast, even on the death of the sovereign, never mind a semi-detached princess, because the Royal Standard is the symbol of the state and the state is ongoing. As the heralds proclaim: 'The King is dead, long live the King.'

Such arcane niceties were of no interest and less relevance to the multitude outside the palace gates, whose lamentations soon became a cacophony of abuse aimed at the royal family. To venture among the crowds in the days that followed and hear the insults was to be caught by a swell of raw passion which threatened to sweep all before it. Most had been drawn to Kensington Gardens and St James's Park by the simple wish to share in the communal sense of sorrow, but as the numbers grew, so the ambience shifted and darkened. Young and old, the well-off as well as the dispossessed who had formed Diana's natural constituency, were asking how the royal family could be so uncaring, so out of touch, so heartless. Her death had turned out to be a catalyst, and resentments that had lain dormant for years came spewing to the surface. A moral audit was being conducted: the royal family was revealed to be deeply into the red and a country that had prided itself on its steadfastness and its stability appeared to be edging to the brink of razing an institution it had been raised to venerate.

By now, the calls to Balmoral had acquired a terrible urgency and the daily bulletins from Prince Charles's household were becoming increasingly bleak. They reported a growing mood of 'real hatred', and urged the prince to try to persuade his parents to order an immediate return to Buckingham Palace.

Reflecting the changing mood, the Queen realised there would have to be a full-blown funeral at Westminster Abbey, so plans were made for a meeting between the Spencer family, Charles's staff and the Queen's men. Sir Robin Janvrin remained at Balmoral trying to co-ordinate everything via speakerphone with the palace. There was a disagreement about what role the boys would play at the funeral – if any. The Queen and Philip were opposed to them being involved, as they were in shock. The Spencers' representatives were saying what they thought the involvement of the boys should be when Philip's voice came booming over the phone: 'Stop telling us what to do with those boys! They've lost their mother! You're talking about them as if they are commodities. Have you any idea what they are going through?!'

Prince Philip had virtually lost his own mother at the age of ten when she was committed to an asylum in Switzerland. He also lost his favourite sister and her family in an air crash in 1937 when he was sixteen. So to some extent he understood what William and Harry were suffering. They both loved their grandpa, who would take them shooting, duck-flighting and watch them speed round the go-kart track at Balmoral. They took no notice of his gruffness and acerbic comments. They just liked being around him, and during that strange, surreal week they were glad of his reassuring presence.

The turreted battlements of Balmoral castle are remarkably resistant to the onslaught of unpleasant reality, however. Queen Victoria hid behind them following the death of Prince Albert, detached from the world beyond, secure in a realm of her own creation which remains very much as she left it, down to the furnishings and the wallpaper. Now her descendants were doing much the same thing following the death of the princess. After the uproar of the first night, Balmoral had settled back into its old routine, and if the atmosphere was muted, everyone still dressed for dinner.

If that was due in part to the royal family's firmly held conviction that in times of trouble, sticking to the rules of protocol offers the best form of defence, it also reflected the antipathy some of them felt towards Diana, because of all the controversies created by her relationship with Prince Charles.

While her sister, her mother and her husband had long given up on Diana, the Queen retained some of her affection for her daughter-in-law. Alone in her family, she found it in herself to sympathise with her problems. Changing the long-established traditions for a woman who, by the letter of the law, was no longer royal was quite another matter, however. She had objected to Tony Blair being represented on the funeral committee, which had been set up under the chairmanship of her Lord Chamberlain, the Earl of Airlie, and it had required another argument to induce her to give way. And it was only when Prince Charles insisted that his ex-wife, as the mother of two princes of the blood, was entitled to (but didn't have) a state funeral that she had given up on her idea for a small, private ceremony.

What she said she was not prepared to do, however, at least not at this stage, was defer to the demands of the mob and go scurrying back to London. Such an action ran counter to the dignity she had been brought up to hold dear. But events were rapidly sliding out of royal control, and even the Queen's resolve was eventually broken. On the Thursday, a Union Jack was hoisted over Buckingham Palace and flew there at half-mast for the first time in British history. That same day, the family came out of their self-imposed seclusion to look at the flowers and letters of condolence which had been lain against the stone walls of the Balmoral estate.

Of greatest significance was the Queen's decision to return to London a day ahead of schedule. It was tantamount to a surrender. The final battle between tradition and modern political necessity was fought out in the Queen's tartan-carpeted first-floor sitting room. Ever since the crisis erupted, the Queen's advisers, including Janvrin and her lady-in-waiting, Lady Susan Hussey, had been monitoring what was happening in London. They had gone by the book, but that had not worked and by midweek it had become clear to everyone but the sovereign that the royal family was going to have to give way if it wasn't going to suffer perhaps irretrievable damage to its reputation. That led to yet more strained discussions.

Matters were brought to a head by the appearance of the bumptious Prince Andrew, who was staying at the castle. Politically naïve but a pedantic stickler for protocol, he walked into the sitting room, heard the arguments flowing backwards and forwards and furiously declared: 'The Queen is the Queen. You can't speak to her like that!' The Queen's word, he said, was their command and it was their duty to carry out any instruction she chose to give. A week before, that might have been true. It clearly wasn't in these circumstances and the sitting room was struck into stony silence. It was broken by the courtier who said that if the Queen did not want their advice, they would leave.

Faced with what amounted to an ultimatum from her own staff, the Queen chose to ignore her favourite son and accept the counsel of her advisers. She had no choice. The discussion was no longer about what was appropriate for Diana. It had come down to the future of the monarchy itself. In the judgement of the men and women whose job it is to guide the monarchy through the storms of controversy, the situation was critical and their advice was blunt and to the point: like it or not, the crowds had to be appeased if a major constitutional crisis was to be averted. This was no longer a simple family matter where the Queen and Prince Philip's opinion was decisive.

The Queen at last agreed. The original plan had been for her to travel south overnight by train and go straight from the station to Westminster Abbey. That was abandoned and instead she flew to London on the Friday, accompanied by Prince Philip,

Princess Margaret and the Queen Mother, who, royal trouper that she was, had categorically rejected her daughter's pleas to spare her health and stay behind in Scotland.

Back in the capital, the Queen drove straight to Buckingham Palace and, with Prince Philip at her side, left the safety of her own forecourt and went out to mingle with the heaving throng gathered beyond the flower-covered railings. It proved to be a disconcerting experience for the 71-year-old sovereign. A chasm had opened between the governed and their governors, and instead of the respect and polite applause which had been her due all her life, she was surrounded by people whose animosity was blatant. 'About bloody time, too,' someone said. 'That gave the Queen quite a turn,' one of her staff remarked later.

With the composure that comes with a lifetime's training, the Queen managed her walkabout with grace and dignity, stopping to chat, asking the right questions, giving the appropriate answers. It was a sterling performance, and to look at her – and the people who came within touching distance looked at her very closely indeed – it was hard to see any chink in her self-possession. It was quite clear to those who knew her, however, that she had been very alarmed by the reception she had received. She could not comprehend why people had been so hostile.

'What do they want me to do?' she asked. No one could remember ever seeing the Queen so agitated, so unsure of herself.

She was more her usual self by the time she went on television that evening to deliver her valedictory to her dead daughter-in-law. Sitting against an open window of the palace, with the crowds on the street providing the backdrop, she spoke simply and movingly in a voice an octave lower than the cut-glass tinkle of her youth and in an accent which had been stripped of some of its upper-class resonance. It was a speech loaded with subtly coded messages.

It offered an explanation for what to many had seemed the

royal family's indifference to the death of a young woman who was being elevated to secular sainthood. 'We have all been trying in our different ways to cope,' the Queen said, adding, by way of apology: 'It is not easy to express a sense of loss, since the initial shock is often succeeded by a mixture of other feelings: disbelief, incomprehension, anger and concern for all who remain. We have all felt those emotions in these last few days. So what I have to say to you now, as your Queen and as a grandmother, I say from my heart.'

She acknowledged, as she had to, the qualities which had touched the hearts of so many of the people who could be seen in the background. 'First, I want to pay tribute to Diana myself. She was an exceptional and gifted human being. In good times and bad, she never lost her capacity to smile and laugh, nor to inspire others with her warmth and kindness. I admired and respected her – for her energy and commitment to others and especially for her devotion to her boys.'

She explained the royal family's decision to stay in Scotland. 'This week at Balmoral we have all been trying to help William and Harry come to terms with the devastating loss that they and the rest of us have suffered.'

And she promised a new beginning. 'I for one,' the Queen said, 'believe that there are lessons to be drawn from her life and from the extraordinary and moving reaction to her death.'

The address was designed to pacify and appease a country which, in the space of a few short days, had become thoroughly disenchanted with its ruling family. It was written by Sir Robert Fellowes and checked by Blair's press spokesman Alastair Campbell, who had added in the sentimental but apposite 'grandmother' reference. It was not quite the wholehearted apologia many took it to be, however.

The Queen had been drawn to breaking point and it had left

her flustered, perplexed – and angry. Her authority had been challenged, her good intentions called into question, the character of her family cast into the gravest doubt. The Queen was spared most of the vitriol; even in this moment of crisis, the British people's peculiar, almost mystical attachment to their monarch still held fast. It was the other members of the royal clan – the amorphous 'them' – who were being blamed for what had happened. But that was hardly any reassurance. The atmosphere in the Mall was charged with hostility and the Queen had just seen and heard at first hand how incensed so many of her subjects were and how thoroughly disillusioned they had become with the family she heads. It was without doubt the worst juncture of her reign. But if the situation was grave, she was still the Queen – 'your Queen' as she reminded the millions who watched her speech – and this elderly lady who had sat on the throne for almost half a century was not going to bow too deeply to the hordes at the palace gates.

As she walked off the makeshift set she asked, 'Was that contrite enough?' It was not a question. It was a joke, but one delivered without a trace of humour and there was steely resolve in her voice.

It wasn't just the millions of mourners who had to be placated, however. There was also the more intimate problem of the Spencers to deal with. Lady Jane and Lady Sarah were willing to fall in with whatever plans formulated by the royal family and Jane's husband, Sir Robert Fellowes. Their brother was not. Charles Spencer, who had succeeded their father as the ninth Earl in 1991, had what might best be called an ambivalent relationship with his famous sister and the two had seen little of each other in recent years. As the head of the Spencer family, however, he claimed the right to have a say – and a decisive one at that – in the funeral arrangements.

Even without his intervention, there were plenty of complications. The royal family is swaddled in ceremonial rituals supposedly drawn from the mists of an ancient past. Most, in fact, are of much more recent fabrication and few pre-date the Victorian era when pageantry became an imperial art form. But this ability to invent a rite to fit the occasion had withered along with the Empire which spawned it. Precedent had superseded improvisation, and by now the House of Windsor and the bureaucrats who serve it had become trapped in the entanglements of their own rules. Without an example to turn to, they had no clear idea of how to honour a princess they had expelled from their fold.

The only model they had available was the one that had been devised for the Queen Mother, and it was in desperation that the funeral committee was reduced to plundering the plans she had so carefully laid for what would be her own last great state occasion. As the last person alive with any experience of organising such an event, following the death of King George VI, she had spent several years checking every detail, down to where the soldiers would be positioned. Without an alternative, this became the template for Diana's funeral. Britain's last Queen-Empress was understandably piqued at having her own meticulous preparations purloined for a woman who had never been a queen. Along with the rest of her family, she was also nonplussed by Lord Spencer's interference in what, like it or not, was now clearly a royal event.

Over the Queen's objections, Lord Spencer insisted that Diana be buried, not at Frogmore, but at the family home of Althorp in Northamptonshire. He also said he should be the only one to walk behind the princess's cortege. Given that they had effectively excluded her, the royal family were in no position to deny Spencer his wishes as to her final resting place. The cortege was quite another matter. In a mark of respect to an ex-wife and a departed mother, Prince Charles wanted to walk behind the cortege with William and Harry beside him. Another of the by-now interminable rows ensued over the telephone, which Spencer ended by hanging up on the prince. This was one point on which the royal family were not prepared to give way, however. It was made clear to Spencer that, regardless of whatever private feelings he might harbour, the prince and his sons *would* walk behind the gun carriage bearing the princess's coffin.

The next difficulty was persuading William to join his father, uncle and brother in the slow walk from St James's Palace to Westminster Abbey. At first William flatly refused. Charles pleaded with him and said that it would be utterly wrong of him not to accompany them. The prince, never comfortable in the eye of a crowd – and certainly not one so charged with emotion and looking at his every gesture – replied that he simply didn't want to. Prince Philip weighed into the argument and eventually William agreed to take part – but only on the condition that his grandfather walked beside him.

Diana had grown to dislike Prince Philip intensely – and he her – but Prince William was devoted to the old man. Philip, in turn, was immensely fond of his grandson. He had taught him to shoot, and William liked nothing better than spending his days with his grandfather out in the fields of Sandringham or wildfowling on the foreshore of the Wash. As football or cricket is in other families, field sports provided the common interest that crossed the generations and bound them together. Now William wanted his grandfather at his side in what was certain to prove the most harrowing public engagement the young man had had to endure. Philip readily agreed and as the cortege trundled under Admiralty Arch it was Philip who put a comforting arm around William's shoulder.

'Walking behind her coffin was one of the hardest things I have ever done,' Prince William admitted in May 2017. 'But if I had been in floods of tears the entire way round, how would that have looked? It was self-preservation. I didn't feel comfortable anyway, having that massive outpouring of emotion around me. I am a very private person, so it wasn't easy.'

If getting there had been fraught, there was still more upheaval awaiting them in Westminster Abbey. Built by Edward the Confessor in 1065, it is the spiritual font of the British monarchy. Kings and queens had been crowned and buried there for almost a thousand years. It can therefore only be construed as an act of calculated revenge for the unhappiness he believed they had caused his sister, that Lord Spencer chose it as the setting in which to deliver a swingeing attack on the family of the sovereign to whom, as a peer, he had sworn 'to bear true allegiance'.

The press came in for a fierce lashing in his address. 'She talked endlessly about getting away from England, mainly because of the treatment that she had received at the hands of the newspapers,' he said. 'I don't think she ever understood why her genuinely good intentions were sneered at by the media, why there appeared to be a permanent quest on their behalf to bring her down. It is baffling. My own and only explanation is that genuine goodness is threatening those at the opposite end of the moral spectrum. It is a point to remember that of all the ironies about Diana, perhaps the greatest was this – a girl given the name of the ancient goddess of hunting was, in the end, the most hunted person of the modern age.'

Spencer himself had once been a part of the media he so savagely lambasted. Indeed, he had once been employed by the giant NBC television network in America specifically because he was Diana's brother. The problems in his own marriage had quickly brought him into conflict with the press, however, and given his anguish and the paroxysm of recriminations it had induced, his remarks were perhaps understandable.

What was far more striking and totally unexpected was his condemnation of the royal family. When he said, 'She needed no royal title to continue to generate her brand of magic,' he was referring to the Queen's questionable decision to strip her daughter-in-law of the designation Her Royal Highness, which reduced Diana once again to the rank of commoner.

His closing remarks were even more barbed. 'She would want us today to pledge ourselves to protecting her beloved boys, William and Harry, from a similar fate, and I do this here, Diana, on your behalf. We will not allow them to suffer the anguish that used regularly to drive you to tearful despair. And beyond that, on behalf of your mother and sisters I pledge that we, your blood family, will do all we can to continue the imaginative way in which you were steering these two exceptional young men so that their souls are not simply immersed by duty and tradition but can sing openly as you planned.'

What Spencer was saying in no uncertain terms was that he considered the royal family unfit to bring up his nephews. It was a stinging rebuke of their father and the values of duty and tradition, which are the bedrock of royal life. The Anglican funeral service allows no place for allegation, accusation or the settling of scores. Quite the opposite: it is a ceremony of remembrance which is designed to bury the woes of this life alongside the body of the deceased. By going against time-honoured form, Spencer was guilty of gross bad manners. Hypocrisy, too, got an airing, because it wasn't Victoria, his wife and the mother of his four children, whom the earl had brought to the abbey that day, but his latest mistress, Josie Borain. Spencer was not the person best qualified to deliver a lecture on good parenting to the Prince of Wales from the pulpit of an abbey in front of a worldwide television audience of several hundred million.

Curiously, the prince's initial reaction was not one of outrage but of relief. Spencer had refused to allow him to see a draft of his address and after the telephone altercations he had had with his erstwhile brother-in-law in the hours leading up to the funeral, he had been expecting a lot worse than the admonition which was finally delivered. The Queen and Prince Philip, on the other hand, were appalled and their indignation was writ large in their stony glares.

As far as the public were concerned, however, Lord Spencer had hit precisely the right note. He had articulated what so many of them were feeling. His address was relayed by loudspeakers to the multitude packing the square outside and as he finished they gave a great roar of approval. It was borne through into the ancient abbey where the congregation, echoing the sentiments of those outside, burst into rapturous applause.

The Queen Mother and Princess Margaret, who had been complaining all morning about the inconvenience of having to cut short her Tuscan holiday because of 'that wretched girl', looked straight ahead. So did Princess Anne, who had viewed the events of the week with all the down-to-earth attitude one would have expected of that pragmatic, no-nonsense woman.

In truth, there was nowhere else to look. The people had taken matters into their own hands. Instead of being told what to do, they had told the royal family how to behave. The monarchy had responded – but only after it had been battered into submission. But now the week was at its end and the beast of public opinion began to settle, its anger vented, its grief expressed. As Diana's coffin made its way up the M1 motorway to her lonely grave on an island in the middle of a lake in Northamptonshire, the crowds began to melt away. A few hardy souls continued to keep vigil in the gardens outside Kensington Palace, but for most the roller-coaster had run its course. There was much talk of a new Britain, in touch with its feelings, cut loose from the restraint of its past, but slowly the country returned to normal, exhausted and exhilarated by the experience it had come through, but embarrassed, too, by its own wanton exhibition of emotion.

There was no retreat to the sanctuary of the pedestal for the royal family, however. The door to the past had been slammed shut. As the Queen had said, there were 'lessons to be drawn' from Diana's life and, first and foremost, from the reaction to her death. The regal system had been put the test – and found to be woefully wanting. Change was vital if the monarchy was going to sail into the next millennium. And the couple who had led their family for so long knew they would have to change with it, but they would also find comfort in maintaining the patterns of the past.

Chapter 12

DIFFERENT INTERESTS

It is 20 June 2013 at Windsor Castle. The Queen is having breakfast alone as Prince Philip is recuperating from an abdominal operation having been discharged from the London Clinic three days earlier. The Queen has forsaken her usual *Daily Telegraph* crossword in favour of the *Racing Post*, which she is studying intently. She has a particular interest in the Gold Cup because her filly Estimate is one of the favourites for the race. The Queen's house guests, among them her grandson Peter Phillips and his wife Autumn, Princesses Beatrice and Eugenie, are also enjoying breakfast in their rooms, having given their breakfast order to the page in charge the night before.

At 12.45 the Queen joins her guests for pre-lunch drinks in the Green Drawing Room before lunch in the State Dining Room. They all sit down to a brisk and, by royal standards, relatively simple meal, the men in tailcoats and the ladies with colourful outfits and extravagant hats. After lunch, they make their way to the Sovereign's Entrance where they all climb into a fleet of cars for the short drive to Ascot before they transfer into open landaus for the final part of the journey. They make their way through Home Park to the Golden Gates at the top of Ascot racecourse.

Once on the course, they trot briskly for the ten-minute drive along the swathe of green turf, taking a slightly different track each day to avoid churning up the racetrack. The Queen is in the first carriage accompanied by Peter Phillips and his wife. As they pass the grandstands, a tremendous cheer goes up for the Queen and top hats are raised. Already some lucky punters are collecting from the bookmakers, having had a successful wager on the colour of the Queen's hat. After dismounting from the carriages in the parade ring, the royal party spends most of the afternoon in the royal box.

It was Queen Anne in 1711 who first saw the potential for a racecourse at Ascot. While out riding near Windsor Castle, she came upon an area of open heath that looked, in her words, 'ideal for horses to gallop at full stretch'. Queen Anne's gift to racing, founding the royal racecourse, is marked by the tradition of opening Royal Ascot with the Queen Anne Stakes. The Ascot summer race meeting officially became a royal week in 1911. Ever since then, the royal meeting has been patronised by the reigning monarch. For the Queen, Royal Ascot is the highlight of the racing year, and she has never missed the meeting since her accession in 1952.

The Gold Cup, a Group 1 race and Britain's top event for long-distance thoroughbreds, is run over two miles four furlongs and is open to four-year-olds and older. It is always held on the Thursday – Ladies' Day – of Royal Ascot. The trophy is one of three cups at Royal Ascot traditionally presented by the Queen. It is the fourth race of the day and the Queen comes down to the paddock in time to look at the runners and meet her Barbadian-born Newmarket trainer Sir Michael Stoute and her jockey Ryan Moore.

The Queen has an expert eye and knows the breeding of every runner in the race. She does not refer to the horses by their names on the race card but by their bloodlines, so a horse may be 'the Galileo colt' or 'the Storm Cat filly'. Her horse Estimate is the only filly in the race and her trainer is not confident, although the capacity crowd has backed her down to be favourite. Sir Michael commented: 'I really felt it was a tough task, I wasn't confident at all with her taking on the boys.' The Queen's racing manager John Warren was also cautious, saying: 'It's a bit like asking whether Martina Navratilova could beat Bjorn Borg.' Adding to the pressure was the fact that no reigning monarch had ever won the Gold Cup.

But, more than fifteen years on from Diana's death, there is little doubt that there would be no more popular winner of the race than the Queen's horse. The intervening years had seen the public regain its trust and affection for the monarchy, as first her Golden Jubilee and then her Diamond Jubilee had been hugely popular occasions. The Queen, now aged eighty-seven, and Prince Philip, ninety-two, have come to symbolise stability in a world that has been rocked by wars, terrorism and a lingering financial crisis that has diminished the status of politicians everywhere.

As the race unfolds, Estimate is lying in fifth place with half a mile to go. Then Ryan Moore drives Estimate into the lead and fights tenaciously to hold off the Irish stayer Simeon to win by a neck. The stands just erupt in celebration and the crowd throws their hats in the air, so delighted were they to see the royal colours carried past the winning post. People rush to get a position around the winner's enclosure so they can get the best view of what is to come. Even the normally staid occupants of the royal box explode with cheering. The Queen is so overwhelmed with delight that her racing manager, John Warren, almost does the unforgivable and kisses her, as they clap their hands with joy as the four-year-old crosses the line.

The Queen had been due to present the trophy to the winner, but instead the Duke of York had to step in to hand the cup to her.

It was one of the very few occasions when the Queen was seen to be overcome with emotion. Peter Phillips said afterwards: 'It's been amazing. This is her passion, this is her life; every year she is here, every year she strives to have winners, and to win the big one at Royal Ascot means so much to her and so much to her supporters. It's the culmination of a lot of investing in sport and to see this result is just brilliant. Sheikh Mohammed came down to congratulate her – racing people understand that these things don't happen every day and to have a win like this is truly, truly special.'

Racing and the breeding of thoroughbreds mean so much to the Queen. The previous year, her Christmas cards showed the Duke of Edinburgh presenting her with the trophy after Estimate, then a three-year-old, won The Queen's Vase at Royal Ascot. The Queen takes a keen interest in the breeding of her horses, and is the patron of the Thoroughbred Breeders' Association. She decides which mares are to be bred to which stallions and makes regular visits to observe and assess her foals first hand from birth.

Her horses are foaled at the Royal Stud in the Sandringham Estate. As yearlings, they are raised at Polhampton Lodge Stud in Hampshire, before being passed on to the training facilities of any one of five trainers. Once they finish racing, they remain in her care into retirement and if they are sick or injured are looked after at Polhampton. As well as thoroughbreds, the Queen also breeds Shetland ponies at Balmoral in Scotland and Fell ponies at Hampton Court. The Fell ponies are used by Prince Philip for carriage driving, which he is still able to enjoy, although not at a competitive level. In 2007, she opened a full-time Highland pony stud at Balmoral to help preserve the breed.

The Queen, who had her first riding lesson at the age of four, still rides out regularly with her groom Terry Pendry at Windsor and Balmoral. She refuses to wear a hard hat and once told trainer Ian Balding: 'You don't have to have your hair done like I do.' She has confessed, however, that in her dotage she enjoys riding only when the weather is decent: 'I'm rather a fair-weather rider now. I don't like getting cold and wet.' Instead of the spirited half thoroughbreds she once rode, she now prefers the safety and width of her home-bred Fell ponies, especially one called Carltonlima Emma.

In 2014, the Queen was honoured with a lifetime achievement award from the Fédération Equestre Internationale (FEI), the International Federation for Equestrian Sports, at a private cere-mony at Buckingham Palace. Hailed as a 'true horsewoman' who has an 'extraordinary bond' with her horses, the Queen was given a white gold and diamond brooch of nine interlinked horseshoes, which had been especially created for her by FEI President Princess Haya, who is married to Sheikh Mohammed Al Maktoum, the world's largest racehorse owner, both of whom are frequently guests of the Queen at Ascot.

Another race meeting that the Queen attends regularly is the Epsom Derby, a race she has never won, although her horse Aureole was placed second in 1953. Prince Philip always goes to the Derby with the Queen, but he has been seen in the back of the royal box reading a book rather than the race card. In the year of her nineti-eth birthday in 2016, the Queen agreed to present the trophies to the winning connections for the first time. On the balcony of the royal box, the Queen could be seen surveying the scene with obvi-ous enjoyment as she chatted with John Warren. Prince Philip was leaning over the edge of the box having an animated conversation with Prince Andrew.

The stands were full and a huge cheer went up from the crowd as the starting stalls opened and the field of sixteen runners started to race the one-and-a-half miles to the finishing post. It was an inter-national field, with runners from Ireland and France taking on the best three-year-old horses in England. The Aga Khan's home-bred Harzand won, ridden by Irish champion jockey Pat Smullen and trained in Ireland by Dermot Weld. The Aga Khan is well known to the Queen, being a Knight of the British Empire and a successful breeder of thoroughbreds. For the current spiritual leader of Ismaili Muslims, it was his fifth Derby winner, extending a tradition started by his grandfather who also had five Derby winners starting in 1930.

After the race, the Queen descended from the royal box to present the trophies in front of the grandstand, where a dais had been erected for the presentation. Each in his turn received his trophy after a few words of congratulations from the Queen. That she took great pleasure in the presentation was plain for all to see.

Meanwhile, 94-year-old Prince Philip was standing erect as always and off to one side of the Queen and the winning group. He shook hands with each one as they mounted the dais, but took no part in the presentation ceremony. The Derby is not a state occasion like the opening of Parliament, so why did he make the trek down from the royal box to the presentation dais, only a week after his doctors ordered him to cancel an engagement because of fears about his health? It was not an obligation, but his sense of duty and a clear indication of his love and respect for his wife made him do it, especially as he has little interest in the sport.

Prince Philip's lack of interest in horse racing stems not from a dislike of 'The Sport of Kings' but rather that, unless one is the jockey or trainer, it is a passive sport. During Royal Ascot, Philip will dutifully be at his wife's side, but he insists on being able to watch the cricket on TV during the racing and has a small office in the back of the royal box where he catches up on his correspondence with the help of a secretary. He doesn't like to be a spectator; he wants to be an active participant. He is highly competitive and the will to win is paramount for him. He has been deeply involved in other equestrian sports including polo, carriage driving and show-jumping. He is the longest-serving president of the International Equestrian Federation, from 1964 to 1986, and as such he has had more influence than anyone on the way international equestrian sport has developed. During his time there, he instigated jumping's Nations Cup series. In 2007, he was inducted into the British Horse Society's Equestrian Hall of Fame, following in the footsteps of his daughter, the Princess Royal.

Although polo eventually became his favourite sport, Philip was slow to warm to it. When he was based in Malta in 1949, he was more interested in the inter-ship sporting competitions such as hockey and rowing. At the command of his own ship *Magpie*, he drove his crew hard, so much so that at the annual regatta in 1949 his ship won six out of ten events, with Philip stroking the whaler class boats. There was a polo ground in Malta where Dickie Mountbatten often played. Both he and Princess Elizabeth wanted Philip to take up the sport, but initially he showed no interest, saying that it was 'a snob sport' and that he preferred playing hockey and diving on the reefs.

Lady Mountbatten wisely advised the princess not to push Philip too hard, saying he would come around to the idea of playing polo in his own good time, which he did. Sure enough, once he took it up, it became his favourite sport and he developed into one of the best players in the country with a five-goal handicap. It did count against him, however, when the question of the royal finances was raised in Parliament from time to time. In Philip's own words: 'Polo is not exactly cheap and anyone wishing to play must be either well-heeled, have a good job or be supported by an indulgent parent or sponsor ... His wife needs to be very understanding and long-suffering.' The Treasury took the view that if Philip could afford to keep polo ponies and grooms, a pay rise in the civil list could not be justified.

As a player, Prince Philip had huge energy – and got stuck into the game not minding what he said or to whom. 'This is also one of the fields in which wives like to take part,' he said. 'Wives have also been known to have very firm views about the way both their husbands and other players conduct themselves on the polo ground.' He was obviously referring to the straight talking during play – which could all too easily waft over to the spectator area, including the royal pavilion.

Playing in the semi-final of the Harrison Cup at Cowdray Park during one Goodwood week, former international showjumper Johnny Kidd, a member of the Todham Team along with patron Ronnie Driver and high goal players Julian Hipwood and Jorge Tassara, remembers playing against the Windsor team of Prince Philip, Patrick Beresford, Prince Charles and the Marquis of Waterford. He recalls 'Prince Philip yelling at Prince Charles non-stop – get a move on, do this, do that – calling him a f***ing idiot and worse. While all the time Prince Charles was quietly polite. He carried on while Prince Philip was steaming with anger.'

Despite or maybe because of his fiery attitude, Prince Philip did much to popularise polo in the 1950s and 1960s. He founded the Household Brigade Polo Club (later the Guards Polo Club) in 1955, which has ten polo pitches on Smith's Lawn in Windsor Great Park where the Queen is often a spectator. She breeds polo ponies along with her thoroughbred racehorses. Philip also promoted bicycle polo, which enabled those who couldn't afford the real thing to get a taste of polo without all the expense. It is now a firmly established sport with international competitions.

However, polo is not an old man's game, and in 1971 Prince Philip gave it up in favour of carriage driving, which involves driving a four-in-hand around an obstacle course against the clock. Philip became so involved with the sport that he revised the rules of competitive carriage driving and wrote on a book on it: *30 Years on and Off the Box Seat*. With his penchant for invention, he redesigned various wooden parts of the carriage that were inclined to break and replaced them with metal ones. Philip's competitive spirit was always seen at the annual Royal Windsor Horse Show. He was still driving at the age of ninety-five, no longer in competitions but going out with his carriage and team of Fell ponies in all weathers.

Unsurprisingly, the Queen and Prince Philip's children and grandchildren have competed in equestrian events with great success, most notably Princess Anne and Zara Phillips. In an essay on horses, he wrote: 'Having a family which seems to be equally willing to be humiliated by the horse, I have to live with the expectation that they too will suffer injury and indignity . . . I am not surprised when it happens to them and I am full of sympathy and useful advice for treatment and recovery.'

However, there are other sports that have had the royal seal of approval. Sailing is an important part of the curriculum at Gordonstoun and was something at which young Philip excelled. His sailing days may be over, but he is still a regular presence at Cowes Week as admiral of the Royal Yacht Squadron, one of the most prestigious yacht clubs in the world, with the Queen as their patron.

Despite this, sailing is a sport where Philip tends to operate separately from the Queen. At Cowes, he would spend his time with Uffa Fox, not his wife. Fox was a boat designer and builder by trade, but also a raconteur, bon vivant and all-round eccentric individual. Prince Philip wrote the foreword to Uffa's biography, including these words: 'His life was one long campaign for the freedom of the human spirit and against the foolish, the stupid and the self-important, the whole conducted with a cheerful breeziness that disarmed all but the hardest of cases.'

He and Prince Philip raced together on the Dragon class yacht *Bluebottle* and in the Flying Fifteen *Coweslip* that was designed and built by Uffa. The 20-foot Flying Fifteen was one of Uffa's most successful post-war designs and *Coweslip* was presented to the Princess Elizabeth and Prince Philip by the people of Cowes as a wedding gift. Uffa and Philip won the Britannia Cup in *Coweslip* in 1952.

Bloodhound is a 63-foot ocean racing yacht built in 1936. She was purchased for the royal family in 1962 at the request of Prince Philip. During royal ownership, *Bloodhound* would accompany the royal yacht *Britannia* in the Western Isles when the royal family had their family holiday every year. She had a permanent crew of three and one skipper was a descendant of Sir Francis Drake. It was during these times that the young royals learned to sail on *Bloodhound*. When not in royal use, *Bloodhound* and her crew were made available by Prince Philip to yacht clubs across the country, and was used to teach thousands of young people how to sail.

Cricket was another sport at which Prince Philip excelled at Gordonstoun. Although he likes to claim he was not particularly good, he became captain of the first XI in his final year. When he was first married, and had a weekend house in the country at Windlesham, he adapted the tennis court for use as a cricket pitch. Always keen to mix with ordinary people, Philip would make up teams from assorted friends, locals, gardeners, detectives and drivers.

In 1949, Philip became president of Marylebone Cricket Club, the ruling body of the sport, and led a victorious English Invitation XI against Hampshire, piloting his own helicopter from Balmoral to the cricket ground at Bournemouth. He possessed 'the perfect action' according to no less a judge than Australian batsman Don Bradman. The MCC, of which the Queen is patron, celebrated Prince Philip's ninetieth birthday with a lunch in the Long Room at Lord's cricket ground, attended by representatives of his sporting charities, at which he was guest of honour. He is also patron and 'Twelfth Man' of the Lord's Taverners, the official charity for recreational cricket in the United Kingdom.

Until 1998, when the MCC voted to admit women members, the Queen was the only woman permitted to watch cricket from the pavilion. Both the Queen and Prince Philip still visit Lord's occasionally during a Test match. The royal family's patronage of Lord's is infused with a hint of scandal, however. Hanging in the pavilion is a painting of 'An Imaginary Cricket Match' at the ground, commissioned to mark the MCC's centenary in 1887. While England bat and Australia field, the Prince and Princess of Wales (the future King Edward VII and Queen Alexandra) stroll around the outfield, while in the foreground, wearing a yellow dress and scarlet bonnet, is the prince's mistress, actress Lillie Langtry.

Ever since Kurt Hahn had impressed upon Prince Philip how physical fitness should be a cornerstone of young people's education, he has been a driving force to get more children into sports and physical activities of all kinds. In 1947, he became the patron of the London Federation of Boys' Clubs. The following year, he accepted the presidency of the National Playing Fields Association, which he held for many years. When the Central Council of Physical Recreation for the United Kingdom appeared close to being disbanded in 1951, Philip assumed the presidency and guided the organisation into its present form as the Sport and Recreation Alliance. These organisations, together with the Duke of Edinburgh Award scheme, have helped millions of young people to make fitness a priority.

Philip would not have been able to keep up his customary punishing schedule of engagements past his ninety-sixth birthday if he were not supremely fit himself. Even in his nineties he follows part of the Royal Canadian Air Force exercise plan, which was created by a doctor in the 1950s. It is a stretching and toning twelve-minute plan designed to keep men and women fit without the use of gym equipment and most of the fashionable simple exercise plans today are based on it.

One of the first things Philip did when he moved to Buckingham Palace from Clarence House was to get the squash court back into working order. He was also a regular user of the indoor pool at the palace. When the Queen was giving birth to Prince Charles, Philip passed the time with a game of squash with his equerry Michael Parker.

Shooting has always been a sport that royalty has enjoyed as a favourite pastime. For example, King George VI was an exceptional shot, and as the Sandringham estate has a particularly fine shoot, a bag of 2000 pheasants in a day was not uncommon in his time. In addition, there was always grouse shooting to be had in the heather at Balmoral. George VI gave Philip a pair of matched Purdey shotguns as a wedding present and taught him the finer points of shooting at Balmoral and Sandringham. Up to that point, Philip's shooting experience had been limited to hunting wild boar in Germany, where all four of his brothers-in-law had country estates. In time, he became a crack shot. After the death of George VI, Philip re-organised the shoot at Sandringham and for many years managed to achieve his target bag of 10,000 pheasant during the annual seven-week stay. He also enjoyed shooting wildfowl from a punt on the Norfolk Broads in the company of the actor James Robertson Justice.

Prince Philip is also an ardent conservationist and for many years has been president of the World Wide Fund for Nature, formerly called the World Wildlife Fund. He has no problem in reconciling his position as president of the fund with his passion for shooting. Nor is he a fan of gun control. After the Dunblane shooting in 1996, when sixteen schoolchildren were shot dead with a pistol, there was a cry for more rigorous laws to control the ownership of handguns. Philip famously said: 'If a cricketer, for instance, suddenly decided to go into a school and batter a lot of people to death with a cricket bat, which he could do very easily, I mean, are you going to ban cricket bats?'

Shooting is very much part of the Queen's life, too – not as a keen shot but as a handler of gundogs trained to pick up the downed birds. The Queen's love of dogs is well known, but it is not just corgis, which she has had as household pets all her life. She also has a deep involvement with the labradors and spaniels kept as working dogs in the royal kennels at Sandringham. Her skill as a dog handler is renowned. She uses hand signals and whistles to control her labradors. Bill Meldrum, who ran the Sandringham kennels for more than forty years, says that she is the best dog handler he has ever seen – 'probably the best in the country'. Glimpsed behind the line of guns on shoot days, the Queen is simply, as one of the keepers recalls, 'a lady in a headscarf with a load of dogs around her, and in a field of sporting people you wouldn't pick Her Majesty out.'

The dogs do not live only at Sandringham. When the Queen travels to Balmoral for her long summer break, many of the labradors and spaniels are put into lorries and driven through the night to be available for the grouse shoots. The Queen prefers the dogs to be worked outside every other day to avoid becoming too tired or getting bruised paws. After the grouse season, they return to Norfolk for the partridge shoots.

Rather surprisingly, the Queen is also an expert on breeding and racing pigeons, and she has 200 of them. Ever since the days when she fed her grandfather King George V's parrot with sugar lumps, she has loved birds. When she lived at Royal Lodge as a child, she and her sister had an aviary of budgerigars. She likes birds in their natural environment and knows the breed and songs of many that inhabit the woods and forests around Balmoral Castle.

The music of nature is not the only form of music she likes: military bands, popular music from her younger days, singing and playing the piano (which she learnt to do as a child) are all things she enjoys. For the Queen Mother's ninetieth birthday, she had the inspired idea of making a cassette of Scottish childhood songs with Princess Margaret. Neither of them played, choosing instead to concentrate on the singing, and to get it right asked

Laurie Holloway, the renowned composer and pianist, to come to Buckingham Palace to help them create the surprise present. When he arrived at the palace, he was shown into a room containing a piano and two microphones. 'There was a sound engineer. We recorded each song in one take,' he recalled. 'I think there were about a dozen songs. The Queen has a nice, sweet tone to her voice.'

At the Queen's request, only one cassette tape was made and the only song Holloway could recall from the recording was 'I Know Where the Flies Go in Winter Time'. 'They sang to me without accompaniment, and I would then play in their key,' he remembered. Sadly, after the Queen Mother's death, the cassette went missing.

'I don't think the title was written on the cassette, so it might be stored somewhere and no one will realise its significance,' says Holloway. Princess Margaret told him that the Queen Mother had really liked the tape – although she had to go into her car to listen to it as she did not own a cassette player. When Prince Charles heard about this, he reminded his grandmother he had given her a sound system which contained a cassette player and all she had to do was pop the cassette in and press the right button. There was no need to go and sit in her car after all!

Another of the Queen's interests is in military history. As head of the armed forces, the Queen feels it is her duty to know every uniform, how it should be worn and with what – which she does – but few realise she is also fascinated by military history. The Countess of Wessex, who is close to the Queen, shares her fascination and loves listening to her talking about great historical events. The pair are apparently sometimes gone for hours, pouring over ancient documents in the royal archives or books in the library at Windsor Castle.

When Sophie visited some of the battlefields and cemeteries of the First World War in France, she told the Queen all about what she had seen.

Both the Queen and Prince Philip have always loved photography, and the Queen was famously filming an old rhino at the salt lick on her cine camera at Treetops in Kenya at almost the moment her father died. Philip had the latest and most professional still camera equipment and used to get very irritated with photographers when they were slow when shooting official portraits. Cecil Beaton was subject to many caustic comments during his sessions, and years later cockney photographer Terry O'Neill recalled Prince Philip's brusqueness at the christening of Princess Eugenie at Sandringham. 'Haven't you taken enough?' he kept asking. 'I can't believe anyone can take so long just to take a few boring photographs.'

More recently Prince Philip was at a lunch at the RAC Club in Piccadilly after a fly-past to commemorate the seventy-fifth anniversary of the Battle of Britain. The duke was in an official photograph together with the Duke of Cambridge, the Earl of Wessex and the Duke of Gloucester and six remaining veterans of the day. Becoming more and more agitated at the slowness of the photographer, he said, 'Just take the f***ing picture.' In the age of social media, the video footage of the moment went viral.

Even in their old age, the Queen and Philip retain their separate interests. The Queen loves walking her dogs, playing patience and completing complicated jigsaw puzzles. She keeps her photograph albums up to date and is meticulous about writing her diary every night. Philip is just the opposite and gets frustrated when he is not doing something physical.

Even he, however, has had to bow to advancing years. In 2011, he received treatment for a blocked coronary artery after he was taken to hospital suffering chest pains. He was fitted with a stent to keep the artery open, because of which he has had to give up shooting. It was considered that the recoil of a gun was too dangerous as it could dislodge the stent. Fly fishing for salmon and trout has since become Philip's favourite pastime at Balmoral. Despite his age, he is still steady enough to stand in the river Dee and, together with a ghillie, can spend hours in the water, wearing chest-high protective waders, only breaking to join the Queen and guests for lunch or tea in one of the huts near the river. The Queen used to be a keen angler, having inherited her love of fishing from her mother, to whom, being a Scot, fishing was second nature, but she has not fished for several years.

In 1962, Prince Philip published a book entitled *Birds from Britannia*. As a keen bird-watcher and more than competent photographer, the book was illustrated with photographs he had taken during his solo tour of Commonwealth countries. His interest in ornithology came about because of his friendship with Sir Peter Scott, the founder of the World Wildlife Fund. Scott was also a gliding fanatic and was British champion in 1956, so he was responsible for involving Prince Philip in gliding; the prince is still patron of the British Gliding Association.

Philip is a skilled and experienced pilot of both fixed-wing aircraft and helicopters. He confessed that he would have rather joined the Royal Air Force than the navy if he had not had his arm twisted by Dickie Mountbatten. In an essay on test pilots, he wrote: 'I have to confess I have frequently speculated whether I would like to have been a test pilot . . . I came to the conclusion that a test pilot has an impossible job.'

Despite opposition from the government, particularly Winston Churchill, Philip started flying lessons in 1952. He learned to fly with the RAF at White Waltham and gained his RAF wings in 1953, his helicopter wings with the Royal Navy in 1956, and his Private Pilot's Licence in 1959. Curiously, he was made an honorary pilot of both the Chilean and Colombian air forces in 1962. He didn't give up flying until August 1997, by which time he had clocked up over 6000 hours as a pilot in 59 types of aircraft in 44 years. He was grand master of the Guild of Air Pilots and Air Navigators from

1952 until 2002. In his centenary address to the Royal Aeronautical Society, he said: 'I find that aviation as a human activity has certain highly individual characteristics. It is as much an enthusiasm as a scientific, technological or commercial undertaking.'

To this day, Philip uses helicopters as often as possible and wrote a tongue-in-cheek treatise on helicopters in which he said: 'I make frequent use of helicopters and indeed I very much enjoy flying them myself but I have sadly come to the conclusion that the time has come to ban the helicopter.' He goes on to state the unfair advantages that helicopter users enjoy, concluding: 'If the disappearance of the helicopter is assured we shall all be able to hold our heads high as we march steadily back towards the caves our ancestors so foolishly vacated such a long time ago.'

With much of his life having been taken up with sporting activities and a full diary of public engagements, it might be thought that Prince Philip had little time for any other pursuits, but he did and still does. His interest in art, both as a creator and collector, dates back decades to when he invited the artist Edward Seago to accompany him on *Britannia* for the Antarctic and later stages of his 1956–57 world tour. On the voyage, Seago gave Prince Philip some lessons in oil painting, adding to his skill as a water-colourist. Hanging in the royal collection is a painting by Seago of Philip at work on deck with his easel and brushes.

Philip confesses to have given much of his work away but one painting remains in his personal collection. Painted in 1956, it is entitled 'The Queen at Breakfast, Windsor Castle'. The painting gives an intimate and detailed view of the Queen in an off-duty moment, reading a newspaper. The breakfast table is covered with a crisp white tablecloth, the plates, cups and saucers are white china, and there is a loaf of bread with a jar of marmalade and another place set for Philip. On the walls are two horse paintings by renowned equestrian artist George Stubbs.

Prince Philip's taste in art certainly didn't appeal to Prince Charles. When he arrived for part of his honeymoon in the summer of 1981 at Craigowan, a small house on the Balmoral estate, he found it had been decorated with the duke's collection of modern pictures, including one of Prince Philip's own efforts – a Balmoral scene. So back on the walls went the Highland scenery and paintings and sketches of Queen Victoria and her children. 'That's better,' the prince said to his valet, Stephen Barry. 'But no doubt Papa will swap them again at Christmas.' He was right. The next time Prince Philip arrived at the house he made the footman change them all around again. And so it went on.

As a patron of the arts, Prince Philip has added many contemporary British artists to the royal collections. He was instrumental in getting the Queen's Gallery open at Buckingham Palace, where the public can view changing exhibitions from the Queen's collection, with the admission fees going towards the palace upkeep. It might surprise some to learn that he is even a fan of Tracey Emin and has said he found her 'interesting' when he met her at the Turner Contemporary Gallery in Margate. The Queen apparently didn't know who she was and asked her if she had ever 'exhibited internationally as well as in Margate'.

Philip enjoys telling a story to illustrate his art expertise. When he was first married to the princess, he was going through the labyrinth of cellars and dungeons at Windsor Castle when he came across a cellar room that obviously hadn't been investigated for years. On the walls were two oil paintings covered in dirt, but with a distinguished familiarity. When he got them out into the daylight and dusted them down, he excitedly realised he had some original Stubbs in his possession. To this day, they hang in his study at Windsor, a reminder that if it hadn't been for his artistic eye, they might never have been discovered and for ever forgotten.

Having a keen eye for art, Prince Philip has also championed improving design in the commercial world. From its inception in 1959, the Prince Philip Designers Prize has celebrated how designers improve daily life by solving problems and turning ideas into commercial reality. Winners have included everything from household products to buildings and great feats of engineering. Having headed up the judging panel and presented the prize since its inception, in 2011 Philip stepped down from the prize as he reduced his royal responsibilities in his ninetieth year.

Prince Philip's high regard for pleasing design is equalled by his admiration for engineers. He has always said they performed such an essential function that it was hard to imagine life without them. He also claimed engineers held the key to the future of humanity and its ability to continue to thrive on the planet. As senior fellow of the Royal Academy of Engineering, he has criticised the lack of a Nobel Prize for engineering. The Prince Philip Medal for Engineering is awarded biennially to an engineer of any nationality who has made an exceptional contribution to engineering.

The Queen, too, has given her name to a prize for engineers. In 2011, the Queen Elizabeth Prize for Engineering was set up to reward and celebrate the engineers responsible for a groundbreaking innovation in engineering that has been of global benefit to humanity, and the generous £1 million prize is awarded every two years.

Prince Philip gave one of his most recent interviews to Radio 4 to talk about the prize he had set up and about the merits of British engineering with former BP executive Lord Browne, who was guest editor on the programme. 'The human population of the world is growing and it's got to be accommodated somehow or other,' he said, adding: 'It's going to be engineers who are going to decide' how to do this without resorting to destroying the delicate balance of nature. To emphasise the point, he commented: 'Everything that wasn't invented by God was invented by an engineer.'

Chapter 13

FROM BANQUETS
TO TEA AT THE PALACE

The Queen and Prince Philip have spent most of their married lives entertaining or being entertained. Even though she has been doing the job for more than sixty-five years, the Queen is still shy and her conversation can be very stilted. If she is with friends or in the company of people who understand breeding thoroughbreds or racing them, she is animated and chatty, but with people she doesn't know or is never likely to meet again, her conversational skills are minimal.

Throughout their married life, it has been Prince Philip who has done most of the talking socially. Occasionally, to liven things up, get a reaction, or just because he is bored stiff, he will make one of his famous gaffes. At times he can appear downright rude, but he can also be very funny, and when he needs to put on the charm he can outshine the most obsequious of courtiers.

Although the Queen is head of state, and many of her duties don't necessarily involve her husband, in previous years when they were travelling or entertaining at one of the royal residences, it was very much a united effort. The Queen has always relied on the Duke of Edinburgh to make conversation not only with the first lady, whoever she might be, but to all the other visiting dignitaries. When he was seated next to former French President Sarkozy's wife, Carla Bruni, at the state banquet at Windsor Castle in 2008, things went extremely well. Philip was at his most charming throughout the evening and his bonhomie was infectious.

Although a state banquet is probably one of the most splendid and awe-inspiring formal events, there can be a few surprises as to how the royal family behave. When King George VI was still alive, as soon as he put down his knife and fork, his page, who always stood behind him, would immediately clear away. This was a signal for every other plate on the table to be taken away, regardless of whether the other diners had finished eating.

The Queen has not exactly ended this custom, but found a way around it. She looks carefully around the table – no matter whether it's a state banquet or a smaller, more intimate meal – and checks on her guests' progress. As she eats frugally, she will often have finished before anyone else, but she has a small salad on a side plate and she toys with it until the rest of the guests have caught up. Once she has finally put down her fork, it's all systems go.

Prince Charles is the slowest of royal eaters, while the Duke of Edinburgh is the fastest and gobbles his food up so quickly he has been known to put more fastidious eaters right off their food. One footman recalls a dreadful night when they were sailing onboard HMY *Britannia* when it was struck by a force nine gale. Everyone retired to their cabins, including most of the ship's company. Not so Prince Philip. He still wanted to eat dinner, and his poor equerry had to sit with him. He was getting greener and greener as he watched Prince Philip, never the neatest of eaters, shovel food into his mouth. Eventually, when he was asked if he would like some rice pudding, he could take it no longer and had to leave abruptly.

Prince Philip was left all on his own in a dining room that can seat sixty, unworried about the discomfort he had caused.

A more common problem than Prince Philip's eating habits is guests simply being lost for words in the royal presence. 'There's a lot of trembling knees – and people can't talk sometimes,' says Prince William. 'It's quite difficult talking to people when they can't talk. You don't get very far. I don't get past the hellos!'

When the head of state from a foreign power is the guest of the Queen and the Duke of Edinburgh, they stay at Buckingham Palace or Windsor Castle. On the day of arrival, which is always a Tuesday, they are given lunch in the Bow Room at the palace or the State Dining Room at Windsor Castle. These state visit luncheons are rather grander than the small and cosy 'meet the people' occasions that the Queen and the Duke host a few times a year. Everything, as the Queen explains, is truly formal.

'A lot of the visits nowadays have a very strong political theme to them,' the Queen says. 'We are the hosts. Basically, we give the entertainment initially and have people to stay hoping to give them a nice time to remember. Obviously, we keep up as many of the traditions as we can, like going in carriages.

'I think that in a way that it's quite an old-fashioned idea that you do put out the red carpet for a guest. I think people don't really realise this. I do tell guests that we put on our best clothes and everybody dresses up and the best china and the glass and the gold plate come out, otherwise it doesn't see the light of day! It's very nice to be able to use it and show it. If you do put out the best china and glass it isn't necessary to make it overwhelming.

'If people are kind to you and make you feel at home I don't think the outward and visible signs matter. It is what goes on inside that really matters. But sometimes it's worth explaining that we put it on specially. That we don't actually live like this all the time!'

The Queen is a perfectionist and as the perfect hostess wants to make her guests feel at ease. When President Lech Walesa of Poland visited Windsor Castle in April 1991 with his wife Danuta, the Queen noticed he was overwhelmed by the grandeur and ordered the furniture to be moved around in the six-roomed principal suite where they were staying and to make it more cosy.

If visitors are staying in London, they are led to the Belgium Suite, where they will be housed for the three-day stay at the palace. All their unpacking has already been done for them and they have half an hour's free time to freshen up before the state lunch. In the meantime, as many royals as the Queen can muster, plus most of her household, will wait in the 1844 Room to greet the guests. Prince Philip would go personally to the Belgium Suite to collect the visiting president and his lady and then lead them to the pre-lunch drinks gathering. He used to bound down the stairs two at a time, but these days his pace is just a little more sedate. Luncheon is served in the Bow Room, which for these occasions is turned into a dining room.

The Queen leads her guests, walking ahead with the visiting president, King or Queen on her right. There are usually sixty seated for lunch, as all the visitors' entourage will be invited. In the case of some less stable countries, this can be a lot of people, as some leaders feel it is safer that way – just in case someone tries to carry out a coup back home while their backs are turned.

Everyone is placed at round tables – six of them, ten people to a table – each of which is hosted by a member of the royal family. Language can be a problem if the guests don't speak English, but the royals can get by in French, which they all speak well, and there are always interpreters on hand for the Queen and the family if French won't do. Everyone else, including the household, has to muddle along as best they can. An awful lot of smiling goes on in lieu of conversations.

Even though it is a very important occasion, the food served will be light. The Queen is aware that there will be a state banquet that night, and that her guests will have a busy schedule that afternoon. No one lingers over the meal. By three o'clock the entire party is back in the 1844 Room for coffee and liqueurs and the ceremony of exchanging presents takes place. The presents that the Queen is given vary from lavish ones, particularly if they are from an Eastern country, down to something as simple as a small piece of furniture. In return, the guests are invariably given a silver salver and a signed photograph in a leather frame of Her Majesty and the Duke of Edinburgh, which the household nickname 'the glums'. Honours are also exchanged after this lunch. Some guests are given honorary knighthoods, and the Queen may be given the highest rank available in her visitor's country. That evening, at the glittering state banquet, the Queen and her visitor will wear the sash of their newly acquired honour.

But these grand occasions are few and far between. The luncheon hour is not normally a time when anything much happens in the royal life. When the Queen is at work, she almost always lunches alone in her private dining room on the first floor. All she eats is a main course and salad, followed by coffee, brought in by her footman. And she usually serves herself from the hotplate that is left permanently in her dining room.

On the rare occasions when she and Prince Philip lunch on their own together, the duke likes to choose something new and different from the chef's suggestions, or something he may have sampled on one of his frequent evening engagements. Even until his ninety-sixth year, he was still attending official dinners, which he enjoyed, despite the huge amount of energy he had to muster to do so. When the royal couple are alone, they often have what they call an 'experiment lunch'. They would never dream of giving guests something they had not eaten themselves. As the duke still takes a great interest in food, it is usually him not the Queen who will write any alterations or suggestions in the menu book.

Apart from family lunches, the midday meal is another opportunity for the Queen and Prince Philip to meet people. Ever since 1956, they have given up to four lunches a year when they do just that. The small gatherings of eight to ten specially selected guests are known as the 'Meet the People' palace luncheons. The guests come from all walks of life and range from jockeys to journalists, actresses to artists, to managing directors of huge corporations. Even editors of the most widely read newspapers have been known to be invited. There is nearly always one of the Queen's favourite comedians present – the late Terry Wogan was much loved and certainly sang for his supper, though he was not expected to.

In 2015, Formula One ace Lewis Hamilton received an invitation and told BBC's Graham Norton about how he sat next to the Queen, and how she ensured that everyone was equally involved in the occasion. 'I was excited,' he explained, 'and started to talk to her but she said, pointing to my left, "No, you speak that way first and I'll speak this way and then I'll come back to you."'

He added: 'She is a sweet woman and we talked about how she spends her weekends, her houses and music. She is really cool.'

It is not just celebrities or famous people who are lucky enough to be invited to these occasions, but often simply those who have made a contribution to their particular walk of life. In March 2016, particle physicist and TV presenter Professor Brian Cox joined the royal couple for one of the lunches. The Queen is fascinated by the solar system and is something of an expert on the stars in the night sky.

Although the lunches are informal by palace standards, they appear very formal to those invited. To stress that this is a business get-together, partners of the guests aren't invited to the lunch. Instead, when they arrive, a footman takes them to the Bow Room on the ground floor for pre-lunch drinks, where they are greeted by the Queen's lady-in-waiting and an equerry. The Bow Room is beautiful, painted cream and gold, but with very little furniture.

People who arrive early can inspect the four display cases – one in each corner – which house some of the Queen's priceless collection of dinner services.

Lunch itself is always held in the 1844 Room next door – the white and gold chamber where the Queen receives visiting ambassadors. On these occasions, an oblong table is wheeled into the room and set with glittering silver and crystal. Also brought in are two sideboards from which the footmen serve the meal. The palace florist does her bit, and by the time the guests, the footmen and the royal family are all assembled, the room looks less austere.

Once all the guests have arrived, the Queen comes to join them, along with her remaining corgis, which as usual stay with her for the entire drinks time and the meal. The corgis have quite an important function on these occasions; they give people something safe and innocuous to talk about, while creating a diversion. Once an old family favourite, Heather, was misbehaving, and the Queen snapped sharply at the dog: 'Heather!' – making the opera singer Heather Harper, who was a guest that day, nearly jump out of her skin.

Lunch is served promptly at ten past one. The palace steward slips into the room, catches the Queen's eye and says: 'Luncheon, Your Majesty.' The Queen nods and then says casually: 'Shall we go in, then?' She leaves a few seconds to give everyone the chance to finish their drinks and then she leads the way into the 1844 Room. There is a seating plan just outside the dining room, and if guests haven't spotted it, the ever-vigilant equerry or lady-in-waiting points it out so that everyone is seated smoothly. The Queen always chooses who she wants to sit beside, and this most important male guest will be on her right, while Prince Philip has the most interesting female guest on his right. People are always somewhat surprised to see that the Queen does not sit at the head of the table. Her place on these occasions is in the middle, with Prince Philip facing her.

As Lewis Hamilton discovered, there is a very definite ritual regarding conversation at the table. Throughout the first and second courses, the Queen talks to the person on her right. While the pudding and cheese are being eaten, she turns automatically and chats to the guest on her left. She has now 'done' two people, and perhaps spoke to a couple in the Bow Room while the drinks were being served. She still has six to go. The point of these lunches is that both she and Prince Philip have some sort of conversation with all the guests.

The polished table gleams with Kings pattern silver cutlery and beautiful crystal glass with the EIIR cypher. Hostess or not, the Queen is still the monarch, and when the food starts to come around the table on magnificent salvers, she is served first. There are two pages serving, and both start in the middle and work their way round. The Queen prefers to help herself to food, and so the pages who serve hand her the salver on her left side, with a large spoon and fork, and wait while the Queen takes what she wants. She helps herself to a very small portion – the royals eat little and often – and her distinctive voice can be heard after every dish saying 'thank you' to the page. This is one of the very rare times when the Queen actually speaks to the staff when they are on duty, and for a new recruit her clipped but courteous 'thank you' can be quite a thrill.

At these 'Meet the People' lunches, the staff remain in the room while the guests are eating and clear away any empty plates immediately. On other occasions – when the Queen and Philip are lunching with friends at Balmoral or Sandringham, for example – the empty plates are all cleared at once, and staff go out of the dining room while they are eating. Then the Queen rings when it looks as if everyone is finished.

There is plenty on offer to drink, though people are very cautious about how much they take, not wanting to go over the top in the royal presence. The Queen always serves a chilled white Moselle or a German hock from the bottle at lunchtime – never heavy wines. Some red wine is also offered in a claret jug. The Queen likes red wine very much, but she doesn't drink it at lunchtime. Prince Philip will usually have a light ale.

Salad is always served with the main course, and the Queen places her plate at an angle if she wants salad, and then the footman brings the crystal salad bowl for her to serve herself. The royals prefer to have plain fruit – such as an apple or a pear – as dessert, which is always offered. The Welsh opera singer Katherine Jenkins, who enjoyed a palace lunch in 2009, admitted she was baffled when she was presented with a fruit platter, a plate and a neat piece of gauze with a bowl of water. She had no idea what she was supposed to do with it: 'Her Majesty caught my eye, helped me out and showed me what I needed to do: wash the fruit in the bowl and clean it with the gauze.'

Everything else is a pudding, and both are available at these lunches. Apple flan with cream from the Windsor Home Farm is often on the menu, as the Queen enjoys pastry dishes. Prince Philip is not the only cook in the family; the Queen used to do a little barbecue cooking and could turn her hand to a Scottish pancake. When she sent the then American President Eisenhower her recipe, which she had tried out on the grill, she advised him to 'use golden syrup instead of only sugar, as that can be very good too'.

After lunch, everyone troops back into the Bow Room for coffee and liqueurs. Some of the Queen's household come through, having eaten their own lunch in one of the staff dining rooms, just to mingle with the guests. The Queen and Philip then have the chance to talk to those they haven't managed to talk with before. At precisely quarter to three, the Queen and the duke take their leave and people say their thanks and bow and curtsey. Then there is a dead silence, followed by an audible exhalation of breath as everyone relaxes.

The Queen and Prince Philip still enjoy a traditional Sunday lunch. At Windsor, the food is not sent up from the ground-floor kitchen until the family and guests have assembled in the Oak Drawing Room. Prince Philip's good friend the late Sebastian Ferranti use to be a regular weekend guest, but sadly for the duke he has outlived most of his contemporaries, including his private secretary Brian McGrath. The Earl and Countess of Wessex are regular guests, as they come from nearby Bagshott Park with their children James and Louise, who often ride with the Queen on Saturday mornings. Now the Duke of York is travelling less, he too is a frequent lunch guest and only has to drive the three miles from Royal Lodge. He never drinks, but the Queen has a pre-lunch sherry, the duke a beer or a weak gin and tonic. As soon as the page sees they are all together, he sends down for the food. When it arrives, he murmurs either to Prince Philip or to the Queen that luncheon is served. The food is all waiting on a couple of hot plates on the sideboard by the windows.

They eat a small first course – usually a mousse – and then it's straight into the roast beef, which the chef has already carved in the kitchen. The roast – medium done, never pink – will be beautifully, thinly cut and served with roast potatoes and greens – either cabbage served in small bundles, or spring greens and fresh peas. Nothing is ever frozen. They are all rather partial to an apple turnover pudding, and this is a favourite finish to the Sunday meal.

Lunch takes no more than an hour. Then they're up and, after coffee, head straight outside. Unlike many of her subjects, the Queen does not have a Sunday afternoon nap. Prince Philip, with his love of cooking, has found a new passion – foodie TV shows – and the Queen makes a great joke of teasing him about his craze for watching all the cookery programmes. Mary Berry is a favourite. 'The Duke of Edinburgh understands cooking,' Berry says. 'I'm very lucky to have had lunch with the Queen. I was seated next to the duke – a delightful man – who talked about barbecuing. He was saying that he took his game birds at Sandringham and stuffed them with haggis but put more breadcrumbs in to absorb the fat . . . you knew he knew what he was talking about.'

Prince Philip certainly knows what he is talking about when it comes to food and cooking. In the days when he used to travel abroad frequently, he would always return with some new dish he urged the Buckingham Palace chefs to try. They dreaded the sound of his purposeful footfall as he made his way to the kitchens to bark out instructions. If the dish didn't arrive at the table exactly as he remembered it, then there would be another visit to the kitchen and a searching discussion to find out what went wrong. Philip always explained what was not quite right and exactly how it could be done in the future. Of course, Philip doesn't just preach, he practises and, according to those who have sampled his food, he is no mean cook.

One of his most ambitious dishes used to be snipe which, after shooting it at Sandringham, he plucked, cleaned and prepared himself. He arranged to be called especially early in the morning so he could get the snipe ready before breakfast. While he was out on his day's duties, the snipe remained in the larder almost under armed guard and when he returned in the evening he quickly changed and set about cooking the bird. Philip has his own cookbook with his favourite recipes he has ordered for himself. One was a casserole of pigeon, cooked according to a Swedish recipe, and he would go out a shoot a brace just because he fancied them.

Philip liked to cook breakfast for himself and the Queen and was famous for his glass-topped electric frying pan, which had to travel everywhere with him. Omelettes were his speciality and he was good at producing quick light supper snacks which he and the Queen enjoyed after the staff had been dismissed. Scrambled egg,

smoked haddock, kidneys, mushrooms and bean shoots with mushrooms and chicken livers were favourites, but nothing is as good to
him as open-aired barbecuing, as Mary Berry testified.

When Charles and Anne were young, Prince Philip would take
them off in a Land Rover, each with a sleeping bag, a supply of milk,
tea, bread, eggs and bacon – and his mobile barbecue. They would
drive high onto the moors and camp for the night in one of Queen
Victoria's little stone shelters. Water for tea and washing was fetched
from a nearby burn and Philip taught them how to make a fire of
dried heather and twigs.

Larger picnics for the royal family and their guests are still frequent at Balmoral. Food is ready to be loaded into the Land Rovers
by ten o'clock and the royal party usually arrive at their destination
by noon. Once his barbecue is going, Philip produces a rapid selection of chops, steaks, sausages and game. He not only cooks for the
family but the chauffeurs and detective in the party as well. If there
is a stream handy, the Queen insists on doing the washing up, but
nowadays they usually lunch at one of the huts on the estate, where
the Queen has better facilities for her dish-washing. When he was
prime minister, Tony Blair was astounded to see the monarch in her
rubber gloves doing the washing up.

'The royals cook and serve the guests,' Blair said. 'They do the
washing up. You think I'm joking, but I am not. They put the gloves
on and stick their hands in the sink. You sit there having eaten and
the Queen asks if you've finished, she stacks the plates and goes off
to the sink.'

No doubt he missed the point and was unable to understand why,
with so many staff available, the Queen should choose to do something as mundane as washing up herself. But both the Queen and
Philip become very attached to their staff, who are like an extended
part of the family to them, and they often take a sympathetic attitude to them when they land in trouble. On one occasion, Philip

noticed that a certain footman had been missing for a few days and asked his page where he had got to. 'He was sacked, Sir,' the page told him. Philip wanted to know what he had done.

'I am afraid they found him in bed with one of the housemaids, Sir,' the page replied.

'And they sacked him?' the duke said, outraged. 'They should have given him a medal!'

When he was younger, Philip's personal staff hardly ever saw him for any length of time as he travelled so much, but now he is much older he is always around and always shouting at them. But, being used to him and knowing he doesn't mean it, they don't take too much notice and behind his back refer to him as 'father'.

Philip was most distressed when two of his valets died from heart attacks, one in the most dramatic of circumstances. Back in 1976, the Queen and the duke were guests at Lord Dalhousie's estate in Scotland and were part of the shooting party. Valet Joe Pearce, who had been with the royal family for many years, was acting as Philip's loader. The Queen was behind watching with binoculars, working her dogs and picking up the shot grouse. She saw a figure fall and for one awful moment thought it was the duke and ran as fast as she could to where the two men were. The duke was fine but Pearce was dead.

Prince Philip had his body sent back to his family and a special memorial service was arranged at St James's Piccadilly, which he attended. This was a significant mark of respect, as the only memorials or funerals the Queen and the duke attend in a private capacity are those of very close friends or staff.

One such occasion took place when Bobo MacDonald, who worked for the Queen for sixty-seven years, finally died. When Bobo's health eventually failed, the Queen hired round-the-clock private nurses to care for her in her suite of rooms at Buckingham Palace. When she died in September 1993, as a mark of her devotion the Queen came down to London from Balmoral for the funeral, which took place at the Chapel Royal in St James's Palace.

Bobo was much more than a dresser, she was a close friend and one of the very few people who could say anything to the Queen that she thought she ought to know. She could mention with great honesty if perhaps the Queen had not put up a perfect appearance or if a colour they had both chosen did not suit her, and there were times when this daughter of a Scottish railwayman did exactly that. Like many of the female retainers who had devoted their lives to royal service, Miss MacDonald, as she was called by other staff, always faintly resented the presence of her mistress's husband. Philip would in turn try to keep her firmly in her place. He believed her role was to open the curtains in the morning and let the dogs in – tasks she had performed every morning for many years before Prince Philip came on the scene. They eventually came to an amicable non-spoken agreement to keep out of each other's way.

On the anniversary of Bobo's fifty years' service, the Queen had a special commemorative brooch made for her by Garrard, the crown jewellers. Mr Summers, who then held the royal warrant, was sent for and smuggled in and out of the palace behind Bobo's back to help the Queen choose assorted designs. The final gift was in the shape of a flower. It had twenty-five diamonds, which represented the crown, and twenty-five gold stamens, which represented the good that Bobo had brought into the Queen's life.

It was a token of love and respect for a woman who was quite simply the Queen's last link with childhood. She had given her life selflessly in service and never expected anything in return. Despite his irritation with her constant presence, Prince Philip knew and respected that sentiment more than he would ever admit.

For the truth of the matter is that socially they still rely on each other, and after seventy years of marriage that will never change. On the weekend of the Diamond Jubilee, when Prince Philip was taken ill during lunch at Windsor Castle after his marathon stint at the cold, wet and windy river pageant the day before, the Queen was heard to say as her husband was taken into the King Edward VII hospital as a 'precautionary measure' for a bladder infection: 'Don't die on me. Not now anyway!'

Of course, she was being facetious and making light of the situation, but it is part of the affectionate and light-hearted relationship they have always had since the days the young Prince Philip used to chase her along the Buckingham Palace corridors wearing an enormous set of false teeth.

That evening, the Queen attended the jubilee concert outside Buckingham Palace without him. She has never panicked or stumbled, and she was not going to start then. But it was a worry for her and when she arrived at the Service of Thanksgiving at St Paul's Cathedral the following day, she looked very alone. It was something she was going to have to get used to as the decade wore on. However together they are as a couple and however much they help each other socially, there will unfortunately come a time when one of them will have to go it alone.

Chapter 14

DEFENDER OF THE FAITH

Throughout their long marriage, the Queen and Prince Philip have shared a life as practising, church-going Christians, but the origins of each of their faiths is very different. Prince Philip was baptised into the Greek Orthodox Church and, although he was educated through the English school system that includes chapel attendance, he was not received into the Church of England until shortly before his marriage to Princess Elizabeth. According to the then Archbishop of Canterbury Dr Geoffrey Fisher, Lieutenant Mountbatten RN, as he then was, 'always regarded himself as an Anglican'.

That the Queen is a deeply religious committed Christian has never been in doubt, and her commitment to her faith runs much deeper. She was christened in the chapel at Buckingham Palace on 26 May 1926 by the then Archbishop of York and confirmed when she was fifteen years old in the Private Chapel at Windsor Castle by William Temple, Fisher's predecessor as the Archbishop of Canterbury.

From a very early age, she was brought up to say her prayers both in the morning before breakfast and in the evening before going to bed. This tradition was instilled by her mother and continued by her nanny Clara Knight. Both Elizabeth and later Margaret never missed kneeling at the foot of their bed with their hands clasped in prayer. It was as much part of their daily life as brushing their hair and getting dressed.

Going to church on Sunday has been part of her routine throughout her life, wherever she happens to be. At Windsor, she has St George's Chapel, which was founded in 1348 by King Edward III as the mother church to the Order of the Garter. The chapel is large and impersonal and extremely ornate, with seventy-six heraldic statues representing the Queen's Beasts on its roof, standing on pinnacles. The chapel has often been used for royal weddings, and the union of the Prince of Wales and Camilla Parker Bowles in 2005 received a blessing there from the Archbishop of Canterbury. The Queen and Prince Philip are not frequently seen on Sundays at St George's, as neither of them enjoy sermons. Philip has instructed the Dean of Windsor that sermons must be limited to not more than twelve minutes long.

Much more intimate is the private chapel in the castle. It was destroyed by the fire in 1992 and rebuilt with only twenty-five seats. The new organ had to be designed to fit into a very small triangular loft. In the grounds of Royal Lodge in Windsor Great Park there is another chapel, Queen Victoria's Chapel, or the Royal Chapel, where the Queen and Prince Philip regularly worship. When the Queen Mother was still alive, it was a Sunday ritual to attend the service at the Royal Chapel and retire afterwards to Royal Lodge for some stiff pre-lunch drinks. Like her daughter, Queen Elizabeth had a traditional and uncomplicated faith and derived a great deal of support from it.

The Queen takes communion only three or four times a year in the old Low Church tradition, and according to her former deputy private secretary, Sir Kenneth Scott, 'She prefers simplicity to pomposity, so when she's at Windsor she'll go to the little chapel in the park rather than St George's, which she considers rather pompous. In Edinburgh, too, she doesn't go to St Giles'. She prefers the Canongate Kirk as she liked the minister who made her laugh.'

When the royal family is staying at Sandringham, the crowds turn out in all weathers to greet them when they go to Sunday services at St Mary Magdalene's Church, 400 yards from the big house on the Sandringham estate. The sixteenth-century church, with its richly decorated chancel and magnificent silver altar, has been the site of many significant christenings, including those of the future King George VI in 1896 and Lady Diana Spencer, whose parents lived on the Sandringham estate in 1961. The most recent one came in July 2015, when Princess Charlotte of Cambridge, their great-granddaughter, was christened there.

When they are in Scotland at Balmoral, the Queen and Prince Philip have the royal pew at Crathie Kirk, a small Church of Scotland parish church. The Princess Royal married her second husband, Timothy Laurence, at the church because she was divorced and, at the time, not permitted to marry in the Church of England.

Even when the royal family were at sea, on board the royal yacht *Britannia* in the days when overseas tours were a regular part of the royal calendar, there would always be a service held on a Sunday. Admiral Woodard, one-time commodore of *Britannia*, said that the Queen preferred not to travel with a chaplain on board because she did not like sermons. Instead, she would ask Admiral Woodard to take the service. He added: 'But she knows her Bible. I'd go to the Queen with suggestions about readings and hymns and she would quote the Bible without bothering to look it up. The prescribed reading might start at, say, verse nine, but the Queen would say: "No, let's start at verse seven, otherwise it won't have the proper sense."'

Time and again in her Christmas Day speeches to the nation

and the Commonwealth, the Queen has stressed the importance of her religious beliefs. In the millennial year address, she said: 'To many of us our beliefs are of fundamental importance. For me the teachings of Christ and my own personal accountability before God provide a framework in which I try to lead my life. I, like so many of you, have drawn great comfort in difficult times from Christ's words and example.'

Again, as part of the television broadcast she made in 2015, she said: 'For me, the life of Jesus Christ, the Prince of Peace, whose birth we celebrate today, is an inspiration and an anchor in my life. A role model of reconciliation and forgiveness, he stretched out his hands in love, acceptance and healing. Christ's example has taught me to seek to respect and value all people of whatever faith or none.'

The Queen gave a rare personal insight when she wrote about her religious faith in the foreword to a book entitled *The Servant Queen and the King She Serves*, published by the Bible Society in 2016 to mark her ninetieth birthday. 'I have been – and remain – very grateful to you for your prayers and to God for his steadfast love,' the Queen wrote. 'I have indeed seen his faithfulness.' She then went on to write about the changes she has experienced during her lifetime: 'The extent and pace of change has been truly remarkable,' she said. 'We have witnessed triumphs and tragedies.'

The Queen also took the opportunity to allude to the current problems in the Middle East, saying the world was experiencing 'terrible suffering on an unprecedented scale'. The foreword was very much along the lines of her Christmas speeches, which are the only ones that she writes herself – or partly herself. Prince Philip, an extremely experienced speechwriter, is known to provide his input to the Christmas speeches and consequently they also reflect his own views and beliefs – another example of how the partnership of their marriage works.

The Queen's faith goes beyond her public pronouncements and private devotions, however. That she reigns through her belief in God is intrinsic to the sovereign. A one pound coin in the United Kingdom bears an image of the Queen's head, surrounded by the words: 'ELIZABETH II D·G·REG· F·D.' It stands for 'Elizabeth II Dei Gratia Regina Fidei Defensor' or 'Elizabeth II, by the Grace of God, Queen, Defender of the Faith'. This notation was first added to British coins in 1714, during the reign of King George I. The decision of the Royal Mint to omit it from the 'Godless Florin' in 1849 caused such a scandal that the coin had to be replaced.

The sovereign holds the title 'Defender of the Faith and Supreme Governor of the Church of England', and this dates back to the reign of King Henry VIII, who was initially granted the title of Defender of the Faith in 1521 by Pope Leo X. It was Queen Elizabeth I who was first proclaimed 'Supreme Governor' of the Church of England, a title that has remained to this day. In her role as Supreme Governor, the Queen is spiritual leader of the 25 million people in the UK who are baptised in the Church of England, though only about one million of them go to church each week. This is mainly a ceremonial role, because in practice the church is led by the Archbishop of Canterbury and other bishops.

The Queen has well-informed opinions and views on many of her bishops and likes those who make her laugh, are straightforward and intelligent. She found George Carey too much of a moralist and disliked the way he criticised her children's behaviour. She might have shared his view, but felt Christianity was as much about forgiveness as morality. She very much likes the current Archbishop of Canterbury, Justin Welby, who employs former royal press secretary Ailsa Anderson as his own director of communications.

Her position in Scotland is slightly different, as there the Queen vows to uphold the constitution of the Church of Scotland (a Presbyterian national church), but holds no leadership position.

Nevertheless, she appoints the Lord High Commissioner to the General Assembly of the Church of Scotland as her personal representative, with a ceremonial role. The Queen on occasion has filled the role personally, as when she opened the General Assembly in 1977 and 2002 (her Silver and Golden Jubilee years).

The Queen's relationship with the Church of England was symbolised at the Coronation in 1953 when Her Majesty was anointed by Archbishop of Canterbury Geoffrey Fisher. He asked her: 'Will you to the utmost of your power maintain the Laws of God and the true profession of the Gospel? Will you to the utmost of your power maintain in the United Kingdom the Protestant Reformed Religion established by law? Will you maintain and preserve inviolably the settlement of the Church of England, and the doctrine, worship, discipline and government thereof, as by law established in England? And will you preserve unto the Bishops and Clergy of England, and to the Churches there committed to their charge, all such rights and privileges, as by law do or shall appertain to them or any of them?' To which the Queen responded: 'All this I promise to do.'

Then, with the Sword of State carried before her, she went up to the altar and made her solemn oath. Laying her right hand upon the Bible, she knelt and declared: 'The things which I have here before promised, I will perform and keep. So help me God.' Then she kissed the Bible and signed the oath. The ceremony continued as these words were spoken to her: 'Our gracious Queen: To keep your Majesty ever mindful of the Law and the Gospel of God as the Rule for the whole life and government of Christian princes, we present you with this Book, the most valuable thing that this world affords. Here is Wisdom; this is the Royal Law; these are the lively Oracles of God.'

The sovereign is 'Queen of England by the Grace of God'. In history, it was used to imply that the monarch has a God-given divine right to rule. 'Dieu et Mon Droit' is incorporated into the royal coat of arms and has been used as the motto of English monarchs since it was adopted by Henry V. The belief in medieval Europe was not that victory in battle automatically went to the side with the better army but, as with personal trial by combat, to the side that God viewed with favour. While of course this is no longer the case, the Queen is very much aware of the religious symbolism behind her role and takes her vows – as monarch and wife – with great seriousness.

For most of her reign, the Queen has appointed archbishops, bishops and deans of the Church of England, who then swear an oath of allegiance and pay homage to Her Majesty. In spiritual and practical matters, the Church of England is led by 108 bishops and managed by a General Synod, which is elected every five years. In 1970, the Queen became the first sovereign to inaugurate and address the General Synod in person at Church House in the precincts of Westminster Abbey. Since then, she has inaugurated and addressed the opening session of the General Synod every five years after diocesan elections.

In November 2015, in her address to the Synod, the Queen highlighted how she saw the role of the church when she said: 'St Paul reminds us that all Christians, as ambassadors for Christ, are entrusted with the ministry of reconciliation. Spreading God's word and the onerous but rewarding task of peace-making and conflict resolution are important parts of that ministry. So too is the Church of England's vocation to work in partnership with those of other faiths and none, to serve the common good in this land. To this end, I was pleased that one of the first events that Prince Philip and I attended in 2012 to mark my Diamond Jubilee was a gathering of leaders of all faiths, at Lambeth Palace.'

The Queen enjoys the music in church and Christmas carols. As part of the Queen's ninetieth birthday celebrations, the BBC broadcast a radio programme featuring her favourite music. Two

Christian hymns made it into the list of her top ten tunes, namely 'Praise My Soul the King of Heaven' and 'The Lord is My Shepherd'. They were featured alongside music from *Oklahoma* and *Annie Get Your Gun*.

The choir of St George's Chapel at Windsor is world famous. Its primary function is to sing the daily services, the Opus Dei, and it has a large repertoire of music drawn from all ages and traditions. The 'Jubilate Deo' was written by Benjamin Britten in 1961 for St George's Chapel at the request of Prince Philip. He also put up money for an organ scholarship at St George's College, although his interest in religion has not always been so apparent.

Looking back to the time in 1962 when the Rt Revd Robin Woods was appointed Dean of Windsor, Prince Philip said: 'I was dragged into religious things by being invited to become involved in the reorganisation of St George's, Windsor. Theological dialogue was really forced on me. I never had any great difficulty in being an ordinary Christian.' Through his father, who was Bishop of Litchfield and as Lord High Almoner had a royal connection, Woods was invited to hold a service for the royal family at Queen Victoria's Chapel in Windsor Great Park.

Together, the Queen and Prince Philip soon formed a close relationship with Dean Woods. They invited him to come up to the castle for discussions at the weekends, which was very flattering for the dean. On one occasion, he was working in his garden behind the chapel when the Queen's page was sent to tell him that the Queen wanted to see him in a hurry. The dean said he would need a few minutes to change into his clerical garb, but he was told to come at once and not to worry about his outfit as the Queen was herself in riding clothes. From then on, their meetings became more informal. However, what the Queen discussed with her chaplain at their weekly get-togethers is not public knowledge.

St George's Chapel is exempt from the jurisdiction of the local bishop and is under the direct control of the monarch. So Woods got the job when the Queen made a personal request for him to become Dean of St George's after hearing him preach. It was at a time when the chapel services were poorly attended. Woods said: 'When I took the job it was made clear that I would be expected to turn everything upside down.' Prince Philip, with his abundance of organisation skills, worked with Woods to raise funds to set up a residential conference centre called St George's House. It opened in 1966, providing a centre where influential people from all walks of life could meet to explore and communicate their views and analysis of contemporary issues against a religious background.

Prince Philip spoke at the first assembly held at St George's House about 'The Role of the Church in Society Today'. This was the first of many discussion groups where Philip expounded his views on religion and the natural world. Philip believed that, as the house was hidden away within the castle walls, it was particularly suitable to attract people in positions of leadership within government, industry, commerce and the churches as a place for discreet discussions of mutual and national interest. Here the Queen and Prince Philip are as one, and every so often indications emerged that she was privately very environmentally conscious and, like her husband, especially concerned about global warming.

One such indication surfaced in November 2014, at a private lunch at Buckingham Palace attended by Dame Julia Slingo, the Met Office's chief scientist, when it was reported the Queen had talked about unprecedented flooding at Balmoral that summer and 'wondered if it was caused by climate change'. This echoes an account reported by Sir Richard Branson of the Queen and Barack Obama 'animatedly' discussing global warming over dinner.

Indeed, her concern goes back a long way, at least to the 1990s. In October 1997, she seriously contemplated including a passage on global warming in her speech to a Commonwealth prime ministers' conference. Experts on the issue were discreetly sounded out on what it might be 'helpful' for her to say, and ministerial aides were told to 'expect something green from the Queen'. In the event, the intervention was toned down to an oblique reference to 'environmental challenges, which especially affect the smaller states'. For Prince Philip, however, conservation has almost become a religion, with his passionate concern for the future of the planet being something he has passed on to his children and grandchildren.

Prince Philip's faith continued to deepen, compared with his attitude in the early 1960s. His correspondence with the Rt Revd Michael Mann, who was Dean of Windsor between 1976 and 1989 ('the best job in the Church of England,' as he described it), has been made public in a book entitled *A Windsor Correspondence*. Mann, who died in 2011 aged eighty-seven, rose to become Domestic Chaplain to the Queen after serving as a soldier in the Second World War and then being told, while working for the Colonial Office in Nigeria, that he only had six months to live. Fortunately, the diagnosis was incorrect. In overseeing the wellbeing of St George's Chapel, he was admired for the adroit way he handled its finances. He also proved a lively preacher, seldom speaking for longer than seven minutes, believing that if a preacher could not make his points in this time he never would.

The dean encouraged Prince Philip to chair the annual St George's House Lecture, which was once addressed by the Princess Royal. Their correspondence began when, in 1982, Prince Philip sent Michael Mann a copy of astronomer Sir Fred Hoyle's lecture on evolution from space, in which he challenged parts of Darwin's theory of evolution. There followed a lively debate back and forth, with Philip taking a more scientific stance against Mann's theological viewpoint.

Philip expressed the view that 'the point of life is to attempt to make it more tolerable and more civilised for the generations we have every reason to believe will live after us'. The dean saw life as a stepping stone to afterlife. He said: 'Heaven is not necessarily guaranteed. It will matter how you have lived this life.' In subsequent correspondence, Philip went on to write about what he described as his hobby-horse – the need to reconcile science and theology. 'I don't think the Church can hope to regain the ability to bring the influence of Christian principles to bear on the formation of opinion and intellectual fashion until the conflict between science and theology has been resolved,' he wrote.

Mann was opposed to the publication of their correspondence, but Philip consulted the Queen, who encouraged it because it showed Philip in a good light as someone who is interested in religion and philosophy.

It would have been impossible to live with someone like Prince Philip without being influenced by his thoughts and beliefs, and of course the Queen has been. Prince Philip has an enquiring mind and if he had a motto it would be 'never give up'. Although the Queen has adopted many of his opinions, she interprets them in a gentler, more understanding way, especially when it comes to their children.

When Lord Mountbatten was killed by an IRA bomb on 27 August 1979, together with his fourteen-year-old grandson Timothy Knatchbull, Prince Charles was devastated. 'I have lost someone infinitely special in my life,' he wrote later, but he never sought comfort from his father. Instead, he turned away from him. When the two of them were due to receive Lord Mountbatten's body from Lydd airport on its way back from Ireland, Philip was at his worst. He masked his own grief with a brusque and abrupt manner, while Charles retreated into himself.

It was decided they should eat a light lunch before leaving for the airport and, much to Philip's irritation, Charles disappeared. He obviously needed to be alone so that he could face whatever lay ahead, but Philip sent Lord Mountbatten's private secretary, John

Barrett, to find him. When Barrett saw the prince standing there, head bowed, shoulders drooping, he didn't have the heart to disturb him. When Charles eventually returned to the table, his father baited him until his son got up and left the room. Both the guests and staff were embarrassed and found it extremely distressing. The duke was trying to stiffen his son's backbone, but for a man who is a Christian he was and still can appear to be very cruel. He simply refuses to accept any weakness, though if Prince Charles had instead discussed some theological point about the soul of the man he so loved, Philip would have joined in.

Over a period of more than thirty years, the Duke of Edinburgh has engaged successive deans of Windsor in wide-ranging philosophical discussions. These have been on the meaning of life, the purpose of man on earth, science and religion, Charles Darwin and the origins of man and, perhaps most important of all to Philip, the relationship between man and nature.

His querying mind has even taken him to some fairly unusual areas. In earlier times, following discussions with Mountbatten, Philip picked up on his uncle's interest in UFOs. He took out a subscription to *Flying Saucer Review* and entered into a correspondence with Timothy Good, a worldwide authority and author of several books on the subject. Philip wrote to him: 'There are many reasons to believe that they exist. There is so much evidence from reliable witnesses.'

In July 1986, Philip, as President of the World Wide Fund for Nature, gathered together representatives of the world's five major religions for the WWF twenty-fifth anniversary conference. At the suggestion of Prince Philip, the conference was held at Assisi, the home of St Francis, patron saint of birds and animals. The idea was to link the secular movement for the conservation of nature with the religious perception of nature as the creation of a supreme being. Philip wrote: 'Most if not all religions allow for some measure of divine intervention in the creation of the world and in the operation of the natural system. Therefore, if God is in nature, nature itself becomes divine, and from that point it becomes reasonable to argue that reverence for God and nature implies a responsibility not to harm it as a duty to the Creator.' The conference was a success in that the leaders of the religions involved each issued a declaration regarding the importance of our relationship with the natural world. Philip believes that there is a moral imperative recognised by all the great religions to support conservation.

Some three years later, Prince Philip co-authored a book with Michael Mann called *Survival or Extinction: A Christian Attitude to the Environment*. The book arose out of a series of gatherings held at St George's House to discuss the Christian attitude to nature. The discussions were attended by a broad range of delegates, including schoolmasters, research fellows, company chairmen and Philip's close friend the Duchess of Abercorn, who is described as a 'Counsellor in Transpersonal Psychology'. The subjects discussed included the danger to the environment arising from scientific and technological advances and from the explosive growth of the world's population. The book talks about the sacred relationship of all Christians to the source of all life on earth and the urgent need for humans to face up to what they are doing to the planet. Philip's religious views are again shown to be tied into nature as the book states: 'Mankind is a fellow creature in symbiosis with the rest of creation, where he has no right to exploit or destroy, but where his kingly status imposes upon him duties to conserve the order of all Creation, for which he is responsible and answerable to God.'

Additional to his views on God and nature, Prince Philip has often stressed the importance of the individual in society, writing in his 1984 book *Men, Machines and Sacred Cows*: 'It seems to me everything begins with the individual and it is people who decide what sort of communities they are going to live in. It is the people who are going to decide whether it will be humanly tolerable and civilised or whether it will degenerate into a human jungle . . . Our first responsibility is to be concerned about our own behaviour, our own relationships with other people and our own attitude to what is right and wrong.'

With the Queen and Prince Philip now both into their nineties, their faith continues to play a central part in their lives. For the Queen, her faith is all-important. 'It's not just a question of duty for her, it's very much part of the fabric of her life,' said a former chaplain at Windsor. 'She loves matins and the words of the Prayer Book have real meaning for her.' For Prince Philip, religion has posed many questions for his enquiring mind, as evidenced by his discourses with Michael Mann. Reflecting on those discussions, Mann said Philip could never accept anything until he had chewed it to pieces: 'When he's in a corner and he's lost a point, he does not stop like other people would and say, "Yes, well maybe you're right," he goes shooting off on something else, but in fact he will come back later and he will have accepted. You know he has been convinced if he's changed the subject . . . he would find it very difficult to say: "I'm sorry, I'm wrong."'

Their different approaches had stood them in good stead through-out their long marriage, and would help them again as they moved into the latter stages of their lives at the start of a new millennium.

Chapter 15

THREESCORE YEARS
AND TEN

The days of our years are threescore years and ten;
And if by reason of strength they be fourscore years,
Yet is their strength labour and sorrow;
For it is soon cut off, and we fly away.

PSALM 90

The Queen and Prince Philip have long outlived the biblical
expectation of life. Now in their nineties and in the seventieth
year of married life, they are in uncharted waters for any royal
couple in history. They retain the mental alertness and physical
fitness of couples many years younger. In recent years, the Queen
and Prince Philip have re-written the record books. The Queen is
the longest-reigning British monarch in history as well as the oldest
reigning monarch; Prince Philip is the longest-serving consort of a
reigning British monarch and the oldest-ever male member of the
British royal family.

On 20 November 2017, the Queen and Prince Philip will celebrate their seventieth (platinum) wedding anniversary. For any couple to reach this landmark is a remarkable achievement. That the Queen and Prince Philip should do so while still working at their public duties is quite extraordinary. It was only in Prince Philip's ninety-sixth year that Buckingham Palace announced he would retire from royal duties in the autumn of 2017. At a royal lunch shortly after the announcement was made, 88-year-old mathematician Michael Atiyah said to Prince Philip: 'I'm sorry to hear you're standing down.'

'Well, I can't stand up much longer,' joked the duke. Having attended 22,219 engagements in his own right since 1952, not including those attended with the Queen, one could understand his sentiment.

He is patron or president of more than 780 organisations and, although he will no longer play an active role in attending engagements, he will continue to be associated with various societies, regiments and charities. He calls himself the world's most experienced unveiler of plaques. Unlike the Queen, whose only speeches written by her are her Christmas addresses, Prince Philip has written all his own speeches which, over the years, run into thousands, particularly on the subject of conservation and his own philosophy of life. Several books of his collected writings have been published on subjects as diverse as ornithology, carriage driving, the environmental revolution, science and religion.

At midnight on 31 December 1999, the peoples of the world welcomed the arrival of the new millennium with some of the most spectacular celebrations ever seen. It came with a general feeling that a better and brighter future lay ahead. In London, attention was focused around Big Ben as the country awaited the first stroke of midnight and a fireworks display called the 'River of Fire' lit up several miles of the Thames. The Millennium Dome, largely funded by the National Lottery and the largest single roof structure in the world, was a centrepiece of the government's planned celebrations.

The Queen and the Duke of Edinburgh joined Prime Minister Tony Blair and other notables at the opening of the Dome, now renamed the O2 Arena, where on the stroke of midnight the Duke was seen to plant a kiss on the Queen's cheek. Such a display of public affection was almost as rare an event as the coming of the millennium itself. The Queen then joined hands with Tony Blair and his wife Cherie and the duke to sing the traditional New Year's song 'Auld Lang Syne'.

The twenty-first century ushered in a new era for the Queen and Prince Philip as old age began to creep up on them. Following the tribulations of the 1990s, the first decade of the new century proved to be one of better times and increasing popularity for the royal family. There was sadness in early 2002 when Princess Margaret, who had been in bad health for some time, and the Queen Mother, at the age of 101, died within two months of each other. The Queen had always been very close to her sister and had been in the habit of telephoning her mother every day. In the days when there was a switchboard, the Buckingham Palace operator loved it when she put them through, saying, 'Your Majesty, Her Majesty, Your Majesty.'

With their children leading independent lives with their own families, the Queen and Prince Philip became more dependent on one another than ever before. They are a unit, isolated from the world around them by their royal status, and they have only each other, especially now that so many of those who had been with them in younger years are no longer alive.

Despite the deaths of her mother and her sister earlier in the year, both the Queen and Prince Philip embarked upon a large-scale series of engagements to commemorate the Queen's Golden Jubilee in 2002. The royal couple travelled more than 40,000 miles, visiting many Commonwealth countries, including Australia and Canada, as well as undertaking an extensive tour of all corners of the United Kingdom. It was to prove the last time they went on an extended long-distance tour. Despite having known him for a longer period, relations with her prime minister had not grown more comfortable. When discussing the celebrations with the Queen, Tony Blair made a faux pas when he referred to 'the Golden Jubilee'. The Queen corrected him with a sharp: 'No, Mr Blair; *my* Golden Jubilee.'

Ten years later, the Queen's Diamond Jubilee was an even more spectacular event and demonstrated throughout the land the esteem, love and respect the population held for their monarch. Thousands of street parties were held up and down the country, with Morecambe in Lancashire claiming the record for the largest event with one of more than one-and-a-half miles long.

The showpiece event was the Diamond Jubilee Pageant on 3 June, when more than a million people lined the banks of the Thames, standing in the pouring rain, to witness the biggest spectacle on the river for more than 300 years. A thousand vessels completed a seven-mile-long voyage down the river to Tower Bridge. The Queen and her family, on the royal barge the *Spirit of Chartwell*, were cheered on by those lining the banks. Prince Philip endured the rain, standing in uncomplaining fortitude despite great pain from a bladder infection for which he was hospitalised soon after.

The following day, after a spectacular Diamond Jubilee concert in front of Buckingham Palace, Prince Charles made a moving speech paying tribute to his mother. He said: 'So as a nation this is our opportunity to thank you and my father for always being there for us. For inspiring us with your selfless duty and service, and for making us proud to be British. The only sad thing about this evening is that my father cannot be here because unfortunately he has been taken unwell. Ladies and gentlemen, if we shout loud enough he might just hear us in hospital.' A huge cheer then went up from the crowd. It was probably fair to say that perhaps Prince Philip had had some misgivings about the elaborate and extensive celebrations in any case. At a press party at Windsor Castle to celebrate the jubilee,

I had the opportunity of having a few words with Prince Philip. I asked him which event he was most looking forward to. 'When it's all over,' he said and turned on his heel and walked off.

On family matters, the Queen and Prince Philip at last had much to be satisfied with. The wedding of Prince Charles and Camilla Parker Bowles took place in a civil ceremony at Windsor Guildhall on 9 April 2005. The ceremony, conducted in the presence of the couple's families, was followed by a Church of England Service of Prayer and Dedication at St George's Chapel, which incorporated an act of penitence. The Queen and Prince Philip did not attend the civil wedding ceremony, but were present at the Service of Prayer and Dedication and held a reception for the couple in Windsor Castle afterwards.

In the years following the wedding of their grandson Prince William to Catherine Middleton, on 29 April 2011 at Westminster Abbey, the Queen and Prince Philip welcomed two more great-grandchildren into their family (George, on 22 July 2013, and Charlotte on 2 May 2015), thus ensuring the direct line of succession of the House of Windsor for generations to come. On 4 September 2017, it was announced that the couple were expecting a third child.

An indication of the possible relaxing of the strict formality that has governed the Queen's life occurred at the opening of the Olympic Games in London in 2012, directed by Danny Boyle. The Queen was seen in her first acting role, with James Bond actor Daniel Craig, in Buckingham Palace. In a short film, Her Majesty was seen to leave the palace gardens in a helicopter with James Bond, before appearing to parachute into the opening ceremony of the games. This rather undignified stunt, which was kept secret from the press, could not have taken place without the approval of Prince Philip, who was extremely dubious about it. At an Irish State banquet at Windsor Castle two years later, the Queen joked: 'It took someone of Irish descent, Danny Boyle, to get me to jump from a helicopter.'

Another reason for satisfaction for both the Queen and Prince Philip was the result of the Scottish independence referendum in 2014. Scotland has always been a favourite place for the royal couple. It was at Balmoral where, as Lieutenant Philip Mountbatten, Philip had proposed to Princess Elizabeth. Their happiest family holidays were spent cruising round the Western Isles in the royal yacht *Britannia*. They are proud to dress in tartan kilts and have often been seen at highland games watching with obvious enjoyment. The Queen is roused each day by her personal piper playing the bagpipes as he walks round underneath her room, and she favours Scottish reels over all other types of dancing.

After Prime Minister David Cameron had telephoned the Queen to inform her that the Scottish people had voted by a comfortable majority to remain part of the United Kingdom, he told former Mayor of New York Michael Bloomberg that the Queen 'purred down the line'. Cameron's conversation was accidentally picked up by Sky News microphones as they walked through an office in the businessman's media empire. This was a serious breach of the convention that the prime minister never discloses anything that is said in conversation between himself and the Queen. Cameron was duly mortified when it was made public.

For all that the recent years have lacked the upsets of the 1990s, this wasn't the only difficult or embarrassing moment in recent years. The subject of Princess Diana would not fade away. Early in the morning of 18 February 2008, an unusually large queue formed for tickets to the public gallery in Court Room 73 of the Royal Courts of Justice, because the inquest into the death of Diana was due to hear from its most eagerly anticipated witness. So great was the demand from both the public and the world's press for access to the court that an annexe was set up in a marquee in the courtyard to house the overflow.

On this day, there was not a spare seat in any section of the court because it was the day that Mohamed Al-Fayed, the billionaire owner of Harrods in Knightsbridge and Fulham Football Club, was due to give his evidence at the inquest into the cause of the deaths of his son, Dodi Fayed, and Diana some ten years earlier in Paris. By then the inquest had been running for some five months before the Coroner Lord Justice Scott Baker.

For years after the accident, Al-Fayed had publicly stated his belief that the deaths had been orchestrated by a group of which Prince Philip was the chief conspirator. Because of his criticism of the royal family, Harrods department store had been stripped of its coveted Royal Warrants as purveyors of goods to the Queen, the Duke of Edinburgh and the Prince of Wales.

While Al-Fayed's testimony was expected to be controversial, it had not been anticipated that his evidence would be some of the most sensational ever heard in the long history of the law courts. For his day in court, Al-Fayed arrived with four hefty security guards who were required to wait outside the courtroom. He was dressed in a checked suit and a blue-and-green checked silk open-necked shirt; this outlandish attire was in sharp contrast to the dark suit, white shirt and smart tie he habitually wore when going about the business of Harrods.

Having sworn in the name of Allah to tell the truth, Al-Fayed first read a prepared statement in which he alleged that Princess Diana had told him that Prince Philip and Prince Charles wanted to get rid of her. He also claimed that Diana told him she was pregnant and was about to announce her engagement to be married to Dodi. He said that Prince Philip and Prince Charles plotted to assassinate Diana so that Charles could marry Camilla Parker Bowles, whom he described as Prince Charles's 'crocodile wife'. He stated that Prince Philip would never accept that his son Dodi could have any-thing to do with Prince William, the future King of England.

Then Mr Ian Burnett QC, counsel for the coroner, asked: 'All this stems from your belief that Prince Philip is not only a racist but a Nazi as well?'

Al-Fayed replied: 'That's right. It is time to send him back to Germany where he came from. If you want to know his original name, it ends with Frankenstein.'

He started waving about a photograph taken in 1937 at the funeral of Prince Philip's sister Cecile. Philip's favourite sister had died in an air crash in thick fog over Ostend, along with her husband the hereditary Grand Duke of Hesse and their children, while en route to London for the wedding of Prince Louis of Hesse. In this photograph, sixteen-year-old Prince Philip is seen walking through the street of Darmstadt, the Hesse family's home town, which was festooned with swastikas, in the company of his brothers-in-law Prince Christophe of Hesse in SS uniform and Philip of Hesse in his brown SA uniform. Prince Philip's uncle Lord Louis Mountbatten followed behind in British naval uniform.

Al-Fayed added: 'Prince Philip is a person who grew up with the Nazis, brought up by his auntie who married Hitler's general. This is the man who is in charge of the country, who can do anything, who manipulates.'

Al-Fayed expanded his theory to include a cover-up by the French police, the British CID and the United States FBI, among others. However, when at the end of the proceedings the coroner gave a detailed summing up of all the evidence, he told the jury that there was 'not a shred of evidence' in support of Al-Fayed's theory that Prince Philip had ordered MI6 to murder Diana, and he questioned Al-Fayed's credibility as a witness. He explained that he had made the decision not to hear evidence from Prince Philip: 'In the light of all the evidence we have heard which provided no evidence whatsoever for the suggestion that he was involved in killing his daughter-in-law and Dodi.' The inquest also shed new light on Prince Philip's relationship with Princess Diana when it demanded that their correspondence be made available, some of which had already appeared in her butler Paul Burrell's book. He was not happy about any of it, but there was little he could do. Once revealed, the letters in question showed that he and Diana – at one time at least – had a very good relationship. She addressed him throughout as 'dearest Pa' and one of the letters began 'Dearest Pa, I was particularly touched by your most recent letter which proved to me, if I didn't already know it, that you really do care.'

According to Simone Simmons, Diana's healer, who knew her better than most, there were other letters that were written in quite a different tone. Prince Philip denied this and issued a statement through his office in Buckingham Palace saying so. He regarded the suggestion that he used derogatory terms to describe Diana as a 'gross misrepresentation of his relations with his daughter-in-law and hurtful to his grandsons'.

Diana had always acknowledged that Prince Philip's letters were helpful in the beginning, but as things became more difficult his tone changed. He had said her actions were damaging the royal family – which indeed they were. She also said that he had insisted that both William and Harry were subjected to DNA tests in the light of her affair with James Hewitt becoming public. There is nothing to prove this is correct, only the hearsay of others, but what was certain was that Prince Philip had moved to the top of Diana's hate list.

The background to the letters was that while the Queen would listen to Diana's woes, she would do little about it, hoping the problems would solve themselves. She would then leave it up to Philip to put his persuasive powers to good use and try to reason with her. He confided in his daughter-in-law, writing to her and explaining that he knew first-hand the difficulties of marrying into the royal family. He tried to make her face facts and deal with the problems within her marriage, and not put her head in the sand. He signed them 'Pa', and in the beginning was sympathetic.

The correspondence between them began in earnest just after the Andrew Morton book was published in June 1992. This provoked a summit meeting at Windsor Castle, with Charles and Diana discussing the state of their marriage with the Queen and Prince Philip. Diana believed the only solution was a separation, but the Queen hoped a compromise would be possible, for the sake of the children and the monarchy. When Diana failed to appear at a second meeting, Prince Philip decided to take matters into his own hands.

He was direct and straight to the point, but not unkind – or at least he didn't think so. One of his fiercest comments was: 'Can you honestly look into your heart and say that Charles's relationship with Camilla had nothing to do with your behaviour towards him in your marriage?'

Philip also told Diana she had not been a caring wife and that while she was a good mother, she had been too possessive with her sons. Like most insecure people, Diana did not appreciate being told off one bit and furiously showed the letters to several of her friends, including Rosa Monckton and Lucia Flecha de Lima, who helped her construct suitable replies. Another letter, which according to Burrell had her leaping with joy, said: 'We do not approve of either of you having lovers. Charles was silly to risk everything with Camilla for a man in his position. We never dreamed he might feel like leaving you for her. I cannot imagine anyone in their right mind leaving you for Camilla. Such a prospect never even entered our heads.'

He also told Diana that jealousy had eaten away at the marriage and that her irrational behaviour after the birth of William had not helped. He added that her husband had made a 'considerable sacrifice' by cutting ties with Camilla and that Diana had not 'appreciated what he had done'. He even went on to suggest Diana's behaviour had driven Charles into Camilla's arms. In one letter, he told her being the wife of the heir to the throne 'involved much more than simply being a hero with the British people'.

He did, however, start one letter with the words: 'Phew!!! I thought I might have gone a bit too far with that last letter.'

Philip also expressed his concern about her bulimia and acknowledged it could have been responsible for some of her behavioural patterns. He tried to play intermediary between Diana and Charles by suggesting to her things they could do together and listing common interests they shared, which is a tried and tested method favoured by marriage guidance counsellors.

In the end, things became so bad between them, as far as Diana was concerned, that she had revealed to her friend Roberto Devorik her fears that Prince Philip was plotting to have her killed. Devorik repeated this under oath, adding that she once pointed to a picture of Prince Philip in a VIP lounge at an airport and said: 'He really hates me and wants me to disappear.' Her other great friend, the American billionaire deal-maker Teddy Forstmann, said: 'She hated Prince Philip.' She told me the same thing when I saw her at Kensington Palace shortly before her death. She explained she had warned her boys: 'Never, never shout at anyone the way Prince Philip does.' Without doubt, having such details of the private lives of the royal family brought out in public – not to mention such outlandish accusations made against Prince Philip – was one of the more extraordinary episodes from the royal marriage.

When the Queen came to the throne in 1952, the United Kingdom was a far different place than it is today. There were no mobile telephones, no internet, no colour televisions and no European Union; the House of Lords was made up exclusively of hereditary peers; homosexuality was illegal and punishable with a term in prison; divorced persons were not allowed into the royal enclosure at Ascot races; and the British Empire still coloured red a large part of the globe.

Throughout the tumultuous changes during her reign, the Queen has remained constant and steadfast in the execution of her duties.

Despite suffering her Annus Horribilis, the divorces of three of her children and other tribulations, including the loss of the royal yacht *Britannia* with its crew of 120 to a tourist attraction in Edinburgh, the Queen has much to be satisfied with. Thanks to her hard work and dedication with Prince Philip, the monarchy now appears stronger than ever, with three new generations waiting in the wings. The Commonwealth, in which she has always shown a special interest, has held together remarkably well and is a force for good in a troubled world.

Yet, despite all of this, for the royal family, much has remained unchanged over the years. Weekends are spent at Windsor, Christmas holidays at Sandringham with its pheasant and partridge shoots and summer holidays at Balmoral with grouse shooting and deer stalking. At Buckingham Palace, footmen wait by every door in case it needs to open for a member of the royal family, although the powdered wigs and breeches have been replaced by military-style uniforms. It is still a world where servants must curtsey and bow to their royal employers, where bedsheets are turned down with the aid of a measuring stick and where rulers are used to set the places on dining tables.

Change may be on the horizon, however. In an interview with *Newsweek* magazine in June 2017, Prince Harry, who is fifth in line to the throne, said: 'The monarchy is a force for good and we want to carry on the positive atmosphere that the Queen has achieved for over sixty years, but we won't be trying to fill her boots. We are involved in modernising the British monarchy. We are not doing this for ourselves but for the greater good of the people. We use our time wisely. We don't want to turn up, shake hands but not get involved.'

On the monarchy, he asked: 'Is there any one of the royal family who wants to be king or queen? I don't think so, but we will carry out our duties at the right time.' It was perhaps a compliment to the Queen and Prince Philip that he should say this, for they have performed their roles and duties so well that they have become a daunting double act to follow.

Prince Philip has been at the Queen's side for seventy years. In the Queen's own words, spoken at the Guildhall in London on their golden wedding anniversary: 'He has, quite simply, been my strength and stay all these years, and I, and his whole family, and this and many other countries, owe him a debt greater than he would ever claim, or we shall ever know.'

The Queen is the central core of the bond which has held their relationship together for seventy years. From the moment she saw Philip in his naval uniform at Dartmouth when she was a teenager, Princess Elizabeth had eyes only for him, persuading her father the King to allow her to marry him at the tender age of twenty-one. She has never wavered from her single-minded devotion to duty, which she pledged in her twenty-first birthday speech to the Commonwealth when she said: 'I declare before you all that my whole life, whether it be long or short, shall be devoted to your service.' She has been sustained in keeping this solemn vow by her deeply held religious beliefs. Every year in her Christmas address she draws attention to Christ's teachings and their importance in her life.

There are many strands to Prince Philip's life as consort, but as his secretary and friend the late Mike Parker always said: 'His constant job is looking after the Queen in first place, second and third.' As consort, he is always two steps behind his anointed Queen and he has performed this role faultlessly.

From difficult beginnings when he was forced to give up a promising career in the navy and when the old guard at Buckingham Palace and at Windsor resented his presence, he slowly but surely carved out for himself a position as innovator, conservationist, speech-writer and promoter of all things British. He suffered the indignity of not being able to pass on his family name to his children, which hurt him deeply. He is remarkably fit for a man of his age and retains the slim figure of his youth and still displays an iron will, a clear speaking voice and a sense of humour. Even in his nineties, when he had a busy day of engagements ahead of him he was known to rise at four o'clock in the morning, summoning his valet, chef, chauffeur and equerry to leave the palace at six sharp.

His sense of humour, so-called 'gaffes' and all, has also been a decisive factor in his relationship with the Queen. He makes her laugh. In earlier days, the shy young Queen would freeze before the television cameras. Philip would defuse the situation with an amusing aside to bring a smile to the Queen's face. When you are under a constant spotlight, as she has been for almost her entire life, this makes a vital difference.

His achievements are many, none more so than the Duke of Edinburgh Award, which has helped millions of young people around the world and continues to do so. He used his position as President of the World Wide Fund for Nature to emphasise the vital importance of conservation around the world and he has been a tireless advocate for engineering and scientific skills in Britain.

Both the Queen in many of her Christmas speeches and Prince Philip in his several philosophical collections of writings have stressed the importance of the individual in society. More than thirty years ago, in his book *A Question of Balance*, Prince Philip wrote: 'In the end, civilised standards still depend absolutely on the way people treat each other as people ... in the final analysis, satisfaction and contentment are created by the relationships between one individual and another.'

Perhaps this goes some way to answering the question of how the Queen and Prince Philip have successfully managed seventy years of married life.

Acknowledgements

I would like to thank Nick Cowan for his arduous work with the research for this book. I would also like to thank him for his expertise in helping me with the construction of the multiple strands it took to compile the manuscript and his endless patience in checking my copy. No royal manuscript would be complete without the forensic eye of *Majesty*'s managing editor Joe Little, whose brilliant memory for royal facts and details is second to none. I would also like to thank Robin Piercy, whose sons Angus and Henry helped with all the technical difficulties I managed to frequently get myself into.

Over the years of writing royal books and especially biographies, I have interviewed many people whose valuable contributions have added to the content of this book. Sadly, some of them are no longer with us, but I would like to thank them posthumously, in particular: the Hon. Margaret Rhodes, with whom I spent a delightful morning at her home in Windsor Park, and James Edwards, the ebullient, eccentric and totally charming former head of Heatherdown prep school, who described so perfectly the Queen's role as a mother.

I would also like to thank my editor Ian Marshall and everyone at Simon & Schuster for their help and support.

Ingrid Seward
London, September 2017

Bibliography

Alexandra, Queen of Yugoslavia – *Prince Philip: A Family Portrait* (Hodder & Stoughton, 1960)

Beaton, Cecil, *The Strenuous Years: Diaries 1948–55* (Weidenfeld & Nicolson, 1973)

Benson, Ross, *Charles, The Untold Story* (Victor Gollancz, 1993)

Boothroyd, Basil, *Philip: An Informal Biography* (Longman, 1971)

Bradford, Sarah, *Elizabeth: A Biography of Her Majesty the Queen* (Heinemann, 1996)

Brandreth, Gyles, *Philip and Elizabeth: Portrait of a Marriage* (Century, 2004)

Chance, Michael, *Our Princesses and Their Dogs* (John Murray, 1936)

Channon, Henry, *Chips: The Diaries of Sir Henry Channon* (ed. Robert James, Weidenfeld & Nicolson, 1967)

Corbitt, F. J., *My Twenty Years in Buckingham Palace* (David McKay 1956)

Cordet, Hélène, *Born Bewildered* (Peter Davies, 1961)

Crawford, Marion, *The Little Princesses* (Cassell, 1950)

Dean, John, *HRH Prince Philip, The Duke of Edinburgh: A Portrait by his valet* (Robert Hale, 1954)

Fleming, Tom, *Voices Out of the Air: The Royal Christmas Broadcasts, 1932–1981* (Heinemann, 1981)

Hall, Unity, *Philip: The Man behind the Monarchy* (Michael O'Mara Books, 1987)

Hardman, Robert, *Our Queen* (Hutchinson, 2011)

Harris, Kenneth, *The Queen* (Weidenfeld & Nicolson, 1994)

Hartnell, Norman, *Silver and Gold* (Evans Brothers, 1955)

Heald, Tim, *The Duke: A Portrait of Prince Philip* (Hodder & Stoughton, 1991)

Hoey, Brian, *Mountbatten: The Private Story* (Sidgwick & Jackson, 1994)

Judd, Denis, *Prince Philip, Duke of Edinburgh: A Biography* (Michael Joseph, 1980)

Kirkwood, Pat, *The Time of My Life* (Robert Hale, 1999)

Knatchbull, Timothy, *From a Clear Blue Sky: Surviving the Mountbatten Bomb* (Hutchinson, 2009)

Lacey, Robert, *Royal: Her Majesty Queen Elizabeth II* (Little, Brown, 2002)

Longford, Elizabeth, *Elizabeth R: A Biography* (Weidenfeld & Nicolson, 1983)

Mann, the Rt Rev Michael, *Some Windsor Sermons*, (Michael Russell Publishing Ltd, 1989)

Nahum, Baron Henry, *Baron by Baron* (Frederick Muller, 1957)

Noakes, Michael and Vivien, *The Daily Life of the Queen: An Artist's Diary* (Ebury, 2000)

Oliver, Charles, *Dinner at Buckingham Palace* (Prentice Hall, 1972)

Parker, Eileen, *Step Aside for Royalty: A Personal Experience* (Bachman & Turner, 1982)

Philip, HRH Prince, *Down to Earth* (William Collins & Sons, 1988)

Philip, HRH Prince, *Men, Machines and Sacred Cows* (Hamish Hamilton, 1984)

Philip, HRH Prince, *A Question of Balance* (Michael Russell Publishing Ltd, 1982)

Philip, HRH Prince and the Rt Rev Michael Mann, *A Windsor Correspondence* (Michael Russell Publishing Ltd, 1984)

Philip, HRH Prince and the Rt Rev Michael Mann, *Survival or Extinction: A Christian Attitude to the Environment* (Michael Russell Publishing Ltd, 1989)

Pimlott, Ben, *The Queen: Elizabeth II and the Monarchy* (Harper Collins, 1996)

Seward, Ingrid, *Prince Edward: A Biography* (Century, 1995)

Seward, Ingrid, *Royal Children of the 20th Century* (Harper Collins, 1993)

Seward, Ingrid, *The Queen and Di* (Harper Collins, 2000)

Seward, Ingrid, *The Last Great Edwardian Lady* (Century, 1999)

Seward, Ingrid, *William and Harry* (Headline, 2003)

Seward, Ingrid and *Majesty* writers, *The Queen's Diamond Jubilee* (M Press Media Ltd, 2011)

Seward, Ingrid, *The Queen's Speech* (Simon & Schuster, 2015)

Shawcross, William, *Queen Elizabeth the Queen Mother: The Official Biography* (Macmillan, 2009)

Sherbrook Walker, Eric, *Treetops Hotel* (Robert Hale, 1962)

Sheridan, Lisa, *From Cabbages to Kings* (Odhams Press, 1955)

Sheridan, Lisa, *Our Princesses at Home* (John Murray, 1940)

Sheridan, Lisa, *The Queen and her Children* (John Murray, 1953)

Turner, Graham, *Elizabeth: The Woman and the Queen* (Macmillan, 2002)

Townsend, Peter, *Time and Chance: An Autobiography* (Collins, 1978)

Vickers, Hugo, *Alice: Princess Andrew of Greece* (Viking, 2000)

Warwick, Christopher, *Princess Margaret: A Life of Contrasts* (Andre Deutsch, 2000)

Wynn, Godfrey, *The Young Queen* (Hutchinson, 1952)

York, Duchess of, with Jeff Coplan, *My Story* (Simon & Schuster, 1996)

Majesty magazine (Hanover Magazines and Rex Publications 1940–2017)
The Queen's speeches and broadcasts (Crown Copyright 1940–2016)

Index

Abercorn, Alexandra, Duchess of, 136, 137, 269
Adeane, Lady, 109
Al-Fayed, Mohamed, 199, 201, 202, 277–8
Albert, Prince, 21, 82, 123–9 *passim*, 131–2, 208
Alexandra of Yugoslavia, Queen, 49, 51, 53–4, 59, 60, 63–4
Alexandra, Princess (Anne's cousin), 117
Alexandra, Princess (Elizabeth's cousin), 15
Alexandra, Princess (Philip's cousin), 136, 143
Alexandra, Queen Consort, 27–8
Alexandra, Queen of Yugoslavia, 65
Alice of Battenberg, 6, 14, 28–9, 33, 34, 47–8, 53, 58, 63, 95, 100, 107
    Anne's godmother, 102
    and Charles's birth, 101
    committed to institution, 50, 208
    and persecuted Jews, 124
    and son's engagement, 72
Anderson, Mabel, 101, 105, 107, 115–16, 144–5, 146, 203
Andrea, Prince, 27–30, 47–8, 50, 53, 123
    Anne's godfather, 102
    treason charge against, 31, 33–4, 35
Andrew, Prince, Duke of York:
    awkward moments of, 160
    birth of, 141–2
    christening of, 142–3
    and Diana's death, 210
    education of, 156
    engagement of, 171
    failed marriage of, 177, 187–8
    infancy of, 143–7
    as lunch guest, 250
    naval service of, 167, 172
Anne, Princess Royal:
    birth of, 81, 102
    Charles's relationship with, 108–10
    christening of, 103
    and coronation, 96, 110–11
    and Diana's funeral, 218
    education of, 116
    failed marriage of, 177, 188
    and horses, 112, 229
    infancy of, 108–13
    remarriage of, 177–8
    at school, 111
    weddings of, 162, 259
    as yachtswoman, 112
Armstrong-Jones, Antony, *see* Snowdon, Lord
Arthur, Duke of Connaught, 26
Attlee, Clement, 19, 91

Baden, Berthold, Margrave of, 51
Baldwin, Stanley, 23
Balfour, Lord Arthur, 32
Beatles, 153–4
Beaton, Cecil, 78, 94–5, 96, 102, 143–4, 235
Beatrice, Princess, 176–7, 221
Benning, Osla, 64–5
Berry, Mary, 250–1, 252
Blair, Cherie, 161, 235, 273
Blair, Tony, 161, 203–4, 209, 235, 252, 273, 274

Bonaparte, Marie, 8, 48
Boyle, Danny, 275
Brabourne, John, Lord, 18
Brezhnev, Leonid, 153
Britannia, HMY, 133, 230, 237, 242, 259, 276
Bruni, Carla, 242
Buckingham Palace:
    couple move into, 90
    public access to, 190
    reorganisation of, 91
Burton, Richard, 153

Cameron, David, 157, 276
Camilla, Duchess of Cornwall, 178, 258, 275, 277
Carey, George, 261
Catherine, Duchess of Cambridge, 275
Chamberlain, Neville, 19, 62
Channon, Sir Henry 'Chips', 63
Charles, Prince of Wales:
    Anne's relationship with, 108–10
    birth of, 78, 99–100
    Camilla marries, 258
    christening of, 100–1
    and dancing, 108
    and Diana, *see under* Diana, Princess of Wales
    education of, 51, 113–16, 117–21
    flat feet of, 104
    infancy of, 101–2, 104
    and Mountbatten death, 267–8
    naval service of, 172
    and Philip's discipline, 105–6
    and polo, 228
    on Queen Mother, 106
    tribute by, 274
    weddings of, 166, 275
Charlotte, Princess, 259, 275
Chatto, Lady Sarah, 184–5
Churchill, Winston, 13, 19, 45, 74, 79, 84, 88, 90, 91, 95, 203, 237
    and coronation, 96
civil list, 127, 190, 227
Clarence House:
    refurbishment of, 18, 19, 76, 80
    royal couple move into, 80
    royal couple move out of, 90
Cordet, Hélène, 48–9, 50, 135–6
Cox, Professor Brian, 246
Craig, Daniel, 275
Crawford, Marion 'Crawfie', 12, 14, 31–2, 44

on Edward VIII, 45
and Elizabeth's education, 38
on Elizabeth's panto role, 61
on Elizabeth's social circle, 45
on Elizabeth's special-child nature, 41
and Simpson, 37

Dean, John, 11–12, 17–18, 68, 70, 75
Diana, Princess of Wales, 164–7, 169–71
    bulimia suffered by, 165
    change to title of, 205
    Charles's engagement to, 164–5
    Charles's marriage to, 166
    christening of, 259
    death of, 197–219 *passim*
        and funeral, 205–6, 208, 209, 214–18
        and inquest, 276–8
        and interment, 214
        and palace flag, 206, 207, 209
    failed marriage of, 3, 138, 178, 185–6, 188, 192–6
    Morton book on, 188
    on *Panorama*, 194, 195
    'People's Princess', 204
    and Philip's love life, 137
    pre-wedding party for, 166
    wedding of, 166
    at William's christening, 169
Douglas-Home, Sir Alec, 152
du Maurier, Daphne, 19, 76, 136
Duke of Edinburgh's Awards, 53, 131, 281 (*see also* Philip, Prince: roles taken on by)

Edward VII, King, 27, 28, 151
Edward VIII, King:
    abdication of, 38–9
    and father's death, 42
    fondness of, for Elizabeth, 44–5
    as Prince of Wales, 25
    Simpson meets, 37
Edward, Prince, Earl of Wessex, 161, 250
    birth of, 147–51
    christening of, 151
    and Duke of Edinburgh's Award, 174
    education of, 156–8
    and Fayeds, 202
    infancy of, 151–2, 155–6
    and *It's a Royal Knockout*, 176
    Marines quit by, 172–4

theatrical enthusiasm develops in,
157–8
Elizabeth II, Queen:
in *Aladdin*, 61
and Annus Horribilis, 190–1
Auxiliary Territorial Service work
of, 67
becomes queen, 86
birth of, 21–5
Charles born to, 78, 99–100
christening of, 26–7
constitutional history studied by, 45
coronation of, 91–7, 110–11, 131
and dancing, 81
as Defender of the Faith, 3, 261
and Diana, *see under* Diana, Princess
of Wales
and dogs, 16, 77, 186, 232–3, 247
and Dome, 273
and emotion, 42–3
engagement of, 2, 7, 69–70, 71–2,
74
and engineering, 239
entertaining by, 241–53
and Fagan incident, 167–8
father's confidence in, 45
and fishing, 236
fondness of, for animals, 26
and global warming, 265–6
godparents of, 26
Golden Wedding anniversary of, 3–4
honeymoon of, 16–17
and horses, 221–6
jubilee years of, 158, 223, 254–5, 262,
263, 273–5
and king's death, 86–8
long life and long service of, 271–2
Malta stays of, 80–1, 82, 104
on meeting Philip, 57–8
and military history, 234
and music, 233–4, 263–4
and Olympics, 275
Philip's correspondence with, 59–60,
67, 70
and photography, 235
and pigeons, 233
and punctuality, 44
Queen's duties of, 89
and religion, 3, 257–65, 270, 280
and Scottish referendum, 276
shyness of, 46, 59
silver wedding anniversary of, 159
stands in for king, 83

tours by, 70–1, 83, 84–7, 93, 103, 141,
171, 179, 259, 273–4
wedding of, 5–16 *passim*, 47, 74, 76
filming and broadcast of, 9–11
and guest list, 7
and king's letter, 14–15
other royalty at, 13
as public occasion, 9
Radio Times cover for, 9–11
as symbol of hope, 8
widening social circle of, 45
and WW2, 43–4
Elizabeth, Queen Mother:
Anne's godmother, 102
and Charles, 106
and Charles's education, 119
and children's education, 38
death of, 273
and Diana's death, 211
and Diana's funeral, 218
diplomatic illnesses of, 186
and Edward's abdication, 39
and Elizabeth's birth, 24
on Elizabeth's engagement, 71–2
Elizabeth's post-wedding letter to, 17
foreign tours by, 43
funeral of, 214
and *It's a Royal Knockout*, 176
and Margaret, 181
song-tape gift to, 233–4
and Townsend, 182, 183
at William's christening, 169
and Windsor Castle fire, 189
Elphinstone, Lady, 26, 71
Eugenie, Princess, 144, 177, 221

Fagan, Michael, 167–8
Fayed, Dodi, 198, 199, 202–3, 277
Fellowes, Jane, 165, 202, 213
Fellowes, Sir Robert, 165, 192, 206, 212,
213
Festival of Britain, 82
Fisher, Archbishop Geoffrey, 257, 262

George I, King of Greece, 27, 33, 47
George II, King, 12
George II, King of Greece, 53, 65–6
George V, King, 23, 26, 28, 31–2, 40, 47,
104, 124
death of, 38, 42
and Romanovs, 33
and Simpson's relationship with son,
37

George VI, King, 23, 60–1, 66, 69–70,
    172, 208, 242
  becomes king, 38–9
  on Charles, 104
  and Charles's birth, 100
  and children's education, 38
  confidence of, in Elizabeth, 45
  coronation of, 43
  death of, 86–9
  and Elizabeth's socialising, 60–1, 69
  at Elizabeth's wedding, 13
  and grandchildren's name styles, 102
  health of, 78, 80, 82, 83–4, 85–6
  letter of, to Elizabeth, 14–15
  North American tour by, 43
  Philip admitted to royal family by, 12
  Philip described by, 62
  Silver Jubilee of, 38
  tantrums of, 40
George, Prince (Philip's uncle), 8, 48, 101
George, Prince (William's son), 275
global warming, 265–6
Great Exhibition, 82, 125, 127, 128

Hahn, Kurt, 51, 52–3, 54–5, 124, 131,
    231
Hamilton, Lewis, 246, 248
Harry, Prince, 195, 279–80
  birth and christening of, 170–1
  and Diana's death, *see under* Diana,
    Princess of Wales
Henry, Duke of Gloucester, 25, 38
Hitler, Adolf, 8, 52, 278
Holloway, Laurie, 233–4
Hussey, Lady Susan, 210

IRA, 168–9, 206, 266

Janvrin, Sir Robin, 198, 199, 208, 210
Jenkins, Katherine, 249

Kennard, Lady Gina, 105, 118, 143
Kennedy, John F., 152
Kent, George, Duke of, 25, 38, 66, 206
Khrushchev, Nikita, 153
Kirkwood, Pat, 134–5
Knight, Clara 'Allah', 26, 41–2, 44, 258

Lascelles, Tommy, 18, 19, 61, 90, 100,
    182
Laurence, Timothy, 177–8, 259
Lennon, John, 153–4
Leopold, King of the Belgians, 126, 142

Lightbody, Helen, 101–2, 105, 108, 109,
    144
Linley, David, Viscount, 184–5
Lloyd George, David, and Romanovs, 32
Longman, Lady Elizabeth, 15–16
Louis of Hesse, Prince, 151, 278

McCorquodale, Sarah, 165, 202, 213
MacDonald, Margaret 'Bobo', 12, 17–18,
    44, 46, 252–4
  and Commonwealth tour, 85
Mabell, Countess of Airlie, 25, 26, 27
Magpie, HMS, 81–2, 103, 128, 227
Major, John, 189–90, 192
Mandela, Nelson, 152–3
Mann, Rt Revd Michael, 94, 176, 266–7,
    269, 270
Margaret, Princess:
  and Anne's education, 117
  Charles's godmother, 100–1
  death of, 273
  and Diana's funeral, 218
  on Elizabeth's future role, 39–40
  at Elizabeth's wedding, 13, 15
  failed marriage of, 160, 171
  flirtatious nature of, 46
  and king's death, 87
  and music, 233–4
  and Philip, 69
  and Philip's love life, 134
  Philip's sparring with, 181
  and practical jokes, 43
  Queen's relationship with, 181
  and religion, 258
  and Townsend, 46, 180, 181–4
  wedding of, 184
  Windsor loved by, 60
  and WW2, 43–4
Margarita, Princess, 97, 102
Mary, Princess Royal, 25
Mary, Princess, Viscountess Lascelles,
    26
Mary, Queen Consort, 26, 28, 37–8, 100,
    106
  Silver Jubilee of, 38
Meldrum, Bill, 233
Milford Haven, Dowager Countess of,
    34, 60, 75, 101
Milford Haven, 2nd Marquis of
    (George), 49, 50, 53
Milford Haven, 3rd Marquis of (David),
    12, 16, 49, 51, 60, 75, 78, 101
Mountbatten, Lady Edwina, 30–1, 189

Mountbatten, Lord Louis 'Dickie', 7, 17, 39, 53, 54, 59, 66, 70, 80–1, 120, 278
  Anne's godfather, 102
  death of, 206, 266–7
  name change of, 124
  wedding of, 30–1
Mountbatten, Lady Pamela, 5, 6–7, 15, 16, 18, 90, 104
  and Commonwealth tour, 85
  and king's death, 87

Nahum, Baron, 78, 96, 133, 134–5
Nehru, Jawaharlal, 153
Nicholas II, King of Russia, 28–9, 32, 39

Olga of Greece, Queen Mother, 30
Olympics (2012), 275

Parker Bowles, Camilla, *see* Camilla, Duchess of Cornwall
Parker, Eileen, 12–13, 64, 78–9, 92, 105, 107–10 *passim*
Parker, Mike, 12, 19, 64, 66–7, 74–5, 79, 80, 81, 89, 132–3, 281
  becomes Philip's private secretary, 91
  and Charles's birth, 99–100
  and Commonwealth tour, 85, 86
  and king's death, 87, 88
  and Philip's birthday, 97
  resigns, 133–4
Paul, King of Greece, 76, 82, 155
Pearce, Joe, 253
Peter, King of Yugoslavia, 65–6
Philip, Prince, Duke of Edinburgh:
  abdominal operation on, 221
  Admiralty and college jobs of, 77
  admitted to royal family, 12
  and Albert, *see* Albert, Prince
  and art, 237–9
  artery problem of, 236
  becomes British subject, 71
  birth of, 29–30
  bladder infection of, 255, 274
  in car crash, 76
  and carriage driving, 224, 226, 228–9
  and Charles's birth, 99–100
  christening of, 30
  and conservation, 232, 266, 268–9, 281
  and cooking, 250–2
  and coronation, 93–4, 96, 131
  and cricket, 230–1

  at Dartmouth, 55, 62
  and design, 239
  and Diana, *see under* Diana, Princess of Wales
  and Dome, 273
  education of, 50, 51–3, 54–5
  at Edward's birth, 148
  and Edward's Marines decision, 172–4
  and engineering, 239–40
  entertaining by, 241–53
  family background of, 27–8, 123–5
  first ship command of, 81–2, 103, 128
  first UK visit of, 30
  and fishing, 236
  and flying, 236–7
  gaffes of, 180, 241
  German connections of, 7–8
  Greece left by, for last time, 34–5
  as helicopter pilot, 79
  high-spirited nature of, 78–9
  and king's death, 87–8, 89
  long life and long service of, 271–2
  and love-life rumours, 132–9
  and Mountbatten death, 266–7
  naval service of, 62–4, 66–7, 68, 80–2, 103, 104, 128
  and photography, 49, 143, 235
  and polo, 81, 226, 227–8
  Queen's relationship and activities with, *see under* Elizabeth II
  and racing, 225, 226–7
  and religion, 257–9, 264, 265, 266–70
  roles taken on by, 91, 129–31
  science address of, 128–9
  and shooting, 208, 232, 236
  and squash, 231–2
  on state occasions, 169–70
  and titles, 125
  tours by, 83, 84–7, 93, 103, 133, 171, 259, 273–4
  and UFOs, 268
  and yachts, 229–30
Phillips, Mark, 162, 177, 188
Phillips, Peter, 162, 163, 203, 221, 222, 224
Phillips, Zara, 162–3, 170, 229
Prince Philip Designers Prize, 130

Queen Elizabeth Prize for Engineering, 128

Radio Times, 9–10
Richard, Duke of Gloucester, 151
Romsey, Lady Penelope, 136, 137–8
Roose, Nanny, 30, 34, 48
    and Philip's upbringing, 47, 48

Sarah, Duchess of York, 171, 176–7,
    188–9, 192
    failed marriage of, 177, 187–8
Sarkozy, Nicolas, 242
Scott, Sir Kenneth, 259
Scott, Sir Peter, 236
Shand Kydd, Frances, 164
Simpson, Wallis, 37, 38
Snowdon, Lord, 151, 160, 170, 184
Sophie, Countess of Wessex, 160–1, 175,
    234–5, 250
Sophie, Queen of Greece, 49
Sophie, Princess, 34, 49, 97
Spencer, John, 8th Earl, 164, 213
Spencer, Charles, 9th Earl, 213, 214
    funeral speech of, 216–18
Strathmore, Cecilia, Countess of, 22,
    24
Strathmore, Claude, Earl of, 22, 24, 26

Taylor, Elizabeth, 153
Thatcher, Margaret, 167

Theodora, Princess, 51, 97
Townsend, Peter, 46, 180, 181–4
Trestrail, Michael, 168

Victoria, Queen, 21, 27, 37, 125–8
    passim, 131–2, 190–1, 208

Walesa, Lech, 244
Warren, John, 223, 225
Welby, Archbishop Justin, 261
Whybrew, Paul, 167–8
William of Gloucester, Prince, 206
William, Prince, 195–6
    birth of, 167
    christening of, 169
    and Diana's death, *see under* Diana,
        Princess of Wales
    Queen's meetings with, 196
    wedding of, 275
Wilson, Harold, 152
Windsor Castle, 44, 60, 90, 189–90,
    258
Windsor name, 90, 124–5, 142
Wogan, Terry, 246
Woodard, Admiral Sir Robert, 259
Woods, Rt Revd Robin, 264–5
World War Two, 43–4, 55, 62–3, 67–8,
    74